BOOM!

LIFE WRITING SERIES

In the Life Writing Series, Wilfrid Laurier University Press publishes life writing and new life-writing criticism and theory in order to promote auto-biographical accounts, diaries, letters, and testimonials written and/or told by women and men whose political, literary, or philosophical purposes are central to their lives. The Series features accounts written in English, or translated into English from French or the languages of the First Nations, or any of the languages of immigration to Canada.

From its inception, Life Writing has aimed to foreground the stories of those who may never have imagined themselves as writers or as people with lives worthy of being (re)told. Its readership has expanded to include scholars, youth, and avid general readers both in Canada and abroad. The Series hopes to continue its work as a leading publisher of life writing of all kinds, as an imprint that aims for both broad representation and scholarly excellence, and as a tool for both historical and autobiographical research.

As its mandate stipulates, the Series privileges those individuals and communities whose stories may not, under normal circumstances, find a welcoming home with a publisher. Life Writing also publishes original theoretical investigations about life writing, as long as they are not limited to one author or text.

Series Editor
Marlene Kadar
Humanities Division, York University

Manuscripts to be sent to
Lisa Quinn, Acquisitions Editor
Wilfrid Laurier University Press
75 University Avenue West
Waterloo, Ontario N2L 3C5, Canada

BOOM!

Manufacturing Memoir for the Popular Market

JULIE RAK

WILFRID LAURIER
UNIVERSITY PRESS

Wilfrid Laurier University Press acknowledges the support of the Canada Council for the Arts for our publishing program. We acknowledge the financial support of the Government of Canada through the Canada Book Fund for our publishing activities.

LIBRARY AND ARCHIVES CANADA CATALOGUING IN PUBLICATION

Rak, Julie, 1966–
    Boom! : manufacturing memoir for the popular market / Julie Rak.

(Life writing series)
Includes bibliographical references.
Issued also in electronic formats.
ISBN 978-1-55458-939-5

    1. Autobiography. 2. Autobiography—History and criticism. 3. Publishers and publishing—United States. I. Title. II. Series: Life writing series

CT25.R34 2013	808.06′692	C2013-900044-5

Electronic monographs.
Issued also in print format.
ISBN 978-1-55458-940-1 (PDF).—ISBN 978-1-55458-941-8 (EPUB)

    1. Autobiography. 2. Autobiography—History and criticism. 3. Publishers and publishing—United States. I. Title. II. Series: Life writing series (Online)

CT25.R34 2013	808.06′692	C2013-900045-3

Cover design by Martyn Schmoll. Front-cover image by iStockphoto. Text design by Sandra Friesen. Photos between pages 89 and 111 by Julie Rak.

© 2013 Wilfrid Laurier University Press
Waterloo, Ontario, Canada
www.wlupress.wlu.ca

CONTENTS

★

GRATITUDE

I'd like to thank my colleagues in auto/biography studies and life writing from around the world, and especially those in IABA (The International Association for Biography and Autobiography). Specifically, I'd like to thank my collaborators, Laurie McNeill and Anna Poletti. I also thank Gillian Whitlock, Craig Howes, my "Paris research assistant" Philippe Lejeune, Julia Watson, Sidonie Smith, Jan Radway, Lauren Berlant, Tom Smith, and Tom Couser for their wise words and practical advice about aspects of the research for this book.

Thanks to all the people working in bookstores across Canada who took time out from their busy work lives to talk to me: Heidi Hallett, Bruce Cartledge, Michael Hamm, Kristen Hogan, Mika Bareket, Gregory King, Ria Bleumer, Gary Crompton, Katherine Connaught, Sheila Koffman, and Sharon Budnarchuk.

In Canada, I couldn't do this work without the wisdom and friendship of my colleagues. I especially want to thank Daphne Read, Corrinne Harol, Paul Hjartarson, Dianne Chisholm, Smaro Kamboureli, Diana Brydon, Daniel Coleman, Andrew Gow, DeNel Rehberg-Sedo, Donna Pennee, and from my writing group, Anne Whitelaw, Lianne McTavish, Sasha Mullally, Liz Czach, Amy Kaler, and Liza Piper. Harvey Krahn, Janine Brodie, Joanne Muzak, Greg Hollingshead, and Bart Beaty all provided specific assistance. I could not have started this project without Joan Waters, and I thank her for her support.

In the United Kingdom, I thank Scott Lucas, Lesley Lucas (and Ryan and Lauren), Steve Hewitt, Ceri Morgan (and Ike, Flora and Gwilly), Anna

Hartnell, the Tilbury Grovers Lynn Abbott and Margaret Robertson, Francesca Carnevali, and Jan Campbell.

The graduate students in the 2008 English 693 course "Life Narrative, Citizenship, Print Culture" helped me to better understand what popular memoir is about, and I thank them for their generosity and enthusiasm as we thought about identity and citizenship together. I also thank these graduate students for their insights as I worked on this project: Cyndi Rasmussen, Jenn Bell, Medha Samarasinghe, Lena Sherstobitoff, Lindsay Scott, Alison Rukavina, Marshall Watson, and Yang Lim. My research assistants provided key work at different points: thanks to Tracy Kulba, Brenda Garrett, Allison Hargreaves, Aloys Fleishman, and Ben Lof.

This book came into being with financial support from the Social Sciences and Humanities Research Council of Canada (SSHRC), the University of Alberta Killam program, the Office of the Dean of Arts at the University of Alberta, and the Faculty of Arts at the University of Alberta. I particularly thank Lisa Quinn, Clare Hitchens, Rob Kohlmeier, and Leslie Macredie of Wilfrid Laurier University Press for believing in this book and for making it much, much better than it was.

I thank Danielle Fuller for her love, her friendship, her keen editorial eye, her belief in this project, and her passion for everything in life that matters. Neither this book nor I would be any good without you.

Boom! Manufacturing Memoir for the Popular Market is dedicated to the memory of my grandmother, Betty Henderson (1903–1983), and my colleague and friend Sharon Rosenberg (1964–2010).

Introduction

IDENTIFYING THE MEMOIR INDUSTRY

In the afternoons, when the sun shone a little lower over Lake Champlain in Vermont, my grandmother would stretch out on a day bed on her screened-in back porch, put on a pair of half glasses, pick up her latest book, and read. She was an avid reader. Every week, she would go to the little Greek Revival–style Bixby Memorial Library in Vergennes, the nearest town. She would pick out her book for that week and if I was with her on a visit, I'd choose a book too. My grandmother did not read romances, or detective novels, or literary classics. Unlike my other grandmother, who liked reading Reader's Digest abridged novels and selections from the Book-of-the-Month Club, she read memoirs and biography. Once I asked my grandmother why she liked reading these kinds of books so much. She said, "I like learning about real people the way they were. I like real stories." She didn't add that she also liked learning about celebrities, but she did. I would sometimes read the books she had already finished and left lying around. Some of them were library books about travel or biographies of political figures, but others were witty paperbacks by famous film stars like David Niven or Mary Astor.

In 1983, when she was eighty years old, my grandmother died suddenly of a heart attack or a stroke. She was found on her back porch by her neighbour Shirley, because Shirley was worried that she had not seen her friend for a couple of days. After phoning her and getting no answer, Shirley went to my grandmother's place and knocked on the back porch door. When she didn't hear anything, she went inside and found my grandmother on her day bed, face down on an open book. It was a biography of Queen Victoria.

When I asked Shirley about how she found my grandmother, she said, "I just touched her once to see how she was, and I knew she was gone."

Then she asked me, "But why was she lying down? Did she feel sick? I don't know if she felt any pain. I'd never seen her lying down before." I told her that my grandmother was doing something she did every day when she didn't have company—she was reading in her favourite spot. Shirley nodded. "So she must have just put her head down for a moment," she said. We were both silent for awhile, thinking about this. Then I asked Shirley, "What page was she on?"

"Page 4. I looked," she said promptly. Shirley was a former Girl Scout camp leader. She was good at keeping her wits about her in a bad situation, and she noticed details. "She must have just started it," she said.

I looked at the day bed where my grandmother had died. Somebody had smoothed it out, so I couldn't tell that anyone had lain on it. But the book was there, off to the side. It was a big hardcover book, more than four hundred pages, and it was covered in the thick plastic the library puts on its hardcovers. I could imagine my grandmother listening to the summer breeze in the cedar trees and looking at the play of sunlight on the water. I could see her finishing her daily cigarette and coffee, putting away a finished *Boston Globe* crossword puzzle, making her weekly hair appointment, and then settling down to read her latest book. It was hard not to think that my grandmother had just stepped out her life for a moment, and that any minute now she'd come back to that porch with a cup of coffee from the percolator and a fresh pack of Camel cigarettes. I missed her then, very much. But I was also glad that she had died there, in the place she liked best of all, at the beginning of a life story just as her own story was ending.

My grandmother was the sort of reader who most scholars of literature and even of auto/biography[1] tend to overlook, if they think about readers at all. She had trained for two years at Wheelock College in Boston to be a kindergarten teacher, and when she was a young woman, that is what she did. After she married, she quit her job to look after her husband, children, and in-laws in a rambling old farm house in Woodbury, a small town in Connecticut. After my grandfather died, she lived alone in their small apartment for the winter, and spent most of her summers at their Lake Champlain place in Vermont. It might be easy to imagine her as Janice Radway's archetypal romance reader, a woman who used reading to escape the difficulties and disappointments of ordinary life and relationships (Radway 1984). But this is not quite right, since my grandmother didn't read fiction after my grandfather died, and by the time I knew her she had little reason to escape the independent life she clearly enjoyed. I believe that my grandmother was fascinated by the lives of the famous because she knew that she was ordinary. Just as she said, she liked to read stories about real people, as long as they and the writing they did were clever, and as long as she knew who they had been in their public lives. She liked her history to be personal, and her stories to be real. My grandmother was not a romantic, although she enjoyed a good time. Her reading reflected this.

This book is about the memoirs that are written, published, sold in bookstores, and circulated by public libraries for people like my grandmother: ordinary readers who are interested in the world around them but who also want to read about places and people that are not accessible to them in their immediate lives. It is also about books that my grandmother wouldn't have had access to yet, the books that are part of what is called the "memoir boom," a period roughly spanning the first decade of the twenty-first century, when the production and public visibility of American and British memoirs by celebrities and by relatively unknown people sharply increased. I do think that my grandmother would have greeted the memoir boom with delight, and perhaps even enjoyed the increasing numbers of memoirs by ordinary people who have led extraordinary lives just as much as she liked reading about the lives of the famous. In this she would have joined the thousands of people who participate in the memoir boom by buying, borrowing, downloading, and reading the memoirs that are part of it.

This book is not about readers, however, because other groundwork about what the memoir boom is, how it is produced, and what it means in contemporary life needs to be laid first. Even though she was not part of the current interest in non-fiction books about the lives of others, the focus I have placed on my grandmother as a reader does make evident something about non-fiction, and especially what critics often call life writing, that often gets overlooked. My grandmother, and readers like her, are the reason that the memoir boom exists, but so far, little critical discourse about memoir has had much to say about the books produced for this readership. The books of the memoir boom are produced by mainstream presses for large audiences, and perhaps that is why critics of autobiography tend to overlook them or not teach them in their classes (Couser 2012, 14). And yet, millions of readers like my grandmother still seek out these kinds of books precisely because they are *not* fictional. What is more, many readers appear to enjoy reading about the lives of others, in apparent ignorance of a chorus of disapproval about the books written for them. Why are so many of these stories produced and eagerly read today? Why are cultural pundits so suspicious of them? How can we understand the ways in which they are produced and received? In mainstream journalism, most analysis of the phenomenon, with the exception of Ben Yagoda's *Memoir: A History* (2009), has taken the form of backlash against aspects of the memoir boom. Other studies, like G. Thomas Couser's recent *Memoir: An Introduction* (2012), try to understand the memoir boom in light of the history of auto-biography production in the United States. In this study of contemporary memoir, I wish to do something a bit different from the other kinds of studies of American memoir in circulation, whether they are by journalists or scholars of life writing. I want to change the way that we have understood memoirs so that we can see them as part of a production cycle as a way to explain how the memoir boom came about, and how it continues. I think that understanding how the book industry works today can help us see why the production of non-fiction has assumed so much importance. I also think that memoirs, particularly those of non-celebrities, have the potential to change the imagined relations their readers have with the lives of others: this is the source of their power and fascination at the present time, and the reason publishers continue to produce them. But exactly what does this change mean? What does it mean to want to enter into imagined relations with others at this time? Does it signify an emergent interest in community? Is it the latest development in neoliberalism that emphasizes the cult of the individual apart from community (Gilmore 2010, 658)? Is it a media industry takeover that sucks the life out of literary production because *anybody* can write a life story as part of a culture of self-help?

These questions are all difficult to pose, since the answers require a shift from thinking about books as mere textual vehicles for an author's thoughts to thinking about books as commodities that are manufactured for a market by an industry. Memoir in particular has been associated with developments in that industry and specifically with writing for the market-place since the eighteenth century in Europe. Before that, memoirs were produced by people who wanted to record their lives in relation to others, whether that meant in relation to the stories of other people, or in relation to a historic event, such as a battle or the holding of an important public office. From the classical period onward, memoirs were written by non-professional writers. Some were published, but others—such as memoirs about families—were not. Like other genres such as diary or written religious confession, memoirs were not strictly literary, and they were written for purposes other than publication. By the eighteenth century in France, however, what were called "scandalous memoirs" were being produced by former courtesans (sometimes anonymously, sometimes not) as a way to pay for their court cases. The "scandalous memoirists" were prostitutes and libertines who published anonymous accounts of their lives with salacious details about liaisons in order to pay for their court cases. These memoirs were very popular during that period (Thompson 2000). Although they were still being written by non-professional authors, this was one way in which memoirs became part of the developing capitalist economy of publishing. They were written in order to sell, and they were bought because they were salacious. Like the novel, which was held in ill repute by many, memoir at the time was thought to be entertaining, but not literary and certainly not morally improving. It was the form for non-professional writers to write about a specific set of experiences or one's own story in relation to the story of another person. Sometimes, as in the phrase "to write one's memoirs," it referred to memoir as the process of collecting personal memories and writing them down, sometimes publishing them privately for family, and sometimes more widely (Rak 2004a).

But when Jean Jacques Rousseau's *The Confessions* was published in 1782 and 1789, something changed. *The Confessions* combines many other genres in its story of Rousseau's life, including the genre of religious confession, the story of the growth of the artist, the road narrative, and the polemic. But it also took many of the conventions found in the scandalous memoirs and changed them. For the first time, the development of a personality was explained in print by relating (or, as Rousseau said, confessing) shameful events. The private world of the individual was then "confessed," exposed, made public, and not kept anonymous. This is an account of the divide Rousseau himself had discussed between the public and the private spheres, where the individual has an obligation to go public with the most intimate details of his life. Memoir therefore could be a way to unite the private life of the self to its public persona. But this account was not a memoir as it had previously been understood. For one thing, *The Confessions* was not written by a non-professional writer but by someone who already had a public reputation. As Christopher Kelly has said, Rousseau was one of the first writers to be known as an author, someone whose personality overshadowed and informed the production of his own works and who was willing to take responsibility *in public* for what he said (Kelly 2003). *The Confessions* was a key document in which Rousseau established this position as an author, because he understood himself as the only person qualified to write about his own life. *The Confessions* also differed from earlier autobiographical writing because it was not written to make money, Rousseau claimed, but as a way to explain himself to the world and to account for his own actions. The "low" tone of the memoir, then, was transformed in *The Confessions* to a literary account about higher issues, such as the reason for human motivations and—in Rousseau's own mind—the need to defend one's public reputation from attack. Just as Rousseau's *Emile* had helped to elevate the perception of the novel to something that could discuss serious ideas, so *The Confessions* made life writing about the self one of the key ways that the liberal subject as unique, autonomous, public/private, and self-reflective was understood. But Rousseau's work was not understood subsequently as the work of memoir or even of confession. Rather, it was characterized often as the first *autobiography*, a term that came into use in the Romantic period when *The Confessions* was published. Autobiography became the way that self writing would be understood as literary, something that could be read and appreciated for its style and substance. It was not a mass-market product, as memoir was understood to be. In a sense, Rousseau contributed to making the form of memoir vanish from public view, as scrutiny turned to autobiography as a literary form.

Memoir remained a minor, market-driven form for more than a century until the advent of the memoir boom in the United Kingdom and the United States. Today, as Couser has pointed out, no one writes something and calls it an autobiography: such writing is now referred to as memoir, for reasons that might never be fully known (18). But traces of that earlier association of memoir with trashy writing by hacks for the marketplace remain, and that may be why memoir is regarded with such suspicion, even as it has become central to understanding how the private life of the self is made to go public. It has, as Ben Yagoda has said in *Memoir: A History*, a dual status as a marketable commodity and as a part of discourses about personal identity that appear in many aspects of American public life. Memoir is now more than just a published product. It has become part of public discourse, and it is ubiquitous. For this reason, it is often regarded with suspicion: "Autobiographically speaking, there has never been a time like it. Memoir has become the central form of the culture: not only the way stories are told, but way arguments are put forth, products and properties marketed, ideas floated, acts justified, reputations constructed or salvaged. The sheer volume of memoirs is unprecedented; the way the books were trailed by an unceasing stream of contention, doubt, hype, and accusations is distressing" (2009, 28). In Yagoda's version of "the culture," memoir is more than a genre of writing: it is the way that rhetoric works in the public spheres *and* in capitalism. But alongside this way to think of memoir as part of self-presentation in a liberal democratic society is the commercial aspect of "memoir" in the form of published memoirs. In that form, it is subject to—and profits from—generic expectations. Memoir is a way of thinking and perhaps even of being public, as it remains a way to construct, package, and market identity so that others will want to buy it. Therefore, it is subject to generic "rules." My grandmother had clear expectations when she picked up a book from the library and took it home, because she wanted a specific *genre* of book to read. She thought and read generically to some extent. At the same time, the way that my grandmother read stories about real people involved wider social assumptions about memoir and biography. They included ideas about what is true (or real) and what is not, who is a celebrity and who is not, what is private, and what is interesting about having private lives revealed in public. And I would guess that my grandmother's pleasure as a reader of memoir also included common assumptions about individuality, memory, and the importance of privacy in the United States, although I am sure that she would not have articulated her reading experience in this way. Her story as a reader of memoir and biography does echo the twin issues about memoir for mass audiences: memoirs turn identities into commodities that we buy or borrow or even steal, but they also participate in the manufacture of public identities as a reader encounters the life of another within the context of his or her own experience, values, and beliefs about what it means to be a person. Both things are true of the production of memoir, and they do not exist without each other.

It has been more than two decades since my grandmother died literally in the act of reading about the life of another. Since her death, memoir has become even bigger business than it was when she was reading David Niven's *Bring on the Empty Horses* or Mary Astor's pithy memoir about the follies of Hollywood in the silver screen era. But one thing has not changed. Readers of memoirs have been characterized as many things: as hungry for dirty details, as star-struck, as voyeurs, as people who are prone to being swayed by cultural authorities like Oprah Winfrey and—most sadly of all—as ignorant and uncultured, bad readers who do not know or care about good writing. Most of the time, these images of mass readership are dematerialized, just as the books they read are often discussed as if they too had no history or context for their material existence. The masses remain a mass in blanket characterizations like this. The "readers" talked about so often in dismissals of memoir in the popular press do not ever seem to have lives of their own. But memoir itself is about individuals, and how private individuals communicate within, against, and to a public—what Paul John Eakin has called "touching the world" in stories about their lives (1992). Readers of their stories are themselves individuals who have chosen to read about the lives of others for many reasons. They are the others to whom memoir is directed, for—in opposition to an opinion about memoir that is often repeated—published memoir is not a narcissistic discourse. The attempt to write oneself into a narrative results in the creation of oneself as "other," a person who exists in a book as a character, in order to turn one's life into a story for others' enjoyment, provocation, and education. It is important to keep in mind the lived lives of those who read these life stories as my grandmother did and think about why stories such as this might matter so much to so many. Therefore, the chorus of accusations that memoir writing and publishing are narcissistic activities does little to address the fact that, to many readers, memoir is a way of discovering the lives of others, not of rediscovering or obsessing about the self.

It appears that many readers do enjoy reading about the lives of others and want to go on reading memoirs. The publishing industry in the United States publishes more than 150,000 new titles every year, and about half of those are purchased and stay in print (Greco 2004, 6). General non-fiction books—the category that includes memoir—were the fourth most purchased books by consumers in 2002 at 7% of the market share. Given that the book industry publishes and sells books in ever-increasing numbers, even a conservative estimate would be that at least five thousand general non-fiction books are published and purchased in a year. Many of those are memoirs. According to Ben Yagoda, Nielsen Bookscan has reported that sales in personal memoirs increased 400% from 2004 to 2008 (2009, 7). In more general terms, sales of "biography," a term that covers all personal non-fiction such as biography and memoir, steadily increased over the period from 1940, when 641 biography titles were sold, to 7,241 titles in 2004 (Greco, Rodriguez, and Wharton 2006, 4–5). These figures do not even take into account the circulation of memoirs in library systems, or the sale of memoirs in the used book trade. Most major newspapers and magazines have a non-fiction book section on their bestseller lists. Awards and prizes now include those given exclusively for non-fiction, and increasingly, nominations include memoirs alongside other non-fiction genres such as self-help books or biographies. It is key to realize that the production of titles in the area of personal non-fiction remains small when compared to the production of fiction titles. For example, 25,184 fiction titles were produced in 2004 compared to just over 7,000 non-fiction titles. And the most recent report on the American publishing industry shows that sales for non-fiction grew by 3.5% from 2008 to 2010, but that overall revenue for fiction sold during these years increased by 9.7% (BookStats 2012). Despite the fact that fiction remains the bestselling category in publishing, it is also clear that the production of different types of non-fiction, including memoir, is now a highly visible and important part of book publishing, and both production and sales are increasing at a rapid rate. This increase in production indicates that readers continue to purchase and read non-fiction in general and memoirs specifically, and the trend shows little sign of abating in the United States.[2]

This surge in the interest in memoirs has been accompanied by another change: more memoirs are being published by non-celebrity authors, with some success. Since the 1990s, the writing and publishing of memoir has undergone a significant shift, although commentators do not always agree on the reasons for it. They agree on the result: the success of memoirs by previously unknown writers is a major reason why memoir is one of the most highly visible and popular non-fiction genres today. In the wake of blockbuster memoirs of the 1990s like Susanna Kaysen's *Girl, Interrupted* (1993), Frank McCourt's critically acclaimed *Angela's Ashes* (1998), Mary Karr's *The Liars' Club* (1998), and, most spectacularly, Mitch Albom's *Tuesdays with Morrie* (1997); which Albom himself calls the bestselling memoir of all time, with 14 million copies sold, memoirs by people who were not celebrities or political figures began to sell in large numbers. Sometimes they even outsold trade fiction. Some memoirists began to be treated like major novelists as they and their books were integrated into the media industries. Some even became celebrities themselves. Kaysen, McCourt, Karr, and Albom appeared on major television interview programs like the *Oprah Winfrey Show* to discuss the issues in their books. Their memoirs were made into films. They became serial memoirists who could command large advances from publishers for new accounts of their lives. Their books moved from the non-fiction section of stores to the front, where bestsellers have pride of place. Suddenly, memoir was hot.

By the early years of the new century, hundreds and perhaps thousands of these kinds of memoirs were being published in the United States and worldwide. Many of them became bestsellers, including Dave Eggers' *A Heartbreaking Work of Staggering Genius* (2001) and David Sedaris' *Me Talk Pretty One Day* (2002). In 2003, many more bestselling memoirs by previously unknown authors appeared, including Azar Nafisi's memoir of a book group she ran in post-revolutionary Iran, called *Reading Lolita in Tehran*, Augusten Burroughs' searing indictment of the manner of his upbringing in *Running with Scissors*, and Alice Sebold's account of being sexually assaulted in *Lucky*. Also in that year, Marjane Satrapi published in English the first part of her critically acclaimed and bestselling *Persepolis* graphic memoir, called *Persepolis: The Story of a Childhood*. The year 2003 also brought *A Million Little Pieces*, James Frey's account of his time at an addiction treatment centre, although its fame and then infamy as an Oprah book would not come until two years later. Although Frey's dramatic exposure as a fraud on network television did create some speculation that memoir was finished as a genre, it was not. Memoirs like Jeannette Walls' *The Glass Castle* (2005), Elizabeth Gilbert's runaway bestseller *Eat, Pray Love* (2006), author Joan Didion's account of the death of her husband in *The Year of Magical Thinking* (2007), and John Grogan's blockbuster *Marley and Me: Love and Life with the World's Worst Dog* (2005) are just some of the most popular memoirs published since the Frey controversy ended. In the United Kingdom, the success of *Angela's Ashes* created a widely recognized subgenre of books about poverty, abuse, and illness collectively called "misery memoirs," a genre that is still popular there today (Yagoda 2009, 8–9).

All of these kinds of memoirs joined other kinds of personal accounts from celebrities, politicians, business figures, and sports stars that they either wrote themselves or had written for them, including a memoir by a relatively unknown lawyer published in 1995 that was re-released in 2004 as he stepped onto the national stage: Barack Obama's *Dreams From My Father*. This increase in the amount and success of memoirs has come to be called by some "the memoir boom." In its wake it has created curiosity about its content, shock about its popularity, celebrations of its power, and disgust at its excesses. In *The Limits of Autobiography: Trauma and Testimony*, Leigh Gilmore described memoir as "*the* genre in the skittish period around the millennium" (2001, 1). Almost a decade after Gilmore identified memoir as an important genre, some journalists acknowledged the "boom" in the amount of memoirs published and in their impact. Jennifer Schuessler calls memoir "perhaps the dominant genre of contemporary literature" (2009, WK3). Leigh Sales wrote about the memoir boom on the ABC web site *The Drum*, noting that there were as many memoirs as fiction that week on the *New York Times* bestseller list for paperback books, with a presence on the hardcover list as well (2010).

But, to return to the core of questions I asked earlier, what is the memoir boom about? Why is it happening? Are rumours of its excesses exaggerated? There are as many answers as there are commentators. Take, for example, Thomas Larson's picture of memoir: "Passionate, contrary, innovative, undefined: memoir today has the energy of a literary movement, recalling past artistic innovations that initiated new ways of seeing.... indeed, we might be living in the age of memoir" (Larson 2007, 21). Larson understands that memoir is a new form of writing that supersedes what he thinks is the more traditional genre of autobiography, a genre that he sees as the stories of the self written by public men, not by ordinary people focusing on an important moment in their lives. He even pictures memoir as the rebellious child of autobiography, which runs away from its parent to forge its own creative path (2007, xi). George Fetherling says much the same thing: "We would never call the autobiography of a politician or other professional public figure a memoir.... a memoir is more tightly focused, more daring in construction, and (its author hopes) more penetrating" (Fetherling 2001, vii). Leaving aside the question of differences between memoir and autobiography for a moment, both of these accounts of memoir see its popularity at least partly stemming from rhetorical innovation and good writing. This form does not need to be supported by the lives of the famous. Instead, the writer crafts a compelling story just as a fiction writer would, but out of real events. The goal, as Larson says near the end of *Memoir and the Memoirist*, is connection from one individual life to another, as the writer thinks about the meaning and impact of history and culture on a personal event and the reader uses that thinking to reflect on his or her own situation. Larson thinks that this change in writing and reading has occurred in the United States since 9/11, when it became difficult for Americans to make sense of what authorities told them. Memoir for Larson is a dissenting voice against propaganda, couched in what he calls the familiar, even friendly, rhetoric of individual experience, but potentially radical in its use of experience (Larson 2007, 188). Even Ben Yagoda—who is suspicious of the memoir boom to a certain degree—thinks that the boom is a good thing because it has allowed important stories to come to light: "the memoir boom, for all its sins, has been a net plus for the cause of writing. Under its auspices, voices and stories have emerged that, otherwise, would have been dull impersonal nonfiction tomes or forgettable autobiographical novels, or wouldn't have been expressed at all" (2009, 240).

One by-product of this defence of memoir is that it endorses the craft of its writing, but not the industry that helps to publish and distribute it. Neither Larson nor Fetherling has much to say about industries that might contribute to the surge in popularity of memoir, including the publishing and media industries, and they offer little in the way of cultural analysis of the phenomenon. Larson does offer an interesting secondary interpretation of the reasons why memoir might be popular with American readers to which I will return, but his main reason is that for him, autobiography is the "traditional" discourse of the public sphere, and memoir is a "new" form that has emerged as the rhetoric of the individual, personal, and private life brought into a public field. The problem is that—as I mentioned previously—memoir as a form precedes the first mention of autobiography by almost a thousand years. Memoir as a term has historically referred both to the writing process and the product of writing, and it has described a writing of one's own life in relation to others, to events, or to the construction of some kind of public identity related to a popular issue of the day. For this reason, memoir became associated with marketable writing about the self.[3] It is hardly new.

Perhaps Larson thinks that memoir is new because its position has shifted since the advent of Romantic forms of autobiography. "Autobiography" was a way to refer to more literary treatments of life writing that involved—for Romantic writers especially—a more nuanced introspection and reflection on the course of a life (Smith and Watson 2010, 2–3). That Romantic sense of autobiography as a form about the interior life that connects an individual story to the human condition has, for Larson and Fetherling among others, become the way they understand memoir to work. Any contemporary distinction between memoir and autobiography might not seem to be relevant since, as Smith and Watson point out, the two terms are often treated as interchangeable (2010, 2). Ben Yagoda—after some deliberation—decides to treat them as the same thing (2009, 1–3). But the argument that Larson and Fetherling want to make is worth considering in terms of its motivations, since it allows both of them to reclaim memoir from market forces and cultural critique while arguing for it as a genre separate from that of the novel. It is a popular line of reasoning, since the argument for memoir's "unique" rhetoric also has been made by autobiography critics who have written memoirs themselves, most notably Helen M. Buss and Nancy K. Miller.[4]

This is one way to see the memoir boom, as a welcome change in the way personal stories are told and as a way for new stories and voices to be discovered, perhaps even as a rhetoric of dissent. But others have not been so kind. Like Larson before him (2007, 180), Yagoda points out that the success of memoir has been accompanied by a backlash against the form: "One of the notable by-products of today's memoir boom, from its beginnings in the early 1990s, has been the anti-memoir screed: periodic complaints about the exhibitionism, unseemliness, and just plain *wrongness* of the genre" (2009, 66). In *But Enough about Me,* Nancy K. Miller notes that it is "difficult to think of a modern genre that comes in for the kind of rhetorical abuse that memoir seems to inspire" (2002, 12). Even Yagoda admits that he agrees with some of the charges, which usually include too much focus on the self, too much representation of victimization, the problem of memoir fraud, and often, the influence of Oprah Winfrey and her popularization of therapeutic culture. As Yagoda says, "the critics were right about some long-term trends that contributed to the memoir boom: more narcissism overall, less concern for privacy, a strong interest in victimhood, and a therapeutic culture … these trends came together in the empathetic 1990s, the era of Bill Clinton's feel for pain, of Oprah Winfrey's furrowed brow and concerned nod" (2009, 238–39). But other criticisms are from professional reviewers and journalists who worry about the failure of the memoir to be literary enough. For example, in his review of *Memoir: A History* for *The Washington Post,* Jonathan Yardley evokes the idea of the boom as the progenitor of a flurry of books, only to dismiss the trend as narcissistic, not literary: "what the memoir boom has in fact given us is too many dull or forgettable memoirs, precious few of which have enriched our literature but most of which have simply encouraged the narcissism of their authors" (2009). The picture of the overproduction of memoir is often equated with the amateur status of their authors as well. Robert Collins in *The Daily Telegraph* pictures memoir as "a literary genre that has been hijacked by a swarm of comedians, television presenters and reality-show contestants who have come to saturate the art of autobiography." The problem with memoir for Collins is that it is written by amateurs and supported by media industries, but thankfully—the author adds—memoir is a genre that is about to be saved by Antonia Fraser's memoir of her life with Harold Pinter (2010).

Other commentators directly link overproduction in the market to amateur and celebrity memoir. Publishers and booksellers are often blamed for this; for example, publishers in the United Kingdom were scolded during an awards dinner with this admonition by crime writer Linda LaPlante: "Publishers, stop spending your millions on this tripe!" The "tripe" referred to here is celebrity memoir (Lyall 2010). After she names it as the "dominant literary genre," Jennifer Schuessler laments in *The New York Times* memoir's decline since Frank McCourt published *Angela's Ashes*: "Today, bookstores are clogged with memoirs, not just about abuse and addiction, but about parenting, cooking and dog rearing. There are B-list (and C-list) celebrity memoirs" (2009). In another image of overproduction, Yagoda pictures the shelves of bookstores "groaning" with memoirs by "the less notable" (2007, 10). The title of Bob Minzesheimer's article for USA *Today* also points to the power of memoir—and its problems with authorship and production: "Everybody Has a Story to Tell, So Memoirs Sell." This article connects the popularity of memoir to the age of reality TV and blogging because "agony sells, especially when touted as a true story" (2008).

And finally, some of these commentators assume that non-professional or just plain bad writers turn to memoir because it is easier to write than a novel, and because it is easier to get commercial exposure for it, as Jennifer Schuessler concludes: "The first-person confessional approach is an easy way for writers to add drama and voice to the most improbable subjects, while increasing their odds of getting booked on talk shows that shun the average novelist" (2009). Ben Yagoda also thinks that memoirists, with some exceptions, are just not as good as novelists: "Memoir is to fiction as photography is to painting, also, in being easier to do fairly well. Only a master can create a convincing and compelling fictional world. Anyone with a moderate level of discipline, insight, intelligence, and editorial skill—plus a more than moderately interesting life—can write a decent memoir" (2009, 24). The picture here is of writers who want to write for the market, and so they choose the "easy" way to get published and get noticed. They are of average talents but they have good stories to tell. And, it is assumed, those who write memoir are crassly commercial artists since writing good stories or writing for its own sake is assumed to be the territory of novelists too. James Frey is often the writer who is made to stand in for this kind of hucksterism in memoir as an object lesson about its dangers. Even he has said publicly in a Columbia University journalism class that he now thinks this about memoir as a genre: "'bunk,' 'bullshit,' a marketing tool that didn't exist until several decades ago" (Mozes 2010). Most of these kinds of dismissals give scant attention to kinds of fiction other than literary or experimental writing that may have similar patterns of authorship. Memoir, like history, must be bunk.[5]

If memoir is bunk, the writers are hacks. Critiques like this conclude that—unlike novelists—memoirists are talentless writers who just want to make money. They are not, in short, real writers. They are just hucksters and narcissists who want to write about themselves and profit from it. This set of assumptions has at heart a utopian belief in the purity of fiction writing: novelists do not need to make money, no novelists are narcissistic, and all write well. The second conclusion is related to the first: it is the fault of publishers and the retail industry for overproducing and over-marketing memoirs by second-rate authors, and for selling them in order to make money instead of producing better books for nobler reasons. When these kinds of comments are made, they reveal that few people can provide concrete evidence as to why memoirs are so popular, how publishing and retail bookselling produce memoirs, and what actually makes the boom happen. The third conclusion, that memoirists are hucksters and narcissists, is an assumption based on the first two: that somehow memoir is popular *because* of its narcissism, and that mass marketing and mass publishing have forced credulous people to consume it. Why else would it be popular, if it is not very good?

Those who have pursued this last line of reasoning and tried to understand the popularity of memoir tend to comment on it in the tradition of those who think in very general terms of media hegemony and models of capitalist consumption. The result can be that the desire of some readers to read contemporary memoir remains unexplained. For example, Yagoda explains the popularity of memoirs only as "the craving we have developed for the literal" (2009, 239) without saying why this might be beyond a few references to Oprah Winfrey's influence on popular culture. Although Leigh Gilmore supplies a list of possible factors for the popularity of memoirs, including the existence of "a culture of confession" and therapy in the United States, literary market demand, the publishing by academics of personal narratives, and the emergence of narratives by writers who have experienced oppression, she concludes that she does not understand "why, exactly, should Susanna Keyser's *Girl Interrupted* and Mary Karr's *Liars' Club* be so successful" (2001, 17–18). Nancy K. Miller in *But Enough about Me* ventures that "the memoir craze feeds the hunger for a different, or at least more interesting, life through literature" (2002, 12), and she goes on to list some possible reasons for the popularity of the genre: selfish baby-boomers, a desire for life stories after the end of postmodernism and experimental narrative, the democratic nature of the form, and finally—with tongue-in-cheek—she suggests that the source for memoir's popularity is this: "it's voyeurism for a declining, imperial narcissism. It's the market" (2002, 12).

Even Miller seems to run out of explanations. Proliferating reasons for memoir's popularity finally collapse consumer "hunger," narcissism, and capitalism together in a familiar grouping. In the same vein, Sidonie Smith and Julia Watson see what they think of as the "commercial" version of memoir autobiography as part of confessional discourse "commodified in daytime talk shows that package the obsessions of popular culture ...

publishers may invite celebrity figures to tell life narratives to a public hungry for vicarious fame" (2010, 65). This kind of analysis assumes that consumer behaviour is about the development of mass appetite within capitalism, and that it cannot be discussed as part of rational discourse. The images of the hungry masses and of the cultural industries eager to feed them portray memoir as the site of consumption and—like celebrity discourse, which is closely related to it—a form based on unhealthy desires for gossip and salacious details. Even Nancy Pearl, one of the most influential advocates for popular reading and librarianship in the United States, recently had to defend the practice of reading memoirs against a similar critique. The online promotional blurb for her December 3, 2010, interview on NPR radio about her favourite memoirs portrays memoir-reading as voyeuristic and—in the eyes of health professionals—possibly unhealthy: "Librarian Nancy Pearl loves reading about other people's lives. And while an unappreciative therapist might call that a predilection toward snooping, it won't stop her from gravitating to the memoir section of the bookstore. Here, for your own vicarious pleasure, are some of her favorites."[6] Pearl's enthusiasm for reading memoir is the basis not for refusing the charge of pathological reading, but for admitting that reading is in fact about desire. She reinterprets memoir-reading as a pleasurable obsession that cannot be helped, even as she tacitly acknowledges that memoir-reading is voyeuristic to some degree.

Other than Nancy Pearl's reference to her own experience as a reader, the critique of the memoir boom and speculation about its readership seem to have difficulty explaining why memoir, if it is such a commodified and/or narcissistic product, is so popular with so many people. And as we have seen, others simply oppose memoir because they assume that the form is not literary, which is to say that it is not enough like a certain kind of novel. This allows critics to argue that as a form and a discourse, memoir is an expression of market forces (in the form of cultural industries such as publishing and television), a claim that is is popular because it responds to widely circulating ideas in popular culture about confession, therapy, self-help, celebrity discourse, and trauma. Such a position at least acknowledges that memoirs are cultural products created by and within a market, but it often fails to distinguish between genre fiction, which has these same features as popular memoir, and other kinds of trade fiction. It also tends to treat celebrity memoirs and memoirs by people who are not celebrities as part of the same tendency, when in fact these texts are produced for different kinds of audiences for different reasons. Celebrity memoir and memoir by people who are not celebrities may in fact share some important features as we shall see, but they often discussed as if they are part of the same shameful urge to profit from one's life story. Such an analysis also can combine the suspicion of the culture industries found in the work of Adorno and Horkheimer with a belief that "mass" behaviour is wholly determined by hegemonic forces. The premise here is that the production of culture and consumption by audiences is not complex, an argument that people studying media industries have begun to contest.[7]

As a result, the popularity of memoir, or at least the high visibility of some of its texts, is largely unexplained except as the result of unhealthy obsessions by a vaguely described "mass" of common people. Those that defend the genre do so by focusing on aspects of its rhetoric, and not on its production or its readership. For those that criticize it, more energy has been spent on dismissing this genre than discovering what the proliferation of books might have to say about American life and culture in the twenty-first century, a pattern that Ben Yagoda says was also part of what he calls the first memoir boom at the end of the eighteenth century in Europe (2009, 66).

MESSING UP THE MEMOIR BOOM: THEORIZING GENRE

I want to stress at this point that both positions on the memoir boom do have merit. The rise in popularity of the memoir as a way for private persons to explain, via an extraordinary experience, something in a public way does seem to describe a new use for an older genre. Memoir has long been part of the way that non-professional writers have created stories for a literary marketplace. The fact that other people seem eager to read many of these stories shows that, as Larson says, something has happened in the American reading publics to make reading these stories attractive, and even urgent. The critique of the memoir boom has merit too, because it focuses on the activities within capitalism that work to turn identity into products to be consumed, and it reads these activities as inauthentic or unworthy of identity itself. But at this point we encounter what Stuart Hall in the wider context of cultural studies has called "that dialectic—containment/resistance" (1981, 228). It is difficult to know at which point a form like memoir becomes entirely captive to market forces, or when it escapes containment and is put to previously unheard-of uses. The result often has been that audiences are either assumed to be producers of meaning with full autonomy, or consumers of meaning with no agency. Like other consumers of low-cultural forms, the readers of memoir sometimes are assumed to be unthinking dupes of the culture industry.

If contemporary memoir cannot be meaningfully distinguished as an emerging rhetorical form or as the sign of the decline of literature, what can be said about it? Before I discuss how we can rethink memoir, it is necessary to take a step back and mess up the terrain a bit by thinking about the conditions by which it appears. In doing this, I am responding to Gillian Whitlock's call to materialize the conditions of production for memoir so that we can see the politics at work in its consumption: "The questions here are simple: Who is getting to speak autobiographically, how and why? To what effect? What becomes a bestseller, and what is remaindered or republished? How do these elicit our attention? What kinds of engagement come into play? How do these appeal to readers, and what kind of consumers are we asked to become?" (2007, 14). The questions may seem simple, but the answers quickly become complex because of the conditions of appearance for any text. One of these conditions is something that is not usually thought to be very messy or complex, although as we shall see, it certainly is. That condition concerns the work of genre. Genre is a powerful organizing set of principles, preconceptions, and practices that without calling attention to itself, drives much of the way memoir is produced, consumed, and received. Understanding the rise in popularity of memoir could benefit from using genre as a heuristic—rather than history, or nation, or gender. Wai Chee Dimock recently made a passionate case for thinking about genre in literary studies just this way, if only because genre is so often caricatured as nothing more than a taxonomic system for thinking about things. There is a long history of antipathy to genre, partly because it has come to represent a constraint on "free" representation. As Dimock points out, theorists as different from each other as Benedetto Croce, Maurice Blanchot, and Jacques Derrida have all said much the same thing about it: genre is a limit artificially placed on aesthetics (for Croce), literature (for Blanchot) or for Derrida, writing (2007, 1377–78). This picture of genre positions it as the grim opponent of creativity and artistic expression. Genre appears most often in the humanities as a system that must be resisted because it is a system: it appears solely under the sign of resistance as the law, the Father's "No," of psychoanalysis, the lie from which any right-thinking liberal intellectual must extricate him or herself. It is common for literature scholars who want to study personal non-fiction to begin by claiming that the example or author to be analyzed "hybridizes" a genre, or breaks generic boundaries, or the work itself is transgressive generically.

Why is genre commonly thought about like this by many scholars? John Frow observes that "perhaps the major reason for this is the continuing prevalence of a neoclassical understanding of genre as prescriptive taxonomy and as a constraint on textual energy and thus the shaping of accounts of genre in terms of the Romantic reaction to that model" (2007, 1627), a reaction that even Derrida had when he portrayed genre as a law or limit that sets the conditions for its own impossibility. Even after the interdisciplinary work on genre by scholars like Mikhail Bakhtin, the study of literature tended to see it—but not other modes of classification such as nation or historical period—as inherently limiting without thinking about the work that genre does.[8] The most common way that genre appears in literary studies—among other disciplines in the humanities—is in its erasure or when it is surmounted, as when authors are said to be making new genres, breaking the boundaries of a genre or mixing genres. This is also, in some critiques, the mark of literary quality because the boundaries of genre have somehow been transgressed or manipulated. The classic understanding of genre as taxonomic and a matter of "pure" classification, particularly in literary studies, has been challenged by theorists in the fields of rhetoric and composition, but this understanding of the dynamic nature of genre has yet to become part of other areas of textual study.[9]

But genre's unpopularity in the humanities in particular also occurs because the notion of genre raises the spectre of the "market," that other enemy of creativity, with its emptying-out of content in favour of pre-digested ways of knowing. What is "genre" fiction, after all? It is mass-marketed novels like mysteries or thrillers, not literature. What are generic drugs and generic foods? They are copies of the "real things" which are cheaper because there are no brand names attached to them. When something is generic, it is worth less. And when the subject is cultural production, it is often assumed to be worthless as well. For example, most scholars who examine genre fiction connect it to the history of the paperback novel, which is how genre fiction such as romances, horror, Westerns, SF, thrillers, and mysteries were first produced. As a result, these scholars have had to contend with lingering opinions about genre fiction that are based on its history as a lowbrow form for ordinary people, not for elites or the avant-garde. This sentiment is best expressed in the work of Q.D. Leavis, who concluded in her pioneering study of British popular novels and reading in the 1930s, *Fiction and the Reading Public,* that the general public reads books, but does not know how (and perhaps has no desire) to read classics of literature as a critic would. Leavis sees this as a misfortune. "The reading habit," she opines, "is now often a form of the drug habit" for poor people because they buy or borrow "greasy" thrillers from run-down shops in side streets for pennies a volume whenever they want to read (1932, 7). Here we see clearly that "bad" books and "bad" reading are to be associated with cheapness and the values of the market, that the urban poor do not understand literature, and—most tantalizingly—that the wrong people reading the wrong things in the wrong way are to be regarded with suspicion and even as a kind of social threat.

Such a view of the nastiness of paperback novel reading and its negative association with the masses might seem to be dated, but as Christopher Pawling points out in *Popular Fiction and Social Change,* Leavis' elitist ideas were widely shared, and they endured in literary studies in the antipathy to genre fiction itself for decades after she first published them (1984, 17). Genre fiction was produced in paperback form at first and so the cheapness of the material production of the writing became associated with generic content. Therefore, literature was assumed to be different from genre fiction because in its paperback form, genre fiction was associated with commercial success and lowbrow readers. That is how genre fiction became synonymous with simplistic, formulaic, or just plain bad writing for the masses. Literary writing was assumed to be more complex or interesting than the writing that disgusted Leavis. The endowment of literature with what Walter Benjamin would have called the "aura" of uniqueness and authenticity given to art objects could not be given to most genre fiction, since much of its appeal comes from the repetitive nature of its plots, characterization, images, and themes, as was the case for mainstream films when Benjamin was thinking about them (1973, 215). Moreover, the traditional technique of literary study is close-reading (a method developed in part by Q.D. Leavis herself). Close-reading was designed to create an aesthetic appreciation of literary works as "well-wrought urns" that could be analyzed for their beauty, complexity, originality, and profundity. Like films that, as Walter Benjamin pointed out, were capable of being repeated and so lost the "aura" of art objects (1973, 221), so genre fiction's repetitious features did not lend themselves to an aesthetic analysis and its assumptions about what literature is supposed to be. Other scholars have defended genre fiction and argued for studying its production within an industry (Hawkins 1990, Karr 2000). Another way to deal with genre fiction differently from classic literature is to study its readership rather than its production. Janice Radway's pioneering work in *Reading the Romance* argued for a change in research methods away from a focus on the texts to a focus on the readership of genre fiction (1984). Other studies in the genres of Science Fiction and Horror have focused on fans, linking the effects of books on readers to fandom in other kinds of media (Williamson 2005; Hellekson and Busse 2006).

Genre fiction is now a legitimate area of study for many scholars, particularly those who are interested in readership and in media industries, including the publishing industry. But the study of non-fiction has not yet followed this path. It is not as if there were no important non-fiction books published: the editors of volume 5 of *A History of the Book in America* say that there have been plenty of bestselling memoirs and biographies about celebrities, non-fiction bestsellers like Rachel Carson's *Silent Spring*, the Kinsey Reports, and studies of social life like *The Lonely Crowd* and *The Organization Man* that were popular and even contributed to debates about public issues (Nord, Rubin, and Schudson 2009, 4–5). Other important non-fiction titles included a self-help book of 1972, *I'm OK—You're OK* that sold very well in paperback, and *All the President's Men*, which Thomas Whiteside says was notable for earning a one-million-dollar advance for its paperback edition even before the hardcover book was published (1981, 19). In *Expanding the American Mind*, book history scholar Beth Luey describes how for decades non-fiction was in fact an important means of popularizing ideas for mass audiences, and how the organization of public libraries in the United States reflects the long fight librarians had against what they saw as fiction's lack of seriousness and educational value (2010, 1–9).

And yet, it is still possible to imagine the study of American writing without thinking about genre very much, and without discussing non-fiction at all. The reason why non-fiction for mass markets has not been studied very much has to do with what I call its triple-threat status. First, it is popular, which means that is not literary. Second, due in part to the desire of American librarians to classify it to elevate its importance, it is diverse: non-fiction includes memoir, biography, self-help, popular history, true crime, cookbooks, gardening guides, and travel narratives, to name a few of its sub-genres, but only novels and short stories are referred to as fiction (Luey 2010). An additional problem connected to the ideological nature of these categories is that they exist in English but not in other languages.[10] Third, like its cousin genre fiction, it would require an awareness of the possibilities of reading for genre before mass-marketed non-fiction could be taken seriously.

For a long time, even scholars of autobiography and life writing did not think about non-fiction in general, or memoirs specifically, because of the perceived problems with thinking about popular and generic works. Auto-biography—and not the material manifestations of non-fiction genres like memoir, biography, essay, letter-writing, or diary—became the dominant non-fiction genre to receive critical attention. Scholars of literature of the 1960s and 1970s worked to make it a genre that could be as literary as the novel itself where the protagonist, like the hero of a novel, was thought to be successful because the writing showed the imprint of his (and rarely, her) personality. The response of many of these early critics of autobiography was to treat autobiography as a genre with rhetorical properties that had to be defined, followed by attempts to create a literary canon and poetics for autobiography that would assure it would have the status of the novel. Like canon-building for literature, the canon included very few popular or generic works. The attempts to build autobiography studies and the cri-tiques of this practice that followed are well documented (Marcus 1994, Rak 2005, Smith and Watson 2010). But the outcome created a major problem that scholars of life writing, life narrative, or autobiography struggle with today: the move to think of autobiography as a genre led to a move to make definitions of it taxonomic, epitomized by the scholarly take-up of Philippe Lejeune's creation of the autobiographical pact. In his original formulation, Lejeune described the pact as an informal "deal" that a potential reader of a text makes with the author. If the protagonist of the text, the proper name of the author on the flyleaf and the existence of a real person in the world match, then the work is autobiography. If any of these elements do not match, the work is fictional (1989a, 44). Lejeune even created a chart to show how deployment of the pronouns I/You/He produces a generic effect. Biography, classic autobiography, or witness narrative, for example, appear when a specific relationship between the pronoun identifying the protago-nist and the identity of the writer is detected (1989a).

The result was that the genre of autobiography was seen to rest upon its truth claims and the correspondence between text and world. This truth-telling quality made it fundamentally different from fiction, although many critics such as the New Model Theorists of the 1970s argued that there were rhetorical differences as well (Rak 2005). Lejeune's early version of the pact was critiqued by many who felt that it was too confining, and he him-self revised parts of it (Lejeune 1983). But the problem of genre remained. Lejeune had created a "test" for genre, and therefore had created a homol-ogy between rhetoric and type that even he has admitted that he did not intend. Autobiography theorists either responded by accepting what Lejeune said, or rebelling against it and not dealing with issues of genre at all. Paul de Man famously argued against Lejeune in "Autobiography as De-Facement" on this basis. De Man concluded that it was impossible to even think about autobiography as a genre because any work of life writing is *prosopopoeic*, an address from the dead that highlights the impossibility of representing the real world in a text. He dismissed autobiography as a "slightly disreputable and self-indulgent" genre and hardly a decent genre at all, and then characterized autobiography as an act of disfigurement, created by tropes, perpetuated by our own misguided desire for verisimilitude in language. Any attempt to fix it generically, he says, cannot work because autobiography is "a figure of reading or of understanding that occurs, to some degree, in all texts" (1979, 921). Here, autobiography is dismissed out of hand as an impossibility, and the *genre* of autobiography disappears, to be replaced by the act of reading across any text.

Paul de Man's critique of autobiography joins many other critiques of genre in its suspicion of typology. He pictures autobiography thought through genre as instrumentalist and formal, the product of institutions at best and the tool of the market at worst. Questions about it are, as Paul de Man says with some irritation, "pointless and unanswerable" (1979, 919). To some extent, de Man's warning about autobiography does make the genre seem to be nothing but typological. As John Frow has warned, this use of genre turns it into a mere description of objects, which results in an endless and ultimately meaningless proliferation of types (2007, 1627–29). In autobiography studies, Sidonie Smith and Julia Watson's second edition of *Reading Autobiography: A Guide for Interpreting Life Narratives* performs this operation in its listing of more than sixty "genres" of life narrative, eight more genres than in the first edition (2010, 4). Smith and Watson are describing the tendency of many critics to coin new terms when "autobiography" as a genre appeared to be too confining or not descriptive enough. Other critics, including me, have attempted to deal with this problem by dispensing with thinking about genre as systemic at all and arguing that autobiography is a discourse or activity that surfaces within many forms or different types of media.[11]

There is obvious merit to thinking about memoir or autobiography as discursive and not generic if we are thinking about how this discourse appears in different forms, for example, how autobiographical or biographical discourse appears in new media or on television. But when we are looking at popular material, it makes little sense to try to ignore the work of genre as it is commonly understood. First of all, there are genres in new media too. Second, there are genres in use in popular culture—like memoir, diary, or biography—that are widely recognized by many people, because genre as an organizing principle is used every day as people go about their lives (Devitt 2004). Is the solution to make more and more terms to try to describe what we are seeing, or should we give up and dismiss genre out of hand? Neither is advisable, especially when we think about how genres circulate, how they are produced within cultural industries, and how they are received and commonly understood. In the case of memoir, it makes more sense to understand what the publishing industry, the bookselling industry, and the public think that memoir means than to coin little-used terms for the types of content that appear in its examples. The former method can expand our understanding of genre so that it can be understood as a dynamic force. The latter risks reifying various works as types. Originally, "genre" merely signified the organization of information into types or kinds. This led to an understanding of any genre as static or as a closed system, with classification as its method (Devitt 2004, 6–7). If genre is assumed to be "merely" descriptive and taxonomic of a text, one of the problems is that taxonomies will proliferate endlessly, and there will always be cases where a work "slips through" the autobiographical pact or another attempt to fix a genre rhetorically. Derrida's warning that genre sets a limit that examples automatically will transgress explains why the problem of limit cases—and how to understand them—is a perennial challenge to autobiography theorists. But it does not have to be this way when we think about what memoir is and what it does.

One way to do this is to return to the much-maligned autobiographical pact and think about its description of what a reader does with a text. Lejeune pictured the pact as a way for a reader to look at any text and decide how it might be read, or even if it should be read at all. The pact is *not* about experts who decide what the content of the writing says, but is about what readers make of paratextual elements and written discourse *before* a text is read. Lejeune does not say where the reader is when this is going on; for instance, it is not clear if the reader is in a store or a library when this operation happens, but he evokes the image of the autobiography as a *product* and the reader as a potential shopper for that product in his discussion of paratext: "In printed texts, the whole utterance is assumed by a person whose *name* is customarily placed on the cover of the book, and on the fly-leaf, above or below the title ... an author is not just a person, he is a person who writes and publishes. With one foot in the text, and one outside, he is the point of contact between the two" (Lejeune 1975 11; trans. Marcus 1994, 252 [italics Lejeune's]). Lejeune emphasizes that autobiography is a manufactured product in the form of a physical book with a flyleaf and a cover. And the author is not just a writer, but also a producer who makes that object. The potential reader then evaluates the book paratextually—in that she or he has to think about the author's name and the *situation* of the book in the world as well as the content within the book, because that information helps the reader to understand what kind of book this is. The material situating of the autobiographical pact is not just a test for typological purposes. It provides an active role for the potential reader, and it materializes the content of the autobiography as the work of a producer, not just an author. It highlights that the book has an industrial existence as a commodity. And the autobiographical pact highlights that it matters how this book has been manufactured and more specifically, what *kind* of book it is. The reader has the power to decide how to read the book. Genre appears here as the materialization of that decision to read. The eventual decision is also the product of a negotiation between the reader and the book, the author and the book, and even the rhetoric of the book. Although Lejeune did not say this, it is possible to deduce that not only does the name of the author and protagonist matter, but also it must matter what is said about its genre, and even where in a bookstore or library it is categorized. As Oprah Winfrey and many other commentators about memoirs have said in the wake of the controversy about whether James Frey's memoir was truthful, any difficulty with genre will inevitably produce disagreement and renegotiation about what a paratext means. In "The Autobiography of Those Who Do Not Write," Lejeune talked about this potential problem, and how readers, as consumers, balance the enjoyment of a text with its truth claims: "What the public consumes is the personal form of a discourse assumed by a real person, responsible for his writing as he is for his life. We consume the full-fledged 'subject,' which we want to believe is true ... the public finds itself in an ambiguous situation, a situation of bad faith, always ready both to suspect the authenticity of a text and to yell 'scandal' ... and at the same time always prepared to lend itself to the games of illusion and not see through the transparent veils that cover the production of the text, the essential being to enjoy it" (Lejeune 1989b, 194).

Lejeune's autobiographical pact can be seen as a site for the production and consumption of genre as a way to read, a site that is open to negotiation and reproduction, since industrial production of genre (here symbolized by the person of the writer) can conflict with consumption (here, the readers who might yell scandal or who might not). In this sense, Lejeune's pact is much like the way that genre is discussed in other areas of cultural production, most notably film and television, as a way for viewers to interpret what they are seeing. Nick Lacey, for example, has pointed out that in media studies, genre "is of little use critically but of great use in 'common sense' terms, which is how mass audience uses the concept" (2000, 212). Jason Mittell in his study of genre and television has argued that genre names the way in which groups understand the medium, not aspects of the medium itself: "instead of asking what a genre means (the typical interpretive question), we need to ask what a genre means *for specific groups in a particular cultural instance*" (2004, 5; italics Mittell's). John Frow has discussed the consumer use of genre as "folk classification, an unsystematically systematic taxonomy which feels intuitive and yet covers most of the difficult and ambiguous cases they are likely to encounter" (2006, 12–13). Therefore, genre is something that helps people to interpret what a cultural product is and how to understand it. It has this quality because in the words of the rhetorical theorist Janet Giltrow, genre provides "background knowledge" about any text, object, or event that forms a type of agreement between the producer or receiver of utterances that is mutual and unsaid (1994, 155). In doing this, genres produce a type of grammar that does far more than merely organize objects. It provides a way to say what constitutes a "legitimate" or recognizable object in a system, and what does not.

But here we come to the other way that genre structures an encounter with a cultural text or product. Because it provides background knowledge, genre also has the potential to set the terms for what can be known. This makes genre one of Pierre Bourdieu's "structuring structures" in a system that creates knowledge as it organizes it (2000, 33–35). Carolyn Miller's work on genre as social action takes this further and claims that genres actually *produce* social knowledge and have material effects because genre provides the terms of recognition for an event, an object, or a text. They exhibit "exigence," which is a "form of social knowledge—a mutual construing of objects, events, interests and purposes that not only links them but makes them what they are" (Miller 1994, 30). In other words, it makes sense to think about genre both as what Tzvetan Todorov famously called "the horizon of expectation" (1975, 18–19), which he saw as the ability of genres to organize knowledge so that it is recognizable, *and* as an industrial set of practices that work to create the horizon. Jason Mittell's approach to the analysis of genre in television acknowledges this dual power for genre, and calls for a movement away from thinking of it typologically for this reason:

"We need to look beyond the text as the locus for a genre, locating genres within the complex interrelations between texts, industries, audiences and historical contexts. Genres transect the boundaries between text and context, with production, distribution, promotion, exhibition, criticism, and reception practices all working to categorize media texts into genres" (2004, 10). Genre, therefore, is central to understanding any cultural industry, because genres work across and through all aspects of the production process, and they contain the terms of recognition for audiences too. According to John Frow, genre is clearly an industrial practice that creates these terms of recognition and negotiation:

> Genre is not just a matter of codes and conventions, but ... it also calls into play systems of use, durable social institutions, and the organisation of physical space. At another level, classification is an industrial matter. It is enacted in publishers' catalogues and booksellers' classifications, in the allocation of time-slots for television shows and in television guides, in the guidelines and deliberations of arts organisations, and in the discourses of marketing and publicity, together with the whole apparatus of reviewing and listing and recommending, that drive so much of film production. The consumers of books, recorded music, television and film are ongoingly schooled, and actively school themselves, in the fine-grained details of genre. (2006, 12–13)

Genres name the intersecting and conflicting means of interpreting not only the content of a product, but the meaning of its production and the intent of its circulation. That is why genres matter, even though they often go unremarked. Their ubiquity disguises their influence because "genre pervades human lives ... people recognize genres, thought not usually the power of genres" (Devitt 2004, 1). As Foucault said in his description of the power/knowledge nexus, an episteme is the name for relations of power that establish themselves as the basis for the producing, accumulating, circulating, and functioning of any discourse (1994, 63–70). Genre is one of these epistemic relations, and it works in the background of all kinds of utterances and acts, constructing, constricting, and allowing what can be thought together.

These two ways to understand genre may dovetail at times. At other times, for example during the Frey controversy, understandings of what genre is and what its cultural force means may conflict. As Nancy K. Miller writes, the problem of genre could be "an old problem with new names and new stakes" (2007, 539) because readers still expect to see certain generic rules in place when they read a memoir, and during the Frey controversy, what readers thought they were reading conflicted with what Frey's publisher thought it was producing. Despite the attempts by writers to reshape the autobiographical project and create hybrid genres or works that defy generic classification, Miller concludes that "the distinction between forms matters to readers" (2007, 541). Therefore, it makes sense to determine not whether a text or object is an example of a genre or whether new neologisms should be coined to describe a rhetorical shift, but to investigate what the social meaning of a genre such as memoir is. If we can see what memoir as a genre means to the publishing industries and bookselling industries that sell them, for the readers who search for them, acquire them, and read them, and the cultural authorities who reflect on them, then it will be possible to understand what memoir is, not in terms of its rhetoric, but in terms of its rhetorical impact. In the case of memoir, that impact is felt publicly.

THE WORK OF GENRE

How, then, does genre go to work? Genre provides the conditions for understanding in everyday life because its operations do not work by a recognition of difference rather in the recognition of elements that are similar to ones that have appeared before. The temporality of these elements generates similar, but not the same, relations. Genres therefore admit repetition as a necessary part of a system (as when someone reads the latest novel in the *Twilight* series and expects the same characters to appear, or when someone buys a tomato each week at a market and expects to get a similar kind of fruit each time), but the operation of time in a system means that no repetition ever means a return of the same (the plot of the latest instalment has similar elements, but there are new developments; the tomato tastes like other tomatoes but it is not exactly the same). Much like Judith Butler's idea of gender performativity as a repetition *with a difference* where gender becomes the effect of repetition (2004, 127–28), generic repetition promises the repetition of an element, or an event, in a recognizable way that often goes unremarked. But, as in the case of gender norms, the repetition of elements is not self-identical, and more repetition is necessary as the performance generates excess meaning that cannot be contained. This argument differs from Butler's in *Gender Trouble*. Butler says that there is something in sexuality that cannot be fully performed, or cannot at least be identified with the performance. That "something" is held back or held in remainder because "psychic mimesis" is thought to have split the subject into being and having as points of difference within the self, a split that she argues is fundamentally unstable. The attempt to repeat gender norms is therefore an attempt to make that distinction between "being" and "having" the object of desire stay discrete and normalized. My argument is based on the idea of desire for the same as something that, due to the presence of time, cannot ever be fulfilled, but the recognition of what is similar creates a desire for what was pleasurable in the past. The pleasure here lies in the recognition of the elements that gave pleasure before and the desire to revisit that experience. The excess creates the need for more repetition, more recognition, and the generation of more meanings that are not identical to what has gone before, but can be *identified*. They are almost, but not quite, the same.

If we think of genre as the non-identical repetition of familiar elements, it is possible to understand why, unlike literature with its features of uniqueness, generic writing is popular with many people. If literature generally works on the principle of difference—a great work of literature must be different from others or the works of an author are similar, but are different in kind and quality from what other authors write—then generic writing works because the recognition of repetition is pleasurable. The act of *recognition itself* creates a measure of participation for the reader who finds similar elements: he or she knows what she recognizes and participates in the act. The work of Philippe Lejeune on the idea of the autobiographical pact can shed light here about the horizon of expectation and the desire for the same, because the reader has an active role as a producer of genre. As we have seen, it is the reader who "signs" the pact, not the author. The reader has work to do. Here, Lejeune's picture of the reader as the guarantor of meaning for any autobiographical text fits with the idea that readers take an active pleasure in their discovery of correspondences, in the discovery *they* get to experience as the shock of the familiar, not the new. The role for readers as the producer of genre and not just as a consumer of it helps to maintain the pleasure of repetition with a difference. It is an instance, in that sense, of performativity where genre, not gender, is the effect of repetition.

As we have seen in some critiques of the memoir boom, the popularity of memoir as a genre cannot be accounted for by its originality. Many examples of the genre repeat themselves, because that is what generic texts are supposed to do. Therefore, it is hard to know why a group of readers, viewers, or consumers becomes attached to a popular genre in the first place. Why would this recognition be so pleasurable for some and inconceivable for others? How is it that people in the United States engage so readily with the genre of memoir as a genre of recognition? What pulls them into telling these kinds of life stories and to consuming so many of them? One way to deal with this problem, as Smith and Watson have done, is to think of auto-biography as a discursive "coaxing." This approach focuses on the cultural text or product as a speech act that calls narratives of selfhood into being as a type of hailing. Smith and Watson understand coaxing as an expectation circulated in a culture to produce a life story as an act. Institutions such as the family, the law court, the educational system and the church all coax life stories from individuals, who produce them in order to exchange informa-tion, get certain rewards from the institution, or get recognition. Smith and Watson also see coaxing as a type of expectation for life stories generated in the mass media and by online communities. Coaxing can be intimate, as in a family gathering, or coercive, as in a court of law (2010, 64–71). It calls subjects into narrative. In this way, coaxing resembles Althusser's idea of interpellation, the way in which a subject is called into ideology and being by being hailed by ideology, into ideology (1990).

But, as Butler has pointed out, it is hard to know how the process of hail-ing is initiated. How does a subject "recognize" him or herself and respond if there is no subject "there" before the hailing process (1999, 337)? In a simi-lar way, coaxing cannot fully explain how someone is hailed into a life story. For one thing, interpellation by an institution could be seen as the con-struction of a certain type of story about identity that produces the identity as a phantom, what Liz Stanley has called an audit self, a construction of identity that exists just for the institution. Individuals are coerced to give false selves to an institution such as the court, the welfare system, or the prison in order not only to survive those systems but also to protect who they really are (2000, 50). This kind of "coaxing" contains strong elements of coercion and Foucauldian requirements for confession that cannot exist in the same way in other kinds of less coercive speech acts, such as those produced in the family or the workplace as Smith and Watson describe them. It is hard to know what is "coaxed," whether it is an idea of liberal sub-jectivity, the imperative to communicate, or the idea of private revelation.

Coaxing might describe different kinds of acts of self-reporting in a cul-ture, but it is less useful as an idea when the relations between mass media and audiences are considered, since audiences often do not interpret mes-sages in the way that they are sent. Coaxing emphasizes what a text or a speaker "does" to someone in the act of communication, and so agency appears to lie with the "coaxer." But do genres really have this capability? Genres themselves do not have agency, and they are not subjects. They are not, as Paul Cobley has said, even things (2001). They mark the ground rules for many kinds of interactions, and they produce the conditions for objects. But like grammar, they cannot invite anyone to speak or write. What, then, does this?

Here we can return to memoir as an example of what does turn people to producing and consuming a specific genre. Since the eighteenth century and its memoir boom, commentators have discussed the attraction of memoir in popular culture as a manifestation of base appetite, like hunger, to which it is often compared. Like hunger, a desire to understand the lives of others is often explained as the desire to consume the other because there is some lack in the self. Nancy K. Miller says this when she observes that even when we read about the lives of people different from ourselves, "they give you just what your own unrecorded history lacks ... a narrative through which to make sense of your past" (2002, 12). This is an interpretation of reading through the private sphere as one self "supplies" a lack felt by another. But memoir is also a public form where private lives circulate. It is no accident that the development of biography and memoir in the eighteenth century in Europe and the United States coincided with the development of modern democracy, capitalism, and the idea that *any* individuals could be private people who act on a public stage. As Charles Ponce de Leon points out in his history of modern celebrity, biography and memoir were important technologies of identity as the idea of celebrity—that is, the idea of fame without inherited titles or wealth—became achievable for anyone. The published memoirs of Parisian courtesans, the autobiographical writing of Benjamin Franklin, and James Boswell's development of modern biography were all connected to this democratic idea of celebrity, that anyone can be extraordinary. Through life writing, private lives could cross a divide and *become public* in a new, media-controlled public sphere:

> Those aspiring to fame, moreover, could "author" themselves, creating public personas that rejected aristocratic models of achievement in favor of an emerging democratic model that would steadily evolve in tandem with changes in values.... this self-consciousness was not confined to dress, demeanor, and choice of public association. It also affected how people presented and came to understand their life stories. By locating their origins and measuring the distance they had traversed since birth and childhood, the life stories that people told about themselves and sometimes published were deeply implicated in their quests for social mobility and vital to establishing a reputation in the public sphere. (2002, 19)

Celebrity became one of the most important ways that individuals not only understood themselves, but understood others to be *like* themselves. The discourse of celebrity that developed in the United States is dependent on this democratic logic, although it also became connected to the idea of "glamour" and the idea that celebrities are not like other people until too much is revealed about them (Gamson 2001, 159–63). The economy of exchange between public and private, focused on the figure of the celebrity, means that celebrities can engender fascination and disgust at the same time (Dyer 2004, 10–13).

The ceaseless movement of this economy for stars undoubtedly contributes to the interest in their life stories. But it is also true that the stories of ordinary people—and these are the focus of much of the critical vitriol about the memoir boom—retains this belief in the democracy of celebrity. As Jean-Jacques Rousseau believed, the development of the private individual as a participant in public life was one of the bases for the Social Contract, in which each person is asked to be private, but gives some rights via the state to the whole society (1975). Rousseau's idea was that a person could remain private but must give away a piece of himself or herself to the public. As Celeste Langan points out in her study of Rousseau, this kind of thinking connected the development of subjectivity in liberalism to the development of the idea of citizenship: "*both* the subject *and* the citizen owe their preeminence as essential units of thought in the regime of liberalism to a metaphorical logic by which one derives its justification from the other" (1995, 31; italics Langan's). The connection between subjectivity, citizenship, and celebrity has become a potent combination, where celebrity can stand in for democracy (anyone can become famous and famous people are ordinary people), but where it is possible for people to become famous because of the stories they tell about themselves. Both types of fame can have political consequences, especially in the United States.

In the United States, it is widely believed that anyone can tell a story of his or her life and connect the story to American ideals. In a speech for the Democratic National Convention in 2004 that electrified the audience, Barack Obama told his life story briefly and then said "I stand here knowing that my story is part of the larger American story" (Obama n.p.). This statement reduced many people in the audience to tears. This is the power of the connection for Americans between the representivity of democracy and the representivity of the self that Leigh Gilmore identifies as the heart of American autobiography, because in autobiography it is possible to "represent" the self and have it stand in for the selves of others (2001, 18). In the United

States, a country that is built on the ideal of democracy and the practice of political representation, memoir becomes one of the technologies for the private self that can be shared. In that sense, the attraction of memoir must lie in both things: it provides the story of others in a way that creates a private self alongside the self of another, and it is the means of *mobility* from the private to the public. In memoir, lives *go public* as they *become public*. It becomes a way for readers to think publicly, but from the private sphere. It creates the possibility of social movement through personal movement. In this sense, memoir as a genre has the potential to create social action. Thomas Larson thinks that memoir has this power as a counter-discourse because it is able to bring private selves and public stories together and critique false public discourse. For Larson, memoir is part of that construction of a counter-discourse of public distrust: "[Memoir] writers and some commentators are telling us to distrust what's telegenically spoken, to recognize that its ring of 'truthiness' and other tricks of the authoritarian dissembler are a kind of devil's bargain. Perhaps memoir's genius is this: to use its intimate-sounding voice, so culturally recognizable already, to cast doubt on the easy believability of that voice. In the memoir itself, this tension is embodied by a willingness to speak of difficult matters and to question what's being spoken" (Larson 2007, 188). That, I would argue, connects the production of memoir to the idea of citizenship as a lived identity, and not as a relationship an individual has with the state. Any study of memoir should take into account its unique quality of connection between private and public worlds. In the conclusion to this book, I take up this particular dimension of memoir as a form of what Lauren Berlant and others have called the affective domain of citizenship, or the feeling that someone experiences through sets of connections to a larger entity, such as a community or a nation. Memoir makes many people *feel* connected, and it connects individual feelings to group ideas. Therefore, citizenship—and not narcissism—should be a key way to understand the popularity of memoirs with many American readers at the present time.

ABOUT METHOD—WHAT THIS BOOK DOES

When I began the research that led to this book, I was faced with several methodological problems. It was hard to know what "popular" memoir is exactly or how to discuss it in general terms. I could have listed, as Ben Yagoda did, as many well-known texts as I could or choose ones I liked, but I thought that this would not provide an accurate picture of what is produced, sold, and read that is mass-produced. I wanted to move beyond what I might think is important and determine what producers and readers think about memoir, as much as I could. But how to choose the texts? As many commentators point out, there are thousands of memoirs in print and more are being made all the time. My other problem concerned genre. Instead of creating a typology of certain kinds of books, I wanted to see how genre works as part of the cycle of book production. Therefore I wanted to understand what the largest publishers, who produce the most books for mass readerships in the United States, think that memoir is, and how booksellers think about genre—and especially memoir—in their work lives as they try to sell books. I was interested too in how ideas about genre flow—or do not flow—between publishers and sellers in the industry. The result would be a more dynamic set of ideas about genre, memoir, and production, and a better picture of the gap between what is produced and how a certain product is taken up and becomes part of the memoir boom.

I decided to create a random sample of the books labelled "memoir," "biography," and "autobiography" by two of the five largest English-language publishers in the world at the time when I started the project: HarperCollins and Random House. I limited my sample size still further by studying a sample of the books produced by these publishers in a single year. I chose the year 2003 at random, and I constructed a database of the 168 titles by these publishers that appeared in that year. The initial list showed me which books stayed in print and which books went out of print after six to twelve weeks—the typical shelf life of most books published in a single year (Thompson 2010). With the help of research assistants, I created a random sample of these texts for a total of sixty-five and had the assistants read them. I designed another database with reading categories so that I could compare these texts to each other and see what elements were unique and marked them as "limit texts" as Leigh Gilmore uses that term (2001). The categories included formalist descriptions such as plot, narrator, tone, the life story or background of the narrator, and the opening/closing scenes. I also had assistants record the gender, racial identification, age, and class of the writers and protagonists, and I asked for information about paratextual elements such as whether the protagonist was famous or unknown, the nature of the back matter printed on the copies, whether the book was a hardcover or paperback, and the cover design. I ran queries about these elements so that I could have hard data about what memoirs for mass markets looked like, how many books called "memoir" (as opposed to "autobiography") were made that year, and how the better-known books in my sample differed from the rest. My close-readings of the texts from the database aim to produce a fuller picture of what autobiography for mass audiences is like and how, especially in the charged political environment of 2003, the year—as it turned out—of the American invasion of Iraq, the memoir boom participated in and reflected changes in how Americans understood themselves as citizens of a public. Two of the books in the sample, Marjane's Satrapi's *Persepolis: The Story of a Childhood* and James Frey's *A Million Little Pieces*, also turned out to be central to public debates in 2003 and later about American attitudes to the Middle East and to the Bush administration's public presentation of the reasons for the war in Iraq, and so I analyzed them—and their reception in print media and on television—in some detail.

I studied memoirs, articles, periodicals, and books about the American publishing industry so that I could learn about that part of memoir production, but available materials about contemporary bookselling were relatively rare, and in the case of issues about genre, there was no material. To assist with this, I conducted interviews at eleven general-interest bookstores across Canada and compared what I learned there about genre with an interview with a manager of the only remaining bookselling big box chain, Chapters Indigo. The cost of doing interviews in a wide variety of regions meant that I could not visit American stores, but the structure of the industry and the nature of the Canadian book business in its dealings with large publishers are similar because, as store owners told me, Canadian bookselling mainly works as a branch plant of American distribution networks for trade and mass-market books. The existence of only one big-box chain in the country (Chapters and Indigo Books merged just as my interviewing began) also made the relationships between independent booksellers, small chains, and the advent of the big box store very clear, particularly since the creation of Chapters had created a vociferous reaction in the English-language Canadian bookselling community, a reaction that was well documented in the popular press. The result of this work is a picture of memoir as part of the cycle of production from publishing to bookselling, an examination of some of the products the industry makes, and an analysis of the ways in which some memoirs have circulated as part of a range of reading publics.

Finally, I turn to texts from my 2003 sample, some well known, some not, to see what they show us about the idea of public identity. To determine if it is correct that people read memoir not to discover themselves in a narcissistic way but to understand something about the other and a larger community, I read some examples from this period to see how memoir reflected and interpreted public events as well as details from private lives. I read paratexts about these books to see how the reception of certain memoirs during the memoir boom did in fact link larger political events closely to the unfolding of individual lives. In texts like *Hacker Cracker*, the story of a reformed computer hacker who survives the World Trade Center bombing or James Frey's *A Million Little Pieces*, it is possible to see how memoir's older function as the conduit between public events and private lives operates today, in the controversy about whether memoirs (and American presidents) should tell the whole truth, or whether the world of computer hacking can provide an unlikely instance of survival and success for one African-American child. I decide to read these public/private stories as stories about what Lauren Berlant calls affective citizenship. Contemporary scholarship about citizenship does much to explain why Americans avidly read the stories of others, and why controversies about these stories become so public.

LIMITS: WHAT THIS STUDY CANNOT DO

As scholars in the field of book history are well aware, there are limits to any study of book production. Relatively few studies of contemporary mainstream American publishing exist beyond memoirs by industry insiders and some studies based on statistical analysis and interviews in the industry. There are two major sources for statistical information about the American book market: Bookscan and the Annual Reports of the Book Industry Study Group, called BookStats. Unfortunately, these sources are not publically owned or funded, and the cost of accessing their data is prohibitive. For this reason, I rely on the work of major scholars in the field of publishing studies who have been able to use these statistics. I also rely on this work because, particularly in the United States, the statistical breakdown for general book sales does not often include separate categories for sales of memoirs or biographies. Non-fiction does not consist of a simple set of categories; rather, it is a diverse classification that includes everything from memoir to history. To complicate matters, biography is the LC classification (also used by Amazon.com) that also includes autobiography and memoir. The scholarly terms critics use, such as confession or testimony, have no equivalent in book industry categorizations. I analyze the politics of these kinds of rubrics in chapter three, but for the purposes of this study, it simply is not possible at this time to arrive at clear statistics that prove how popular memoir is compared to other classifications of books. The statistics that are accessible, however, do show some consistent trends in the production and consumption of memoir that show that the memoir boom is not in any danger of destroying the predominance of fiction in the book industry, and that the upswing in the production and sales of memoirs continued throughout the first decade of the twenty-first century. It is also not possible to determine in any simple way how publishers decide to publish more memoirs, because publishing companies do not make this information available to the public. What is possible is to trace the relationship between agent, publisher, and author in personal accounts of the industry, interviews of industry members by scholars, and when incidents such as the Frey scandal expose some of the complexities of these relationships. However, my more general discussion of the structure of the publishing industry does show how some industry practices have resulted in a change in attitude toward publishing categories, profitability, and the operations of what in the industry is called "the long tail" of a book's influence and profit. As other scholars of publishing have pointed out, the book business is not as organized as it might appear. Many decisions are still made based on a feeling that a book could be successful, as Nan Talese's support of James Frey's *A Million Little Pieces* clearly shows. In the publishing chapter, I work toward understanding the publishing culture that relies on these judgments so that it is possible to appreciate further how memoir has become more popular, more visible, and more "legitimate" in the marketplace. But additional work remains to be done on this subject, particularly as it pertains to publishing categories, rubrics, and the idea of genre that helps to inform them.

Finally, although this study begins with a single reader, my grandmother, this book is not about reading memoirs and it is not about how readers select certain memoirs to read. It focuses on the industry that creates products for readers like my grandmother. The developing area of reading studies in the United States, first pioneered by Janice Radway and Elizabeth Long, would no doubt put together an analysis that would include social history, interviews of readers, surveys of reader habits, and an examination of reader ephemera such as online book reviews and review sites. Such work could join the work of Nancy K. Miller, Helen Buss, and others who are interested in recording and analyzing their own responses to reading and writing memoir in what promises to be a rich area of enquiry. Such a rich study of memoir reading would be fascinating, but of necessity, it exceeds the scope of this book and its focus.

WHAT FOLLOWS

The first two chapters are about two aspects of print cultural production: the mainstream publishing industry in the United States and bookstores. In the first chapter I connect the impact of the memoir boom to developments in the publishing industry that changed the nature of what I call industrial demand for certain kinds of genres, including memoir. The environment of American publishing has undergone major change in the last three decades, going from a set of family-owned businesses based mainly in New York City to the era of buyouts from the 1980s to 2005 that created the large, multinational, and foreign-owned companies that we see today. Harper-Collins and Random House Ltd. are different examples of what the mergers of publishing produced. In many cases, publishers that bought out smaller houses maintained the identity of those publishing houses as "brands." Smaller publishers were not erased entirely and in some cases, their identity and even their backlists were preserved. This practice shows that fears of the decline of publishing—symbolized by the publication of mass-market non-fiction, or the hope that publishing would be vertically integrated with other media industries—did not occur as extensively as some industry insiders predicted. But the changes in profit-generation, including the impact of the paperback book revolution and the rise in importance of best-selling trade books did alter the types of writing that was published, particularly when bookselling chains began to drive changes in the business. To a large extent, the memoir boom has been maintained by these changes in industry practice.

The second chapter focuses on the other major node of book production: the bookstore. As in the case of publishing, the changes in the bookselling industry in North America since the 1980s have created upheaval in the industry, but not always in as apocalyptic a way as some commentators have imagined. The rise of independent bookstores in large cities can be traced directly to the fact that publishers did not exert control over distribution networks for books after the end of the nineteenth century. Almost since their appearance, these independent bookstores have been presented as constantly under threat from mass-market distribution systems, from the Book-of-the-Month Club to drugstores, department stores, mall chains, and big box chains such as Barnes & Noble. However, the picture of the threatened independent bookstores is not an accurate representation of the story of the American book market. As s Janice Radway, Laura J. Miller, John B. Thompson, and Ted Striphas—among others—have pointed out, the availability of books in large urban centres meant that there were large parts of the United States that did not have access to books. Alternate distribution systems for books appeared in order to service these areas. Additionally, bookstores were intimidating places for many Americans at first. Customers who either did not have access to independent stores in major centres or who did not feel welcome in the environment of the early twentieth-century independent bookstore turned to other places to purchase books. These customers found books in department stores, made use of mail-order services like the Book-of-the-Month Club, or bought paperback books that began to appear in drugstores or bus stations. By the 1970s, mall chains had begun to appear across the country, and smaller independent stores were stocking paperbacks. Working-class and middle-class Americans became book buyers, and the influence of older independent booksellers as purveyors of cultural value began to wane. The 1990s saw the introduction of big box stores, with their larger selection and buying power but also their use of elements of store culture found in the shops of independents. In interviews conducted with store managers and owners, I ask how these changes in the book industry have affected what stores do to sell books, how they relate to publishers, and how genre (and especially memoir and biography) figures in everyday work environments in the industry today. My findings about the enduring importance of store culture and the social role of the bookseller—an image that is important to independent sellers and chain managers alike—show that independents are sometimes able to survive and even thrive in the wake of big-box bookselling, and that their understanding of genre as a spatial concept contributes to the maintenance of store culture.

Chapter 3 looks at larger patterns my research shows in the production of memoir, and it examines lesser-known examples of memoir published by Random House and HarperCollins to see how those books negotiate and articulate the idea of private and public life in the first decade of the millennium. I begin with an analysis of the structure of Random House and HarperCollins in 2003, the year in which these memoirs were produced, and I analyze how "memoir" as a genre is articulated through their use of cover blurbs, reviews and endorsements, and categorizations meant for booksellers to use. With assistance from my data set and selections from memoirs about such disparate subjects as bartending, war, and computer hacking, it is possible to see how myths about the lives of memoir writers are articulated in specific ways in order to sell books. We can also see that some memoirs do attempt, as Thomas Larson had hoped, to provide thoughtful commentary about current events, and to work against corporate ways to understand the value of private lives and stories as they go public. In that sense, the authors invite Americans to respond to their lives in an intimate register, and also implicitly encourage Americans to read about their lives as citizens, even in texts that are not specifically about citizenship.

Chapter 4 is about two memoirs that have become well known: the English translation of part of Marjane Satrapi's graphic memoir, called in English *Persepolis: The Story of a Childhood*, and James Frey's memoir of his time in an addiction recovery centre, *A Million Little Pieces*. Both of these memoirs participate in the idea of an intimate public that came about as a response to the 2003 American invasion of Iraq. When Satrapi published *Persepolis*, she changed many of the paratextual elements in order to make the story more palatable for an American audience, and to appeal to the interest liberal Americans had in a historic "enemy" of the United States as the invasion of Iraq began. James Frey's *A Million Little Pieces* is often used as an example of the excesses of the memoir boom. The bestselling account about Frey's time in rehabilitation as he battled drug and alcohol addictions became synonymous with literary fraud when it was discovered that Frey had exaggerated or falsified some aspects of the narrative. It has been discussed with an equal amount of bemusement and contempt in the popular press, and is associated with the limits of Oprah Winfrey's philosophy of transformation when Oprah Winfrey berated him on national television and forced him to apologize for lying to the American public. But the circumstances that led to Frey's account being published as a memoir in 2003, and the reception of the book in 2005 when it was chosen as an Oprah's Book Club selection, are more complex than most journalists and other commentators have pointed out. *A Million Little Pieces* was originally intended to be a critique of the twelve-step addiction and recovery model, itself a powerful model for many life stories that are published in the United States and the way, arguably, that many Americans understand themselves as recovered addicts. But when Frey was accused of fraud, an unprecedented firestorm of criticism linked this book to a discussion of lying in public sphere and what the Bush administration was claiming about the existence of weapons of mass destruction. In this way, Frey's memoir came to symbolize the difficulties of truth-telling and the clash between different ways to understand the genre of memoir when stories become public and the public sphere seems to be composed of what could be untrue stories.

Finally, I consider what reading for citizenship reveals about the production of memoir in the twenty-first century. *Boom! Manufacturing Mem-*

oir for the Popular Market is an early attempt to bring approaches from media and cultural industrial production to a consideration of memoir and its impact on the way that Americans think about public events and think about themselves as citizens of a powerful imagined community. I have sought in this book to think more critically about the production of the memoir boom and to think more empirically about what its texts say about the construction of identity. In order to do this, I have not chosen the texts that for some, might encapsulate the excesses of the boom, and I have not examined its most recent productions. My limitations with respect to space and expertise mean that I could not provide a section about libraries and non-fiction, although there are many scholars who are beginning to develop an interest in this area. I do hope that I have provided a way to think about the way that texts made in the memoir boom are produced, how they circulate, and how they are received, so that others can analyze what it means to be and think as a citizen during the time of late capitalism. This desire to read memoir as an expression of belonging is articulated clearly by Nancy Pearl, who said in *Book Lust* (2003) and *More Book Lust* (2005) that reading is a positive expression of a desire for connection. As she says in the introduction to *Book Lust*, "because I am incurably interested in the lives of other people, both friends and strangers, I read to meet myriad folks and enter their lives—for me, a way of vanquishing the 'otherness' we all experience" (ix). In this sense, reading memoir about all kinds of lives is a way to create the conditions of belonging to others. Memoir-reading, in its openness to others, can potentially be an act of citizenship, although it is necessary too to understand the conditions that produce the products that engender this sense of belonging, and to evaluate what they mean. I end this introduction and begin this investigation with Gillian Whitlock's invitation to think of autobiography as a political and ethical act that is intimately connected to what it means, in the twenty-first century, to be a person among others. It is part of the reason why I think that my grandmother, a solitary, unknown (except to me), and ordinary reader, read life narratives for most of her life, until her life ended:

> This is the world we inhabit, and where we engage in our own most intimate work of self-invention. This contemporaneity establishes beyond doubt that autobiography is fundamental to the struggle for recognition among individuals and groups, to the constant creation of what it means to be human and the rights that fall from that, and to the ongoing negotiation of imaginary boundaries between ourselves and others. Life narrative plays a vital role in the public sphere as it deals in and through private lives. (2007, 10)

41

Chapter 1

"MORE BOOKS!":
PUBLISHING, NON-FICTION,
AND THE MEMOIR BOOM

But if you're publishing [a book] as a memoir, I think the publisher
has a responsibility because as the consumer, the reader, I am trusting
you. I'm trusting you, the publisher, to categorize this book whether
as fiction or autobiographical or memoir. I'm trusting you.

– Oprah Winfrey, interview with Nan Talese and
James Frey, January 26, 2006

The story of the memoir boom is at its heart a story of publishing. Oprah
Winfrey's comment to Nan Talese, James Frey's editor and publisher,
during the height of the controversy about Frey's book *A Million Little
Pieces* bears this out. On the Oprah Winfrey Show episode called "A Million Little Lies," Winfrey called Frey to account because she felt that he had
"betrayed the trust of millions" when he published an addiction memoir
with some false details. Winfrey asked him to explain to her audience why
he would lie about events in his life, but she reserved her comments about
problems with genre for the representative of industry: Talese. Winfrey
blamed Talese and all of publishing for failing to do the work of classification. For Winfrey, the "rules" that govern memoir are clear and absolute.
A memoir is an accurate picture of events that really happened. A memoir should be read not just because it is believable, but because it must be
believed. A work of fiction, although it might contain higher truths, is not

read in the same way. Since Winfrey has dedicated much of her career to encouraging emotional and ethical responses to events of various kinds, the idea that a memoir cannot be trusted appears to her in that moment to be a betrayal of what she values. Although she does not say this, the Frey controversy, as it came to be called, also served to call into question Oprah Winfrey's position as a trusted mediator between her audience and specific sets of ideas. This is why Winfrey tried to deflect the work of mediation away from herself, as the host of Oprah's Book Club, to the publishing industry, as the mediator between books and the reading public. The publishers' job of categorization, she said, can have implications for the way in which a memoir is received by the public because it is the publisher who decides—for others—what is true and what is not. For Winfrey, these implications move the work of generic classification into economic and political spheres. This makes classification appear to be linked to ethical concerns and to consumer rights. And because Winfrey thinks that books (and especially true books) have the power to change lives, the publishing industry's use of genre has political implications for her as well. "I'm trusting you," she said to the world of publishing. In that moment on her show, she meant it.

In chapter 5, I will discuss how the Frey controversy is linked to other aspects of public life in the United States during the beginning of the Iraq invasion. But for now, Oprah Winfrey's comments serve to highlight something important about memoir in the twenty-first century: memoir is produced, and not just written. Memoir is a creative product, but it is still a product and—if Winfrey is right—the genre to which it belongs can even be regarded as a brand produced by the publishing and book retailing industries. This is a far cry from general thinking about how literature is made. Since the Romantic period, literature has been widely thought to have been primarily a creative production by the author, who then has his/her book published. The power of the author is understood to be primary, and the work of publishers and others is thought to be secondary or supplementary, especially in the case of classic or avant-garde literature. This kind of belief in the power of the author can have the effect of branding the author's persona and proper name and connecting the brand to a certain kind of style and content. Through a set of changes that included the rise of individualism and the attachment of individualism to the idea of creativity, the detachment of authorship from the patronage system and the invention and development of copyright for an author's works, what we might now call the cult of authorship and author celebrity became the most important way to read and understand literary writing. In his essay "What Is an Author,"

Michel Foucault discusses this phenomenon as the "author function," and he sees its primary goal—the idea of the author—as the granting of unity to a set of texts (1984, 101–120). In *Expanding the American Mind*, Beth Luey says that in the case of non-fiction, it is often the literary agent or the publisher who creates the idea for a book, and that this rarely happens in the case of fiction: "in most cases the author of a nonfiction book is far less important than the novelist in determining the content of the book and the style and form in which that content is delivered to the reader" (2010, 19).

The industry that helps to bring the works of a "literary" author into being, when it is considered at all, remains of secondary importance to most of us who are not interested in the history of the book or print culture. As one agent says in an interview conducted by John B. Thompson—the first scholar to write a monograph about publishing in the United States and the United Kingdom in the twenty-first century—no one goes to a bookstore to find books by a certain publisher. Readers go to purchase books by their favourite authors, because "the writer is the star, much like the movie business. Nobody goes to see a Paramount movie, they go to see a new Tom Cruise movie" (Thompson 2010, 63). But this is not true of all books. The cult of the author that appears to lift some books away from considerations of them as commodities tends to operate when books become "literary" as opposed to generic, or when their authors become famous enough to be known as authors, rather than just the writers of certain kinds of books. In the case of memoir, the history of the genre as something not fictional and not quite literary means that it is harder to forget that memoirs are commodities produced by an industry. The rules that govern what a memoir is, why it is not fiction, and what its relationship to certain values in the marketplace is have quite a different history and have created different expectations in its readers. In this chapter, I will discuss the role of publishing, one part of the memoir production industry, in the tricky business of truth-telling and narrative, and examine how the publisher's role in that work of classification—as Oprah Winfrey guessed—can be closely related to the ways in which identity makes its way into a marketplace and even into the public sphere.

At its limits, when the genre appears to be doing a work other than truth-telling, the power of memoir appears. And along with it, the power of publishing to turn identity into an industry becomes apparent too, as it did during the Frey controversy. Surveying a dizzying list of hundreds of memoirs published in the first decade of the twenty-first century in the United States and the United Kingdom, Ben Yagoda, in *Memoir: a His-*

tory, says that all these books have one thing in common. All of them "were evaluated, accepted, physically produced, and marketed by a publishing house. This apparatus was capable of putting into print many hundreds if not thousands of memoirs a year" (19–20). Yagoda makes an interesting connection here between memoirs and publishing. If we are to take popular memoir seriously, then we should take seriously the conditions of cultural and material production that have made memoir and other forms of non-fiction into important commodities that are produced, bought, and consumed in the United States and worldwide. It means that publishing has to be considered (as it is in the fields of book history and print culture) as an industry that creates non-fictional stories about identity *as commodities* and not just as aesthetic objects. It is also necessary to think of publishing as an industry that itself has undergone many important changes since the major publishing mergers and buyouts began in earnest in the 1980s. The changes in the industry as a whole have affected what kinds of non-fiction material is produced and how much of it is made. In order to tell the story of the memoir boom and publishing in the United States, I do have to provide a considerable amount of backstory about the development of publishing, changes that took place in the role and purpose of non-fiction titles in publishing, and, finally, what kinds of current practices in publishing and book retailing help to produce the memoir boom itself. It might seem easier not to do this backstory and to just get on with talking about the books of the memoir boom. But without this story of publishing, the memoir boom appears either as Oprah Winfrey saw it—as an initiative by publishers to get consumers to buy books—or it appears as many autobiography critics and media pundits have seen it—as a response to insatiable (and unmeasurable) consumer demand. Both views depend on a certain hegemonic view, either of corporate power or of mass culture. Neither is accurate, because it is not strictly true that publishers have the power to dupe the public. Nor is it true that there is a hungry mass readership that somehow fuels demand via a magical process. In reality, the publishing industry in the United States has undergone some profound changes that have made larger publishing companies look less like gentlemanly enterprises where craft is prized over profit and more like other cultural industries. But it is also still accurate to say that publishers look for what sells in ways that continue to rely on intuition about what readers might want to purchase. The journey of a book from the mind of an author (or agent) to the hands of a reader involves a conglomeration of factors, some of which cannot be fully known because we cannot eavesdrop on the conversations between agents, writers, publishers, and booksellers. But it is possible to look at how, since the 1950s, first non-fiction and then memoir as an aspect of non-fiction steadily rose in importance to publishers and then to consumers. Although this picture can never be complete, the backstory here will establish how industrial changes have allowed this to happen to one form of writing and then to a specific genre of writing.

David Hesmondhalgh has pointed out that like the music industry or film industry, publishing is a cultural industry whose product is symbolic capital and whose activities are indicative of social, economic, and cultural change in the economies where publishers are active (2007, 6). Studying such an industry can aid in understanding what the memoir boom in the United States looks like beyond Ben Yagoda's tantalizing yet unsubstantiated estimate that thousands of books have been published in its name (19–20). Almost all scholars who conduct research in the area of contemporary book production and consumption are aware that there are many social factors that materially influence how books move through cycles of production and become endowed with all kinds of cultural meanings. One of these factors is genre, including what the nature of industry "demands" to write in a certain genre can mean for the production and circulation of memoirs. The role of genre and the horizon of generic expectations in the publishing industry deserve special attention in this process because, as we shall see, the long association of genre with lowbrow book production has affected how memoir is understood in two ways. First, books identified as generic have long been associated with inferior publishing values via what has become known as the paperback revolution. Second, genre itself creates what I call a horizon of expectation used by publishers as they attempt to market, distribute, and ultimately sell books. Looking at publishing and genre in this way involves changing the emphasis in our analysis away from books as literary objects. Instead, I aim to highlight some of the material processes that bring ideas (and their objects) into being and helps some of them to endure. In this light, it is possible to understand why Oprah Winfrey said so earnestly, "I'm trusting you," to an entire industry, and what role ideas about genre play in building, maintaining, and even eroding that trust.

PUBLISHING AND INDUSTRIAL DEMAND

I'd like to tell a story about publishing that highlights the importance of industrial demand to the production of memoir, a demand that occasionally makes it seem like Oprah Winfrey's expectations for the publishing industry are in fact part of the work of publishing. One of my colleagues at work came to my office door one day and asked me what I was thinking about at that moment. "Publishing," I said promptly. I was reading a wide variety of books about the publishing industry at the time. My colleague is a very well-known and respected fiction writer, and so I asked him what his thoughts were about publishing and the writer's role within it. He told me this story in response. In 2002, Dave Eggers, the author of the bestselling memoir *A Heartbreaking Work of Staggering Genius* and the founder of McSweeney's publishing house, began with a collaborator a series of non-profit tutoring centres and writing workshops for young writers in San Francisco. In order to abide by the bylaws for the storefront they had purchased for the centre, the building had to have a business in it. In a dazzling display of lateral thinking, Eggers and his collaborator created what they refer to as a pirate supply store because they needed to show that they had the required business in the front of the building. The store does sell pirate supplies such as glass eyes, hooks, and peg-legs, and it has facilities for writing workshops and after-school tutoring in the back. This model was wildly successful, and is now found in other large American cities today. Run by an umbrella organization called 826 National, other programs include other kinds of stores: 826michigan in Ann Arbor has what it calls a Robot Supply and Repair Shop, for instance; 826NYC in New York has a superhero supply store; and 826LA is a time travel store.[1]

One of the programs in the original San Francisco centre is a writing workshop for young children. The kids are given pens, crayons, paper— anything they need for writing. They write something with the help of volunteers (dressed as pirates, of course) who guide them through exercises that help them to write dialogue, description, and plot. The volunteers help the children staple together and bind their writing into "books," complete with a picture of themselves on the back. At intervals, a trapdoor in the ceiling opens and a basket is lowered to the main floor. The children fill the basket with their writing, and the basket is pulled up through the trapdoor. Once in awhile, Mr. Blue, an unseen and very grumpy editor who is rumoured to be 600 pounds and covered with boils, opens the trap door and shouts down "More books!" at the children, who happily make some more to fill the basket. If Mr. Blue doesn't like what he gets (he dislikes unoriginal stories based on cartoons or television shows, for instance) he rips out the offending pages and throws them back. Eventually, Mr. Blue approves the work and the kids get their bound copies to take home. Many of the kids come back another time, because there are no writers alive who do not love to see books they wrote themselves, in print and in their own hands.[2]

I was instantly delighted by this story. For one thing, it is evocative. Who would not want to go and see that pirate supply store and attend one of those workshops? Who does not like the idea of filling that basket as Mr. Blue roars for more? But on reflection, what I like best is my colleague's description of the workshop itself. Dave Eggers' writing workshops are unique in lots of ways, but one of the things that I think is particularly noteworthy about them is that they stress how writing is not an isolated act of creation, but a *process* that includes editing and publishing as part of the cycle of production. The children do not just compose something on their own, but are taught the basics of professional writing. And they inevitably learn that professional writing can be a response to what an editor or publisher asks for. *"More books!"* shouts Mr. Blue, the archetypal dissatisfied editor who must be appeased, as rejected pages flutter down. The busy writers get back to work, trying to make the invisible person happy so that they can see their work in print. This model of publishing as an industry is simplified and made comic for the purposes of the workshop, but it does get at an important aspect of writing and publishing at the present time: writing is a craft that often involves responses to the demands of others, whether they are the demands of an editor, a literary agent, an industry, a market, or a public. The work of writing itself is shaped by those demands: there is even pleasure to be had and (if an author is fortunate and willing to work very hard) a livelihood to be made by answering them.

The workshop does not address the nature of Mr. Blue's demands, other than identifying his preference for original stories. Mr. Blue is also the only one who can demand anything. In publishing, the nature of market demand is much more complex. It is what, in the words of Alfred Greco, makes book publishing "at times, a bitter mystery" (2005, 2004), because even those in the publishing industry cannot always predict what will make a book enduring and profitable, and because there are many factors in play (including the existence of similar books, the marketing a book receives, the timeliness of the topic, the role of the agent, and even the existence of cultural authorities like Oprah Winfrey) when a book is produced and marketed. The unpredictability of publishing and the uncertainty of marketing leads to complaints both within and outside the industry that publishers want what will sell, and yet so many books have brief shelf lives and the majority of books do not see a second printing (Thompson 2010, 266–68). Since its inception, the publishing industry in the United States has not put much emphasis on market research or advertising beyond work done for some bestselling authors (Scott 2009, 77–78). Therefore, it is not accurate, as some journalists and reviewers have assumed, that publishers either "force" material on readers or publish books that are certain to sell. Publishing is hardly an exact science. What then can we say about how non-fiction, and especially memoirs, are produced and come to market? What role do publishers play in this process? In order to get at the mechanics of the increased visibility and popularity of memoirs as they make their way onto bestseller lists, to the fronts of bookstore shelves and into the hands (and e-readers) of the public, it is important to remember that publishing is part of a complex system of book production and distribution. As many of the theorists of book history and print culture have pointed out, publishing itself is part of a complex and interrelated series of cultural and economic systems made up of sets of factors that influence each other. These factors are hard to isolate and analyze. Pierre Bourdieu, for example, has described the literary field not as the backdrop for the operations of individual genius, but as a field of production in which social agents of various types occupy different positions at different points, and where each position affects the other (2000, 29–30). John B. Thompson says in his study of the British and American publishing industry in the last decade that publishing can be best understood as a field of cultural production in Bourdieu's sense because Bourdieu's model emphasizes the relational basis for action within the industry. Editors, agents, writers, marketing personnel, and many others all work to create, distribute, and sell books. These actors are dependent on the kinds and quantities of what Bourdieu called capital, which Thompson sees in publishing as the power an actor has to act and accomplish things (2010, 4–5). Robert Darnton's communications circuit with its cycle of book production also understands publishing to be part of a larger system of book circulation because it is related to other aspects of economic and cultural production. For Darnton, "book history concerns each phase of this process and the process as a whole, in all its variations over space and time and in all its relations with other systems, economic, social, political, and cultural, in the surrounding environment" (2002, 11). Darnton's communications circuit admittedly has been critiqued, most notably by Adams and Barker who attempt to reclaim Darnton's emphasis on communications for the area of bibliography, but few scholars have disputed the importance of understanding systems of production for books or print culture more generally. If anything, scholars like Jerome McGann and Juliet Gardiner have critiqued other theorists who do not think systemically enough about book production and who do not emphasize enough that books are material artifacts and commodities made within specific social contexts (Finkelstein and McLeery 2005, 12–15).

Although the publishing industry is complex, consisting as it does of multiple (and conflicting) fields of action, each with actors with access to varying amounts of economic, cultural and symbolic capital, John B. Thompson says that it is still possible to think of publishing as a chain of production. In other words, the construction of a book is mainly a one-way process whereby an author writes a book, an agent markets the manuscript or idea, a publisher picks up the book and then the book makes its way through various channels of production and distribution until it ends up as a retail item (2010, 15–16). However, the chain of production can be disrupted, particularly in the case of non-fiction where authors, agents and publishers work together to shape a book project. Thompson calls this process one of interaction and negotiation (2010,16). As Beth Luey points out in *Expanding the American Mind,* publishers, agents and editors play less of a role in the generation of a novel's content than they often do in the case of a non-fiction book because "if composition is ever to be viewed as a social or communal process, nonfiction is the place" (2010, 20). Luey's larger argument has to do with the importance of content in the production of non-fiction rather than in the importance for readers (and publishers) of the author as the unifying personality who creates a unique work. But her comments can be read as another aspect of the demands that publishers and agents make when a book is non-fiction, demands that do not exist in the same way for most authors of fiction. Some of these involve requirements that a non-fiction book be timely and in tune with contemporary issues. Others involve expectations that a non-fiction book has to contain elements that will make a book sell well in the marketplace. Still others are jurisdictional, in the sense that Oprah Winfrey means it: a work of non-fiction, including memoir, is supposed to be true and accurate (2010, 20–21). Therefore, changing demands for non-fiction titles in the publishing industry do affect how many and what kinds of personal narratives make their way into print and—in some cases—stay in print for many years.

Here is where industrial demand can be seen clearly for a book to appear under highly specific conditions. We can sense the roar of Mr. Blue as the demand not just for "more books!" but for more of a certain *genre* of book that might be able to sell, if writers produce within the rules. Memoir does have a long history of being treated as a commodity connected in just this way to market demand. The long association of memoir with the marketplace and its "demands" for timely, truthful and sometimes sensationalized non-fiction continues today, as does the backlash against this kind of writing as trashy, lowbrow, and not worth reading.[3] Oprah Winfrey's expectation that the publishing industry is supposed to produce a consistent memoir "brand" that she can consume has its roots in this kind of association of memoirs with the idea of commodification. But there is another set of reasons why Oprah Winfrey might see the problem of genre as a problem for publishers. Before we can look at how the memoir boom developed and why memoirs have become a mainstay on the front and backlists of publishers, it is necessary to see how different things once were, when memoir (along with other kinds of generic writing in the areas of non-fiction and fiction) was held in disrepute, and publishing it was seen as a necessary evil, not a pleasure. The backstory of memoir, then, lies in the history of American publishing and the paperback revolution, and it is to some aspects of this history that we now turn.

LOWBROW: AMERICAN PUBLISHING AND THE PROBLEM OF GENRE

Contemporary scholarship on American publishing has begun to address many of the key factors that influence how books are produced, circulated and consumed. For example, historic events (such as the cold war and the civil rights movements), the growth of academic institutions, changes in religious beliefs, the actions of government, economic developments, changes in distribution systems, and the expansion of the importance of mass media since World War II have all received consideration within the study of print culture in general and contemporary publishing in particular (Nord, Rubin and Schudson 2009, 1–5). But there is another factor vital to understanding how publishing works. It is the economic role that assumptions about genre in the world of publishing have played in the writing, publishing, and selling of books.

Although an awareness of the work genre can do is something that is found more in the study of television, new media, communications and rhetoric than in print culture, there is evidence that some scholars are interested in these questions in relation to the production of fiction, and especially in fiction that is not usually thought to be literary. This connection seems to be a natural one because in the United States, novels produced for mass markets are often referred to as "genre" fiction, a moniker that refers to the qualities they have in common, or the formulas used to write them. Romances, horror, science fiction, westerns, and mysteries are all called genre fiction. The appellation is also applied to a sense of the commercial value of these texts, not their artistic value, because of a long-standing equation of "formula" with "formulaic" writing that is not literary. Such writing is thought to be for lowbrow readers who do not read for quality. It is not for nothing that Stephen King, a prolific author of horror novels, once said, "I am the literary equivalent of a Big Mac and Fries" in reference to his ability to write genre fiction that—like fast food—is cheap, easy to produce, enjoyable to read but also not all that good for the consumer (2000, 222).

There are compelling reasons why genre fiction has been regarded as lowbrow and cheap and why it has been associated with the mass production of writing. For one thing, there are times when this actually has been the case. Most often, genre fiction is understood to be part of the production of mass-market paperbacks that began with introduction of Penguin paperbacks to the United States in 1939, the same year that the Pocket Books publishing company was founded: these companies were joined by many other publishers who produced paperback mysteries and detective thrillers, westerns, romances, horror, and SF (science fiction and fantasy). When paperbacks such as these first appeared, they were thought to be "trash" because hardback publishers would not publish them and bookstores would not stock them. Since pulp books were so cheap and easy to produce, paperback publishers turned to the magazine distribution networks to sell their books, and they began to appear in drugstores, train stations and newsstands, all places where "legitimate" literature was not sold, but where many lower-income Americans went to shop. Although a few publishers like Penguin and Pocket Books published reprints of what they called "serious" non-fiction and literary works, some of the early paperback publishers like Bantam or Dell also sold romance or detective magazines, and so they began to commission similar kinds of stories in book form. They used the same artists to create lurid book covers that would attract the magazine readers to this new medium. The idea worked, but it also meant that "respectable" publishers and literary critics, among others, viewed these affordable books with some suspicion (Scott 2009, 79). That is how the cheap, easy-to-access and (for many) enjoyable texts of genre fiction became associated with bad, formulaic and non-literary writing.

Within the publishing industry itself, genre fiction and less "serious" non-fiction were part of the economics of running the business before the industry began to experience profound changes. But they played a supporting role in the minds of many editors. Before paperback and imprint publishers actually became part of the larger publishing companies, editors depended on the sales of cookbooks, coffee table books, self-help books, and bestselling hardcover fiction to subsidize the production of the books they really wanted to publish. For example, the 1950s and 1960s are recalled as a "golden age" by Jason Epstein as the time when publishers introduced cutting-edge modernist writers and their ideas to American audiences (2002, 100), a period when expatriate Europeans sold rights to American books overseas, and published translations and reprints of major European authors such as Jean-Paul Sartre or Simone de Beauvoir. The editor André Schiffrin's own father had been this kind of publisher when he started Pantheon with other expatriate intellectuals (Schiffrin 2001, 4–5). Publishers also sold rights to paperback book publishers and imprints, so that profitable hardcover books could turn another profit when they reproduced in mass-market formats. These altruistic publishers saw publishing as "a break-even proposition" (Schiffrin 2001, 104) where better-selling books subsidized what they saw as the more important, less-popular works. During the 1950s and 1960s, the trade book publishing industry in the United States was subsidized by sales of scientific books, medical books and textbooks internationally (Luey 2009b, 29–32) and by the sale of textbooks, children's books and religious books domestically (35–40). Publishers made some money from price markups of hardcover books to cover the cost of book returns. They also sold publishing rights internationally and to the burgeoning paperback imprint publishers. Such mass-market/trade books like cookbooks or gardening guides should, in this story of the publishing industry, exist only to subsidize the rest of a serious publishing operation (Schiffrin 2001, 5). Non-fiction is seen as either "serious" or money-making. In this version of the state of American publishing, the former is worthwhile to publish, and the latter is a necessary evil for the industry. In their well-known and influential memoirs about the publishing business, Jason Epstein and Andre Schiffrin make distinctions between what they each term important non-fiction works that take years of research and a considerable amount of editorial vision to bring to the reading public, and non-fiction that pays the publishing bills. Important non-fiction could include a biography of business titan J.P. Morgan (Epstein 2002, 14–15) or what Schiffrin calls serious non-fiction books featuring "new, controversial ideas" (2001,7). Both editors are thinking of trade hardcover books, which for a long time were considered to be at the heart of the American publishing industry. This type of book was considered to be of superior quality and more challenging than better-selling books. But its importance was paramount. This is why serious non-fiction and literature was understood to require the help of subsidies from bestselling fiction, bestselling non-fiction like the multi-million-selling self-help book *The Purpose-Driven Life* and niche books such as cookbooks (Luey 2009b, 42). The latter were seen as a necessary evil so that publishers could publish better books. In publishing, this is how a high/low cultural split was maintained for decades. In this system, political memoirs by major figures such as American presidents were understood to be serious, important books worthy of consideration, books that had to be produced as hardcovers. But memoirs by relatively ordinary people who had done something exceptional such as survived a major disaster, recovered from an addiction or—in the case of Malcolm X's *Autobiography*—were about a controversial public figure, were not published in this way. Memoirs and biography by Hollywood stars were also not considered to be serious enough to merit publishing in the trade hardback system. Memoirs did not make bestseller lists in the way that biographies of the famous or historical studies did. They were relegated to the status of cookbooks and travel guides, unless their authors were worthy-enough figures to merit serious treatment. Books like these were published, but not as trade hardcovers. They were often released as cheap hardbacks or, in some cases, as paperback books without ever having been hardcover. As we shall see, this changed the system of distribution and retailing for these books, and it ensured that they were bought (so it was assumed) by readers who were not serious about what they read. Memoirs, and their authors, were as "cheap" as the paper they were printed on.

The system of publishing trade books worked as long as publishers remained relatively small and family-run, with relatively little overhead costs and a dedication to a certain kind of publishing vision not entirely based on turning a quick profit. But during the 1970s and 1980s, publishing as editors like Epstein and Schiffrin had known it began to change. Even as early as the 1960s, the predominance of small and medium-sized family-run publishers in the industry had started to shift. Publishers who had built the family-run publishing businesses located in New York City began to retire. In some cases, their heirs did not want to continue the business and decided to sell. In others, publishers found that their companies were not turning much profit and were undercapitalized. These owners wanted to raise more capital to expand their businesses, and began to seek to merge with other companies (Thompson 2010, 103). At the same time, the growth in revenues from subsidiary rights and expanded sales made publishing companies attracted to other media conglomerates looking to increase their profits and holdings. The result was a series of mergers and acquisitions, including the purchases of Knopf and Pantheon by Random House in 1959 and 1961 respectively. In 1962 Harper & Brothers merged with Row, Peterson & Company: this latter merger allowed Harper & Brothers to enter the textbook industry. Times Mirror, a newspaper company, bought Abrams and New American Library in 1963 as a way to diversify its holdings, while Simon & Schuster was sold to the multinational corporation Gulf & Western in 1975 (Luey 2009b, 47–48).

In the 1980s and 1990s, foreign companies were able to enter the American market by purchasing a publisher, as the German conglomerate Bertelsmann did in 1998 when it bought Random House, a publisher that itself had already bought many smaller publishers and imprints. Another example is Rupert Murdoch's Australian media company News Corp., which bought Harper's and Row, Petersen and Company and in 1989 merged it with children's book publisher William Collins and Sons Ltd. to form HarperCollins. The purchase, vertical and horizontal integration and merging of publishers—in some cases by companies that did not have direct links to the publishing business but were involved in entertainment industries—has been viewed with alarm by editors working in publishing for decades. It has created narratives of lament for the lost golden age, when the publishing of quality books mattered. In a specific aspect of this narrative of lament, the system of subsidy was abandoned by publishing houses which began to produce more mass-market books (bestsellers, genre fiction, and mass-market non-fiction) in order to boost profits, but the revenues were not used to support the kinds of books some editors wanted to keep making.

Jason Epstein observes that many of the companies that had bought publishers found that the book business could not be made to be profitable. Some of them sold the companies they had acquired, and others tried to make the book business generate more profit, a strategy that he says leads to a decline in quality and reliance on bestsellers and popular non-fiction books to generate revenue (11–12). Schiffrin agrees with Epstein that the strategy was not profitable (2001, 119). According to him, the results were disastrous: "Until quite recently, publishing houses were for the most part family owned and small, content with the modest profits that came from a business that still saw itself as linked to cultural and intellectual life. In recent years, publishers have been put on a procrustean bed and made to fit one of two patterns: as purveyors of entertainment or of hard information. This has left little room for books with new, controversial ideas or challenging literary voices" (2001, 7).

In this version of events, subsidy gave way to profit-making as publishers began to publish more lightweight non-fiction books with mass-market appeal (Greco 2004, 201). One of signs of the decline of the publishing industry for Schiffrin and Epstein is the move they see to publishing as a for-profit industry to generate revenue rather than a break-even enterprise. The result, as Epstein points out a bit sardonically, are non-fiction books that can be marketed on television and whose authors act as reliable brand names for publishers. Such non-fiction books were successful because they could be marketed on television in the popular talk-show format, which was seen by publishers and television producers alike as an easy way to create programming (Whiteside 1981). During the 1990s, talk shows were still seen by publishers as a major vehicle for author promotion: Ben Yagoda suggests that authors of memoir were particularly good on these shows because most memoirists had "a dramatic or unusual story" to tell about themselves and that this was easier to present than authors talking about their works (2009, 238–39). For Epstein, this is lamentable because writers like this are not real writers. They are: "royal princesses, health faddists, reformed mafiosi, discoverers of the twelve secrets of financial or romantic success, politicians, Eastern mystics, wrestlers, inspirational football coaches, body builders, diet doctors, gossips, evangelists, basketball stars and so on (Epstein 2002, 105)." What Albert Greco has called "the disaster narrative" of the publishing industry often sees the publishing of mass-market non-fiction or more popular forms of non-fiction just as Epstein does, as symbolic of the publishing industry's more general decline in editorial and literary standards, and its embrace of market values (2004, 203). Mark Crispin Miller's analysis of publishing in the 1990s concludes in a similar way that publishing standards have fallen, and the signs are that biographies about famous people, cookbooks, gardening books and interior design books as well as film adaptations, memoirs by royalty and political memoirs are being produced. All make for substandard reading, but at least in the "old days," publishers "did their share of the eternal dreck, for for them it was a necessary evil ... they did the high-yield trash in order to be able to afford the gems they loved" (1997, 117). The "gems" were serious non-fiction and literature.

The problem with this kind of narrative, as David Hesmondhalgh points out, is that it is almost impossible to substantiate because it is based on aesthetic criteria (2007, 293). It also relies on a heavily nostalgic narrative arc. In fact, the kind of publishing that some editors remember with such fondness was not friendly to the concerns of women or members of minority groups, and it treated authors as celebrities who were part of a cozy club of publishers and editors, almost all of whom were men fortunate enough to live and work in New York City. As Albert Greco says, this kind of lament works to obscure problems with the publishing industry before the time of mergers: "Although critics of the existing marketing system raised important issues, one must wonder about their highly romantic depiction of the 'good old days' of book publishing. One should not forget that this industry, during the time period they found so endearing, was essentially a white male WASP province. African Americans, Hispanic Americans, and Asian Americans were rarely found in the corridors of power or in editorial or sales meetings ... perhaps the critics are right; perhaps their world was better, filled with individuals reading Camus, Proust, and Dickens; but perhaps their lost firmament was not so grand" (2004, 207).

Eva Hemmings Wirtén writes that the publishing environment in this period was also sexist. Underpaid women ran much of the business, as British editor and publisher Diana Athill observes in *Stet: A Memoir*, but they rarely received credit for the work they did. The lament for publishing before the era of mergers is often "a *male* story" (2009, 403). It also pays little empirical attention to how many and what types of books are being published now by academic presses, small presses and major publishers (Greco 2004, 207). As Beth Luey observes, "the lost golden age, [was imagined as] a time (usually between 1920 and 1960) when publishers did not worry about the bottom line, when good books reached an eager public with no obstacles, and when editors did not need to know the meaning of the word 'spreadsheet.' There never was such a time" (2009b, 52).

Finally, the disaster narrative of publishing assumes that non-fiction can be divided into "serious" and "light" offerings. And it makes generic distinctions: between literature and pulp, "serious" non-fiction and non-fiction that is not about ideas. It assumes that mass-market non-fiction *itself* is somehow suspect, and therefore is the symbol of an industry in decline. The connection between the rise of the mass-market paperback in the United States, the suspicion of certain kinds of non-fiction and the problem of genre as a sign of the decline in literary quality all coalesce in the belief that memoir and biography for mass markets (along with other types of non-fiction) is not worth examining beyond its status as a necessary evil for publishers, more than seven decades after Q.D. Leavis pictured the advent of the mass-market paperback and its impoverished readers as the sign of contagion in the modern world. In this kind of suspicion about certain types of non-fiction it is possible to see the more contemporary expressions of contempt for the memoir boom and the kinds of books it produces.

But what did the paperback revolution actually signal, and what was the role of non-fiction within it? Paperbacks, with their lurid covers and cheap production values, were the target of censorship campaigns, but they continued to grow in popularity. Some publishers, such as Penguin and Pocket, only reprinted classics, or contracted with hardcover trade publishers for a print run in paperback for a specific amount of years. By 1959, paperback sales had exceeded sales of hardcover trade books, even though paperbacks were cheaper than hardcovers (Luey 2009b, 42–45). In *Two-Bit Culture: The Paperbacking of America*, Kenneth Davis suggests that the popularity of the early paperback had a democratizing influence on American life, and could in some cases even be credited with facilitating social change. As I pointed out earlier, paperbacks began to be published in the United States in 1939 with the introduction of Pocket Books and from the United Kingdom, Penguin paperbacks. During World War II, paperback books were shipped to American servicemen overseas because they were easy to send. When these soldiers returned to the United States after their tour of duty, they continued to read paperbacks. Since these types of books were, as I mentioned, easy to buy in railway stations, drugstores and supermarkets, lower-income readers began to read when they would not have done so before. In fact, the popularity of paperback books meant that the reading of books by Americans actually *increased* after 1945, although the reading of what could be termed high literature decreased (Scott 2009).

As the popularity of paperback books rose, some paperback publishers began to do more than reprint bestselling trade hardcover titles. They began to solicit material from authors directly, and they also began to negotiate more lucrative deals for paperback books (Epstein 2002; 4; Luey 2009a, 375). One of the results of this increase in visibility and revenue for paperback book publishers was the first wave of publisher buyouts in the 1970s: Random House bought paperback publisher Ballantine, for example (Whiteside 1981, 18). Market convergence and the negotiation of large author advances the 1970s helped to create "blockbuster" non-fiction titles in paperback form, such as *I'm OK, You're OK* (Whiteside 1981, 19).

According to Kenneth C. Davis, the cheapness and easy availability of the paperback book in this form meant that some non-fiction works reached lower-income readers and became highly influential. For example, Dr. Benjamin Spock's *The Common Sense Book of Baby and Child Care* of 1946 was the first bestselling mass-market paperback. It changed how many Americans looked after their babies and young children because it was produced as an inexpensive paperback by Pocket Books and sold in places where young parents went to shop. This book is an example of how non-fiction sometimes could and did have a major impact because of how it was distributed.[4] Social movements like Black Power and the women's liberation movement were similarly influenced paperbacks such as *The Autobiography of Malcolm X*, Eldridge Cleaver's *Soul on Ice* and Betty Friedan's *The Feminine Mystique,* all of which were cheap and readily available in stores where lower-income Americans shopped regularly (Davis 1984, 308). Suddenly, members of oppressed and marginalized groups who could not imagine going to bookstores had access to non-fiction books about social change offered to them at prices that they could afford. A great many of these were memoirs by people who were not members of elite groups. And their readers were the kinds of people who did not frequent bookstores necessarily, but who saw books for sale where they did their shopping. Davis says that the cost and accessibility of paperbacks meant that "universally priced at twenty-five cents in its early years, the paperback democratized reading in America" (1984, xii). There were problems with the distribution system, however. Paperbacks were successful at first because they were sold in all kinds of outlets. But some news distributors who handled them found the depictions of race, sexuality or political views objectionable, and so they either refused to carry some books or they deleted offensive words or passages before books were sold (Luey 2009a, 375). This type of activity worked to blunt the democratizing power of paperbacks to some extent, but it also was an early sign of what William Shatzkin was to critique a few decades later: the success of paperbacks lay in their *distribution*, not in their production of content. Distributors in this kind of system are able to control content if they wish. Nevertheless, the cheapness and availability of paperbacks changed who read books in the United States and why books were read. As Beth Luey concludes, "like the expansion of higher education, they [paperbacks] democratized learning and book ownership" (2009a: 376).

As influential as it was, the unique character of the paperback revolution was relatively short-lived. In the 1950s and 1960s, trade paperbacks (mainly reprints of classics by companies like Anchor and Penguin) already were beginning to be included in reading lists for elementary school, high school, college and university courses. Like the servicemen and women before them, students became used to reading paperbacks and continued to buy them after they graduated. They also had a place to buy them: as I discuss in chapter two, bookstores run by counter-cultural entrepreneurs were beginning to stock the paperbacks that established bookstores would not sell. By the 1970s, the "revolution" was over and paperbacks were no longer regarded as lowbrow in content. Due to buyouts and then what Thompson calls "the hardcover revolution" when hardcover book sales began to rise in 1980s and 1990s, mass-market paperback sales began to sink. Publishers began to publish trade paperbacks as a response (2010, 39). By 2005, trade paperbacks had become more popular than mass-market paperbacks themselves, and sales of mass-market genre works began to decline (Luey 2009b, 46–47).

The story of the paperback revolution and the role of non-fiction within it forms a counter-narrative to the disaster narrative of publishing as a story of the decline of the literary, and the ascendancy of lower-quality works of fiction and non-fiction for the masses. And yet, it is the latter story that is the most popular and quietly influences much of what is said about the memoir boom. There is little doubt that the mergers of the 1980s and 1990s changed the publishing business rapidly, and that large companies did begin to change their publishing strategies. One of the reasons was that during the period of mergers, the ideas that drove paperback revolution became part of the culture of the major publishers as they began to publish a hybrid form: the trade paperback (Thompson 2010, 40). The economics of publishing "genre fiction" and mass-marketed non-fiction began to affect the business and the culture of the publishing industry itself.

PUBLISHING MORE BOOKS: A LOOK AT THE INDUSTRY

Nan Talese's response to Oprah Winfrey's earnest entreaty that publishers must act as custodians of genre was to describe how she understands the process of book acquisition to work. Her answers during her interview on the *Oprah Winfrey Show* provide us with a view of publishing a book selection that is almost never made public. In her response to Oprah Winfrey, Talese said, "'Well, I can only tell you how the book came to me and how I read it. And I read the manuscript as a memoir. I thought it was this extraordinary story of a man with drug addiction going through the hell of both the addiction and the recovery and the process. I thought the book was absolutely riveting'" (Oprah's Questions). For Talese, the decision to publish *A Million Little Pieces* as a memoir and not an autobiographical novel was founded on *her* sense of genre and the fact that she was moved by what she read. The decision to call Frey's work "non-fiction" was about Talese's own judgment as an editor. Talese revealed an important aspect of publishing in these comments that is not always obvious: American publishing today might *appear* to be controlled by large multinational corporations like Random House, the publisher that produced *A Million Little Pieces*, but in fact it still operates in some cases like a cottage industry. Editors like Talese—who has published major authors like Margaret Atwood through her own highly respected imprint within Doubleday, itself an imprint within Random House—do have a measure of control over what books to publish, how to market them and even—in this particular case—what the genre of the book could be. Oprah Winfrey's address to "publishers" does not and cannot take into account how complex the structure of American publishing is, and how changes in the industry have resulted less in a monolithic corporate culture than a dynamic field of production. But the story of the changes to American publishing in the last forty years has much to tell us about how a memoir like *A Million Little Pieces* could become a bestseller, and why Nan Talese appeared on a major talk show to defend her industry and her decisions.

The prevailing picture of the publishing industry since the 1960s, according to the accounts of industry insiders, is of mass buyouts of family firms and market consolidation, with disastrous effects on what is published. Some industry commentators, who Albert Greco calls "the industrial complex school," charge that publishing since the 1980s has been bought out "by nonbook people uninterested (and in some instances downright hostile) to books, reading, or culture. In essence, "barbarians" with MBAs pierced the sacred veil, breached the protected gates, and are now in the boardrooms controlling what we read and think" (2004, 200). The flurry of mergers for the last twenty or thirty years has created a profit-motive in publishing that was not there before, these commentators say. The result has been the vertical integration of publishing with other cultural industries such as the Hollywood film and television industry, the music industry, and even professional sports. Publishing has therefore been turned into a culture industry as Adorno and Horkheimer would understand it, because "this process integrates all the elements of the production, from the novel (shaped with an eye to the film) to the last sound effect. It is the triumph of invested capital" (1997, 107). In this version of events, the industry itself has become subject to market concentration: for example, Schiffrin wrote in 2001 that publishing was becoming concentrated in the hands of very few companies (2). As we have seen, some commentators have charged that the mergers have directly affected the content and type of books published, resulting in a flood of low-quality material, including memoirs, that can be easily hawked on television. This strategy failed to turn a profit, flooding the market with books that had to be returned when they did not sell (Shatzkin 1982, 200). Deep discounting by chain bookstores and by general retailers has also been suggested as the source of falling publishing revenues (Shatzkin 1982, 9), as has competition with former paperback imprints for publishing rights (Whiteside 1981, 18–19) in what could be called a failure of the publishing industry to control what Wirtén calls "horizontal convergence" (2009, 401). In order to make profits in this kind of environment, publishers began to chase the dream of the "blockbuster" by paying very high advances to bestselling authors in the hopes that books by these authors would yield profits quickly (Whiteside 1981, 21–22). By the mid-1990s, in the wake of the success of a memoirs by Lee Iacocca (*Talking Straight*) and Frank McCourt (*Angela's Ashes*), they paid these advances to memoir writers as well, particularly if they were famous public figures. This practice is part of what fuels the memoir boom, as memoirs become a fixture of bestseller lists alongside novels. The strategy of endorsing bestselling books occurred at the cost of maintaining publishing backlists, some have argued because books on those lists were not as immediately profitable, even if the list contained some steady sellers (Shatzkin 1982, 204–205).

Is this an accurate picture of what has happened to the publishing business? Yes and no. During the 1960s and the 1970s, large publishers began to adopt mass-marketing strategies used by the paperback publishers and imprints and other cultural industries that, like the publishing industry, had been affected by globalization. Publishing was one of the last industries to adopt "the practices of publicity and marketing characteristic of monopoly capital" (Ohmann 1996, 22). The early result of this shift for the publishing industry was two sets of mergers and acquisitions. First, there was an early set of publisher mergers and acquisitions of publishing houses by larger media empires. These mergers changed the publishing industry in profound ways. Until this time, there had been dozens of small and medium-sized publishing houses in the United States, mainly located in the intellectual centres of New York City and Boston. Many of these houses were family businesses that had been started by energetic, iconoclastic men, "and they nearly always were men" (Thompson 2010, 101). When publishers like Alfred Knopf realized that their children were not interested in running the family business, other publishers (in this case, Bennett Cerf of Random House) bought them out and created a publicly traded company to raise more capital. As Random House expanded as a result of this and other acquisitions, larger corporations began to take an interest. In the end, RCA, a large media conglomerate, bought Random House, and Bennett Cerf stepped down as president, marking the end of an era for American publishing (Thompson 2010, 105–106). The goal for buyers like RCA was to vertically integrate different media platforms in order to boost efficiency and profits (Finkelstein 2009, 337). These acquisitions were also a way for corporations to position themselves as print and electronic media heavy-weights. They hoped to achieve synergy, which was thought to be a way for corporations to control media content across any number of media plat-forms. In another early example from the 1960s, Xerox bought University Microfilms and textbook publishers in an effort to control media content and hardware in schools, because it was thought that schools would begin to rely heavily on technology for teaching (Finkelstein 2009, 338).

This type of synergy did not materialize, and Xerox sold its holdings when it became clear that "the profit margin in book publishing was not adequate to satisfy the share-holders of technology companies" (Luey 2009a, 377). RCA also sold Random House in 1980 when it became clear not only that synergy was a myth, but that vertical integration did not guarantee that "content" could be migrated from books published by RCA-controlled publishers to films made by RCA-controlled movie production companies. Movie rights are often controlled by agents, not publishers, and so the idea that movie adaptation would be profitable failed to materialize (Thompson 2010, 106). Profits in any case were not certain, and this remains true. But mergers changed the landscape of publishing from individually controlled, sometimes iconoclastic family-run houses, to publishing as an *indus-try* with a profit motive. In this respect, the fears of editors who had been trained in the older model of publishing came true as parents companies began to require that all books turn some profit, rather than assuming that some books turn a profit in order to pay for the existence of others (Wirtén 2009, 403).

The second wave of mergers began in the 1980s and changed the indus-try yet again. When synergy and vertical integration failed to make enough profits and American corporations began to divest themselves of publishing houses foreign-owned companies began to buy them. German companies such as Bertelsmann and Holtzbrinck, the French conglomerate Lagardère, the British media conglomerate Pearson, and Rupert Murdoch's Austra-lian News Corp. all sought to acquire trade publishers located in the United States. According to John B. Thompson, there were four main reasons for this level of interest. First, European publishers had limited growth oppor-tunities in their domestic fields. By buying an American publisher, they could expand their holdings and acquire a major stake in the globally domi-nant English-language publishing industry. Second, media conglomerates that already operated in English, such as Pearson and News Corp., wanted to be part of the American market. Third, the publishing market was relatively stable, and so one way for these conglomerates to grow quickly was to acquire more publishers. And fourth, it was a way for publishing houses to achieve vertical integration within their own industry by purchasing or merging with paperback publishing companies in the wake of the paperback revolution (Thompson 2010, 109–10). This move did change what was published, and why. It would directly affect the publishing industry's attitude to certain kinds of memoir writing, and decisions about publishing it.

But before we discuss what happened to memoir, here is the story of the mergers that rocked the publishing industry and made it operate more like other cultural industries, so that it becomes clear how macro developments in the industry affected micro issues connected to what kinds of titles went into print. Between 1960 and 1989, a twenty-nine-year span, there were 570 mergers in the publishing business. Between 1990 and 1995, that figure was approximately 300. Between 1996 and 2001 the figure jumped to 380, a pace that Greco calls "staggering" (2004, 77). Some industry insiders were afraid that the result of the mergers would be market concentration and monopolies, as the host of smaller and medium-sized companies were reduced to four large and powerful publishing groups: Random House (owned by Bertelsmann), Penguin (owned by Pearson until Bertelsmann merged it with Random House in 2012), HarperCollins (owned by News Corp.) and Simon & Schuster (owned most recently by CBS).[5] But Greco concludes that the mergers did not significantly affect market concentration in the book business. Publisher mergers occurred at a relatively low rate compared to other kinds of mergers of the time (2000, 321), and market concentration in the publishing industry actually declined between 1995 and 1996 because new publishers entered the market (2000, 329). The effect was that the scale of publishing became divided between the large umbrella companies containing formerly independent firms, and small independent firms that specialized in particular kinds of publishing. Mid-size publishing companies do not survive well in such a competitive atmosphere (Thompson 2010, 146–70).

The structure of the large companies did not have the effect of destroying the commitment to quality that some editors feared, because most acquisitions that occurred in the 1980s merged business functions, but larger companies were not willing or able to combine editorial offices, even for imprints. Smaller publishers with large amounts of social capital operate as brands that ensure quality. This remains important in the world of publishing. Even during the time of the most frenetic mergers, "book publishing remained essentially a cottage industry" as smaller publishers were bought by larger ones (Luey 2009a, 378). Although Bertelsmann owns it, Random House is in fact an umbrella enterprise that owns dozens of smaller publishers and imprints. These smaller "publishers" maintain their own editorial staff and identity. In the case of smaller companies, Beth Luey points out that buyouts are not always negative: when the heads of smaller family-owned publishers such as Knopf or Pantheon wanted to retire, buyouts were a way for these publishers to leave the field without ending the lives of their companies. At the same time, smaller presses did not disappear, but made money by serving niche markets such as regional audiences, religious groups, minority groups, museums, historical societies, and the academic world (Luey 2009a, 377–78). Moreover, some of the large media companies that bought publishers were subsequently bought out themselves, as was the case with Time Warner when AOL bought it in 2000 (Greco 2004, 61). Therefore, the tendency of smaller publishers to preserve their identities inside of larger conglomerates did not affect what these publishers continued to produce, even though their owners were often large, foreign-owned corporations. After 2001, in the wake of the September 11 attacks and the collapse of the stock market, merger activity slowed. Large media companies such as Viacom, Vivendi, and AOL-Time Warner began to sell off assets, including publishers such as Simon & Schuster. The promise that new technologies would mean a convergence of media hardware technologies into single systems where content could simply "flow" from one form of media to another still had not materialized (Wirtén 2009, 402). Although book sales have remained strong and more titles are in print than ever before, the publishing industry has to compete for consumer attention with other media while book prices have not kept pace with the rising costs of publishing (Greco 2000, 334).

In this competitive environment, where publishers were expected to run profitable operations and to make the sales targets of their parent corporations, one aspect of the business became very important: bestselling titles, sometimes called "blockbusters." This is the source of the memoir boom, because the industry's reliance on blockbusters began to include memoirs. The increased importance of bestselling fiction and non-fiction in general was caused by three factors. First, as I mentioned, corporate mergers had created larger publishing companies with more capital to spend on publishing advances. At the same time, the head offices of these publishers began to require that more titles perform well. As early as 1981, Thomas Whiteside argued in *The Blockbuster Complex* that the mergers of paperback publishers and hardcover publishers had created the capital for huge advances to be paid to authors for potential bestselling books as houses competed for contracts. The bidding wars happened for major authors, but they also happened for individual non-fiction titles. One example of a non-fiction blockbuster is the self-help book *I'm OK, You're OK*, which became a bestseller in the 1970s after Harper & Row sold the paperback rights for the book to Avon for one million dollars, a large sum of money at the time (1981, 19). Some publishers, it has been argued, chased bestselling books at the expense of backlists, although this has been disputed (Shatzkin 1981, 204–205; Schiffrin 2001, 112–14). But it is accurate to say that bestselling books represent a gamble for publishers, and so smaller and medium-sized publishers often cannot bear the expense of that risk. Large publishers, however, began to compete for promising titles in the hope that they would become bestsellers and help their operations. Potentially bestselling books were also helped by two other developments: the importance of television talk shows as a marketing tool for "big" books, because publishing houses do not put much money into marketing (Whiteside 1981, 21–22, Scott 2009, 77), and the existence of bestseller lists in newspapers and magazines. The latter, as Laura Miller has pointed out, are more useful as marketing tools in the book industry than as indicators of which books are actually top sellers (2000).

In addition, developments in the retail and distribution sector of the publishing industry began to make the pursuit of bestsellers more lucrative for publishers: a case of the "tail" of production (retail) wagging the proverbial dog. Early in the 1980s, Thomas Whiteside had already blamed what he thought of as a crisis in the book business on the advent of the paperback revolution and its distribution system in drugstores and other non-traditional venues (1981, 18). A lesser known fact is that mass-market hardcover books—especially bestselling titles—became important in the 1960s and 1970s because chain bookstores (unlike more traditional independent booksellers) were willing to stock them. By the 1990s, big box retailer bookstores like Borders and Barnes & Noble were able to ignore what publishers wanted to charge for books and apply the practices of deep discounting, selective ordering, and charging high prices for display space in their stores. One of the results of this change in the business of books was the rise of the blockbuster because large bookstores were able to move many more copies than smaller stores could in earlier decades (Thompson 2010, 36–37). More recently the entrance of large general retail chains into the book market, such as Costco, Target, and Walmart, also had the effect of supporting the market for bestsellers in hardcover and paperback (Thompson 2010, 48). As the sales of bestselling titles increased exponentially from the 1970s to the present—Thompson says that by the 2000s, a hardcover book by a brand-name author would often sell more than a million copies in the United States alone (37)—the publishing of big frontlist books began to be crucial for publishers, despite the risks involved. Publishers had to respond to the demand for bestsellers by trying to produce more of them.

The third factor that contributed to the pursuit of potential bestsellers was the rise of literary agents in power and influence. The role of the agent is extremely complex in contemporary publishing, and so it is not possible to detail what agents have come to mean for the production of books in the United States.[6] When what Thompson calls "super agents" began to advocate for their clients in the 1980s, they were able to win large advances for their books. Increasingly, editors have come to rely on agents to determine what books could become good sellers, and agents themselves have become acquisitions editors, looking over manuscripts and in some cases suggesting the genre for a book, asking an author to write a book on a particular topic (Thompson 2010, 74–75, 96), or even making suggestions for improving the writing (Hart 2010, 39–40). Particularly in the case of non-fiction, agents also create what is called the "platform" for an author, which is the type and amount of public identity that a certain author has. Agents try to enhance the author's platform on television and in other venues in order to create a pre-existing audience for a book (Thompson 2010, 86). Agents have become key to the hunt for a potentially bestselling book: they are mediators in their own right in print culture, just as they are in other media, such as television or film (Finkelstein 2009, 336). In light of what Thompson calls "passion and belief" in the book industry about what might prove to sell well, agents are able to drive up bidding for potential blockbusters (98). They too are responsible for creating the environment for potential bestsellers that fuels the memoir boom.

These factors for the production of blockbusters are the reason why authors such as Jackie Collins and Tom Wolfe rose to prominence, so much so that their names became brands and appeared in larger print on their books than the titles did. But the increased reliance on blockbusters and the new tendency to publish all books as paperbacks also meant that in some cases, memoirists such as Mary Karr and Frank McCourt (and earlier, the autobiographer and biographer Alex Haley) were able to also command large advances because of their presence on bestseller lists, their visibility when they were interviewed by the media, and the high sales figures for their books. Like their novelist counterparts, memoirists like these could and did produce blockbusters. The larger publishing companies began to rely on them to produce, as the story about the children's writing centre illustrates, "more books" of a specific type, because these authors were able to present *themselves* in public and in print in ways that meshed well with the new pressures the industry was facing: to produce bestselling authors and faster release times for titles with immediate public relevance and appeal.

PUBLISHING AND THE MEMOIR BOOM

Until the time of mergers the publishing industry had made distinctions between cheap paperback generic fiction such as Westerns, detective novels or romances, and literary fiction produced by the trade industry. It had also made distinctions between popular non-fiction in paperback—which could be everything from celebrity memoirs to cookbooks—and what is still called serious non-fiction in trade hardcover—which was anything from "literary" memoirs, political biographies, books about current events, or philosophical books. But after the merger activity died down in 2001, these lines became increasingly difficult to draw. Popular non-fiction was no longer expected to pay for serious non-fiction, for example, since many more books were now expected to make a profit. The mergers of paperback and trade companies meant that the values of the paperback revolution had become part of these larger corporations. The changes in the retail environment, the increase in the influence of agents, and the need for the publishing corporations to turn greater profits meant that increasingly, companies looked for profitable books that could become bestsellers, or that could be the product of brand-name authors, whether these were fiction authors like Jeffrey Archer or J.K. Rowling or authors whose public personae (what could be called their platform) would sell non-fiction books. At the same time, the book publishing industry is producing more books than ever before. In 2002, more than 150,000 new books were published, which is about seventeen books per hour (Greco 2004, 6). Consumers buy roughly half of these books (the rest are returned), and from 2001 onward, half were in popular fiction. But in 2002, sales in general non-fiction were strong (fourth place), and most other sales categories (except for children's literature) were non-fiction as well (Greco 2004, 216). But what is even more important than these statistics is that the *visibility* of non-fiction titles, especially those by celebrities, was very high at the same time (2004, 136–37). Even though popular fiction sold better as a category than any other, the visibility of memoirs on bestseller lists, in bookstores, and in the media meant that from the early part of the decade onward, memoir and biography at least *appeared* to be important, and life stories began to circulate at a higher level of visibility. The source of the memoir boom, then, is not just higher rates of sales for the genre, but higher rates of visibility for some of its books and authors.

Although non-fiction has always been produced, the higher rates of visibility that bring in larger book advances, better book deals and bestselling titles mean that more memoirs are produced than before, more are selling, and (perhaps) still more are being acquired as writers, agents, publishers, and sellers realize that there is a steady demand for them. Like their hardcover fiction equivalents, trade hardcover and paperback memoirs by authors who can operate as brands or have a national platform are central to the book business today, particularly since the competitive environment requires that more books need to be potential bestsellers (and few books can be risks) than before. And that means that non-fiction often has to feature life stories by people who are already in the public eye as celebrities, political figures, or both, because they are the people who have a platform (Thompson 2010, 192, 203).

The memoir boom is supported by such books, but they are by no means the only memoirs produced. As Thompson says, new books are often sold by agents and adopted by publishers because they are *comparable* to others. This means that a book is often sold because it might be "like" another solid-selling book. This is one way for editors to try "hedging the indeterminacy of the new" as they try to get a book adopted by their publisher. Another is to use platform to sell the book within the organization (Thompson 2010, 203–204). Comparability in the case of a memoir involves comparing it *generically* to another book that is like it (for instance, Vicky Myron's 2008 memoir about Dewey the library cat might be the next *Marley and Me*, the bestselling memoir about a man and his dog—and in fact it was a sensation).[7] This is a strategy that can help unknown memoirists get published. Platform, on the other hand, is well suited to selling celebrity memoirs, because these are already about public image, and the potential for the author to increase their public image. As Yagoda points out, memoirists can exhibit their platform more easily on television than fiction writers can, something that he thinks caused the memoir boom to take off during the late 1990s: "In the publishing environment of the time, promotion was seen as the key to commercial success; the key to promotion was getting on talk shows; and the best way to get on a talk show was with a dramatic or unusual personal story. Once a novelist answered the 'Is it autobiographical?' question, the only thing left to discuss was No. 2 pencils versus Microsoft Word.... Julie Grau, the editor of *Girl, Interrupted,* explained to *Vanity Fair* in 1997 why memoir trumped fiction in the marketplace: 'You can send the "I" out on tour'"(Yagoda 2009, 239).

Memoirs, therefore, can exhibit either or both of these features: they are capable of being comparable because they are generic, but their authors—if they are known or could be famous—can also easily exhibit platform. Memoirs can be produced quickly if required. Why might this be important? What publishers call "the gap" between the profits they expect to make and the additional margin required by their corporate owners in a given year has to be made up by sales from books produced outside the usual publishing cycle. Thompson calls this measure "extreme publishing." It "works particularly well with certain kinds of non-fiction books," including celebrity memoirs and topical works that can be produced and marketed quickly, taking advantage of author platform or timeliness. Many memoirs exhibit both of these qualities (Thompson 2010, 225–226). Some of the jump in the production of memoirs can be attributed to this kind of gap publishing.

Even in the wake of Oprah Winfrey's questions of 2005 about whether publishers can be trusted to deliver memoir as a product, the wave of memoirs shows no sign of cresting. As I mentioned in the introduction, Nielsen Bookscan has reported that sales in personal memoirs, childhood memoirs, and parental memoirs increased more than 400 percent from 2004 to 2008 (Yagoda 2009, 7). There is no reason to suppose that this trend has slowed or reversed. The Bookscan statistic supplements Albert Greco's earlier finding that celebrity memoirs were already doing very well in the early part of the decade, with books by financial advisor Suze Orman and Fox news presenter Bill O'Reilly, for example, topping more than a million copies each (2004, 136–37). But memoirs by authors who are not famous also appear to be popular. In the words of Susan Shapiro, memoir by anyone is worth writing, as long as the story is dramatic: "Even in this bad economy, first-person books are more popular than ever. The public is hungry for passionate personal narratives, whether they're about marital meanderings, blog projects (like Julie Powell's *Julie and Julia*), or Afghan adventures. You don't have to be a celebrity, politician or daredevil to sell your story. In fact, I've published three memoirs chronicling stupid substance abuse and bedroom and career blunders from my past, and my journalism students have recently signed book deals about obsessive-compulsive disorder, sex and single motherhood" (2010, 46).

What is interesting about Shapiro's comments is that, like other commentators, she pictures a hungry public who want to consume printed lives of many kinds, but she sees this hunger as positive. The changes in publishing in the last four decades have allowed that hunger to be satisfied, until the call for "more books" is heard as an industrial and public demand, within publishing houses and—as we shall see in the next chapter—as part of the retail environment as well. The story of the publishing industry's transformation from family-owned, interest-driven businesses to their position as members of larger media conglomerates has—to a large extent—changed the visibility and number of memoirs available. In the next chapter, we look at the next piece of the puzzle, the sector of the book industry that now also works to influence what is published and how the public buys books: the book retailing industry.

Chapter 2

BOOKSTORES, GENRE, AND EVERYDAY PRACTICES

> Bookshops—real and virtual—are a reminder that critics of the contemporary must hold things together: books on the shelf, production and consumption, addressee and addressor, and our own imaginative work of self-identification.
>
> – *Gillian Whitlock, Soft Weapons: Autobiography in Transit*

I have been looking at how genre is an important aspect of book publishing, because a consideration of memoir necessarily involves thinking about what kind of book merits publishing, and why certain kinds of stories become public. But in the book production and distribution cycle, it is important to consider the stage between the book's publication and its reading, that is, the selling and purchasing of books. Before a book can be read, it must be acquired in some fashion, and there are many ways to get books into the hands of readers. The transaction is not always monetary. Books can be given as gifts, awarded as prizes, borrowed from libraries, or even stolen. But at some point in the journey to readers, a book must be bought and sold like any other commodity before it is read, and unless it is bought directly from a publisher, it must be purchased from a book retailer. Although most readers do not think of their books as ordinary commodities, and many academics who study books—with the notable exception of book historians and publishing historians—do not think very much about the material circumstances of book acquisition, the scene of bookselling is an important part of the cycle of book production. Scholarship, too, is sparse in this area, especially when it comes to the study of contemporary bookselling. With some significant exceptions such as Laura J. Miller's study of American bookstores, *Reluctant Capitalists* (2007), and a shorter study she did with a research team about the Chapters superstore (2001), sections of Claire Squires' book about publishing and marketing in the United Kingdom, *Marketing Literature* (2007), Juliet Gardiner's examination of the online bookseller Amazon.com (2002), and John B. Thompson's chapter "The Growth of the Retail Chains" in his book *Merchants of Culture* (2010), there is little sustained research available about the role of the contemporary bookstore in publishing and reception, or the nature of the book as a commodity in the environment of bookstores, whether they are online, in a mall, or on a city street. As Miller notes, most material "tends to lack a critical edge" because it comes from memoirs of booksellers and publishers, reports, and hagiographies of industry titans (2007, 6). What field work there is has been undertaken by journals that serve the publishing industry directly: these are a valuable source of information about the ongoing conflict between major chain stores and independent bookstores, for instance. Government publications like those produced by the Department of Canadian Heritage can provide a snapshot of a national publishing industry that includes bookselling in its research, but their focus is necessarily national, and can look more like reports from the front than analyses of what bookselling means.[1] My study of bookselling aims to contribute some field observations to the burgeoning study of bookstores and the important role they play in the production and distribution of books in late capitalism, paying particular attention to the idea of genre and how it affects the way books are marketed and sold. These investigations will help to explain what role memoir and biography play in the book retail environment, and how these books reach their audiences.

Genre plays a central role in the management of consumer expectations. In *Reluctant Capitalists,* Miller mentions that "decisions about where to shelve individual titles influence which readers will pick up a book.... the simple act of book classification [in a bookstore] may predetermine a book's audience" (2007, 96–97). Miller's observation is key to understanding how genre works in a bookstore. As in the case of book publishing and classification, generic expectations do more than create a passive backdrop for the exchange of books: they actively participate in the process of exchange, even influencing where readers will pick up books, and which ones they might read as a result. Genre therefore can be understood in the context of bookselling to actively participate in the social world of bookstores and to help shape the worlds of the customers and/or readers who frequent them. Genre takes on the function of social action (as it is understood by theorists in the field of rhetoric) in this last aspect of book production before books pass into the hands of readers and are consumed—that is, before they are read.

My point of entry into this discussion of genre is this: if genre can be understood as a social action that is part of daily life and as an organizing principle for the production of books themselves, what kinds of roles does genre play in the daily life of a bookstore and in its position in the cycle of book production? If we understand Gerard Genette's sense of paratext as a zone of transaction between authors, publishers, and readers (1997, 1), then the bookstore can be seen as another zone of transaction, where ideas about paratextual elements, including ideas about what a book is and what is it for, are exchanged. Understanding the book's journey from publication to the hands of potential readers is includes recognizing the role that genre plays in the environment of bookstores themselves, since as we have seen, publishers use elaborate strategies—including the use of generic identifications—in order to sell a book. In order to examine this, we need to understand genre not as a taxonomic category or even as a classification strategy, but as a social production that organizes knowledge in space and time.

I began my research with a few questions about genre and bookstores. When a customer enters a bookstore, how and when does genre come into play? Do generic expectations and principles structure the working lives of bookstore employees? Is there a spatial aspect to genre that influences the layout of bookstores and the flow of customers through the store? Is there a difference between what independent bookstores do with classification systems and what large chain stores do, and if there is, what can that difference tell us about store cultures? To explore these questions, I conducted interviews with bookstore workers (who were owners, managers, and book buyers) at a total of eleven English-language bookstores in Canada: ten independent stores across the country, and one chain store, Chapters Indigo.[2] I summarized the results of these interviews and categorized similar features with these rubrics: the store brand or culture, how the interviewee understood the category of non-fiction to work, shelving practices, whether the publisher's generic categories on the back covers of books were used, the process of ordering books, and who the store viewed as a competitor. I also recorded my observations about the store interior and exterior, and I took photographs when I was given permission to do so. The questions I asked about store culture and practices enabled me to draw some conclusions about the role of genre in the daily working lives of bookstore employees, and about the horizon of generic expectations that customers have when they are in a particular store's environment. I also learned first-hand in a Canadian context about what Laura J. Miller calls "shopping for community," which is the way independent retailers often talk about the differences between the service provided by chains and big-box retailers, as opposed to the service that independents say that they can offer (2007, 119). The importance of community, at least in a symbolic way, is what makes booksellers appear to act differently from many other retailers, and it makes the customers of bookstores act differently too. In the current climate where most bookstores see their role as serving communities, or as active participants in communities, genre as a social category becomes a way to structure the bond between customers and sellers, particularly as independent booksellers strive to remain in the book market alongside chain and big-box retailers. Since I conducted my research, some of these stores have closed, including Frog Hollow Books in Halifax, Duthie Books in Vancouver, the Toronto Women's Bookstore, and Pages in Toronto. However, Ria Bluemer, the former manager of Duthie, opened her own store, Sitka Books, in 2010, and the store Type, which is on Queen Street west of where Pages was in Toronto, has opened a second location. Although closures of independent bookstores like Frog Hollow, Duthie, and Pages are often seen as a cause for alarm, I would argue that the re-emergence of general and independent bookstores in the wake of some closures shows that the retailing market remains dynamic, and independent stores are still viable in the book market, partly because of the emphasis on community and store environment found in most independent bookstores that do survive.

GENRE AS SOCIAL (BOOKSTORE) ACTION

As I discussed in the introduction, genre is much more than a neutral or even a conservative way to classify objects and keep them in place. In that sense, although I sometimes refer to classification as an aspect of genre, the term "genre" means much more than the act of classification alone. Carolyn Miller and other New Rhetorical theorists of genre have pointed out that genres can also be a type of social action that can enact practices counter to the status quo, depending on how they are deployed. A genre *acts* in the

world because its effects of restriction and allowance are spatial and tem-
poral. Genres do "put things in place," but the effect of this can be to create
new arrangements, and therefore new possibilities, of knowledge. Much as
the rearrangement of objects can change our understanding of spatiality as
it transforms the objects, genre has the ability to actively transform how we
know what we know and how we know it (Miller 1994). An example of how
this works can be found in Beth Luey's discussion of American librarianship and the development of non-fiction as a category. Anyone entering a
library encounters what Luey calls "the Great Divide" between fiction on
one side of a library, and non-fiction on the other. The Dewey Decimal
System of classification created this divide to categorize non-fiction in the
nineteenth century, because "like most librarians of his time, Dewey dis-
dained fiction and did not really care how it was catalogued" (2010, 8).
The spatial division of the Great Divide separates the two areas, but the
attention the Dewey Decimal System pays to non-fiction created complex
generic distinctions as well as value judgments about what good writing is.
In a time when cultural authorities actively campaigned against fiction as
evidence of moral decline, the spatial arrangement of libraries and the use
of rubrics to distinguish non-fiction seemed to emphasize the importance
of the latter. Today, those categories implicitly serve to support the cult of
the author because (unless it is genre fiction), fiction is shelved alphabeti-
cally by author, but non-fiction is not. The spatial arrangement of genre in
libraries helped to create the terms for which each type of writing was to be
understood.

According to Claire Squires in *Marketing Literature*, genre plays an
active role in the physical layout of bookstores in the United Kingdom,
particularly in terms of what David Duff calls the "conscious" component
of genre. Squires' examination of genre in bookstores shows how three
chain bookstores in Oxford, UK—Blackwell's, Borders (now defunct), and
Waterstones—placed fiction in or near the front section of their ground
floors, with generic fiction figuring prominently and bestselling non-fiction nearby. Other non-fiction sections, including computer books and
gardening books, were located on other floors, although Squires says that
beyond these general observations, the three chain stores had such different layouts that it is hard to keep the differing classification systems straight
(2007, 94–95). The single independent she saw, the QI bookshop in Oxford,
did not use fiction or non-fiction categorizations to organize its books.
QI had categories like "The Good Life," "Modest Proposals," "Ice," "Lives,"
"Secret Lives," and "Relations." Within these categories non-fiction and fic-

tion appear to "encourage ... the potential reader to browse and to ponder the links between categories and individual titles. Niche bookshops such as QI are a reminder that layout—and categorization—could be done entirely otherwise" (Squires 2007, 96). Squires' observations show that genre is part of the marketing strategy for bookstores, and that generic classification also serves to underscore a specific store culture with cultural values that its consumers may choose to share.

Understanding store culture is central to understanding how booksellers sell books today, in part because booksellers have long considered themselves to sell culture, not "just" books. Books are not commonly thought about as commodities, despite the fact that they are objects that are bought and sold. Because of this, booksellers have, since the advent of mass distribution systems for books in the nineteenth century, been seen (and have seen themselves) as different from other kinds of entrepreneurs. In the United States, before the American Civil War, publishing evolved "from a genteel, artisan trade supported by civic patronage, religious groups, and local businesses to thriving, modern, cutthroat profit-driven national industry" (Zboray and Zboray 2005, xviii). In a move that will appear familiar to those who watch the attempts of big-box chain bookstores and mall chains to corner the book market, larger publishers bought printing companies as well as book and magazine outlets in a form of market vertical integration. Through a system of book peddlers, rail deliveries, and guaranteed returns for unsold books, publishers were able to distribute books more quickly and cheaply than before, although peddlers and other local sellers found it hard to make money in a market where free materials also circulated widely (Zboray and Zboray 2005, 128–42).

While peddlers roaming the countryside found it hard to sell materials, the American bookstore became a place of social interaction, where authors and readers could gather and feel at home with other like-minded people (Zboray and Zboray 2005, 142–44). This picture of the early bookshop as a small-business haven and social gathering place for book-lovers is an interesting one. The bookstore as a refuge from the market, a refuge that resembles a social institution more than a business, is an image mostly sustained by a market-driven and cutthroat big-business system of book publication and distribution. And so, this image of the early bookstore is remarkably similar to the picture of the modern bookstore or, at least, to the independent bookstore as a cherished ideal. The debates of the 1990s in North America and the United Kingdom about the advent of big-box chain stores and online retailers, the attempts of independent shops to compete with them, and the pervasive sense that competition between stores should not happen because books are not like other commodities are the latest signs of an old phenomenon (L. Miller 2007, 5–6). In an economic environment that separates culture from commerce, bookstores occupy an ambivalent middle ground in which culture and commerce are, from necessity, yoked together. As David Wright observes, the book trade is one of the "culture industries" in which the connections between consumption and production are understood not to work precisely along capitalist lines. The fact that cultural industries often do work like other industries means that there is significant public ambivalence about what it means to treat the commodities of culture as if they were like other commodities: "Consuming 'culture' is of a different order of meaning from consuming other commodities. Alongside the powerful narratives of the triumph of consumerism in contemporary society, there are equally powerful narratives of ambivalence to consumerism as evidence of shallow engagement with the material market place and crass commercialism. The consumption of culture somehow stands askance from, or is indeed seen as the antidote to, these kinds of criticisms, as if this type of consumption isn't consumption at all despite the persistent reliance on processes of economic or commodity exchange" (Wright 2005, 106–107).

The story of the contemporary book industry in North America and the United Kingdom, and the role of the bookstore in that story, embodies this sense of ambivalence about capitalism and consumer culture. There is an elegiac quality about it, which David Hesmondalgh relates to the tendency of critics and pundits to evoke a narrative of decline in the selling and production of books without providing any hard evidence for the existence of this trend (2007, 292–94). As Laura J. Miller points out, with no little sense of irony about the American publishing industry, this ambivalence often appears as nostalgia for a conveniently vanished golden age of bookselling: "it is striking how frequently people will comment that the book business is just not what it used to be. With great regularity, members of the industry wistfully hearken back to a golden age when individuals entered this line of work because they cared about books, not money; when publishers engaged with writers, not bestseller lists; and when the American public supported the neighborhood bookseller, who worked so hard to make a living. However, if one actually tries to locate this bygone era, it keeps receding further and further into the past" (L. Miller 2007, 23).

But Miller also points out that it is important to understand the context of that nostalgia. As independent booksellers try to imagine an economy where large players are not always the most successful, or when booksellers think of consumption as something that is not only about instrumentality, this contemplation of the complexity of consumption and its politics offers ways to imagine capitalism differently, and to see how daily consumption is not always inherently about pleasure, or about profit (224). And if it is not, then like other aspects of popular culture, the buying of books is a complex cultural activity subject to the centrifugal power of powerful corporations, and the centripetal actions of ordinary people and local companies whose activities cannot be controlled by the actions of the centre (Fiske 1989). The bookstore itself has long been understood as the place where ambivalence about consumerism and even about capitalism itself is enacted. The politics of genre within bookstores highlights how this ambivalence works. Before I go on to discuss these issues, I will provide some background about the situation of bookselling in the United States and Canada from the 1990s to the present time.

INDEPENDENT AND BIG-BOX RETAILERS: BOOKSTORES IN NORTH AMERICA

The story of bookselling in the United States traces a trajectory that shares some similarities to the terrain of bookselling in Canada today. According to Laura J. Miller, after the advent of book subscriptions, general stores that sold books, and the era of book peddlers, bookselling in the nineteenth century was dominated by independent retailers who developed a sense that bookselling was not like other kinds of mercantile activity, and that quality bookstores should sell quality books—which meant not selling cheap paperback fiction like dime novels, romances, or thrillers. Those were left to drugstores and other venues that did not specialize in books. Over time, booksellers adopted the attitude of major publishers in that they too promoted high culture as opposed to "popular culture," which was associated with commercial activities and market forces. Bookstores like these sold "literature," an increasingly more narrowly defined way to mark a difference between commercial books and books that were thought to promote higher learning (Radway 1997, 142–43). Booksellers, therefore, actively tried to dispel the idea that they were commercial enterprises, even though that is in fact precisely what they were. This is one reason why, unlike the magazine industry, the book industry did not use wholesalers to quickly get books to stores, because sellers and publishers prized the trust-based relationships they had with each other. A business based on mutual regard did not look or act as big business might (L. Miller 1997, 27–32).

Threats to this system before the advent of World War II came from drugstores and stationery stores that sold increasingly popular paperbacks. Starting in the 1920s, the popularity of the Book-of-the-Month Club, which sold books directly to readers, helped create the idea that books could be sold in places other than highbrow bookstores. At the same time, department stores began to sell books in order to create a more highbrow image for themselves in the eyes of the public (32–36). As Janice Radway has discussed in detail in *A Feeling for Books*, the direct marketing system of the Book-of-the-Month Club posed a threat to booksellers, who saw the club as a middlebrow incursion into the highbrow values of the bookselling world and its genteel association with publishers (1997, 198–210). Department stores were seen as another threat to traditional bookselling, since stores like Macy's in New York City marketed books much like other commodities, and even sold similar commodities—such as cookbooks and cookware—together (L. Miller 2007, 36).

The postwar baby boom brought many changes to the book buying habits of Americans and Canadians alike. Higher enrolment in universities brought an increase in textbook sales for publishers across North America. Because they became used to reading paperback books at school, postsecondary and secondary school students also began to buy classics in paperback issued by companies like Penguin in the United Kingdom, Pocket Books in the United States, or the New Canadian Library in Canada. This new buying habit changed how North Americans saw paperback books. No longer were paperbacks associated only with the lowbrow world of dime novels sold in drugstores; they could now be the way that literary classics and paperback non-fiction books could reach wider markets (Davis 1984). Bookstores began to carry more of them until, by the 1960s, there were independent stores that specialized in paperback books. These stores were often run by maverick retailers who had participated in the countercultural movements in universities in North America. At the same time, Walden Book Company opened its first mall chain bookstore in 1962, tapping into the growing suburban market. B. Dalton followed, and by 1982 Waldenbooks and B. Dalton had 24% of the retail market in the United States (L. Miller 2007, 45).

In Canada, the homegrown chain Coles Bookstore and the British chain W.H. Smith also moved into malls and, until the 1990s, were both significant players in the book trade. With their commitment to serving mall customers and suburban markets by providing deeply discounted books in their brightly lit almost supermarket-like environments, the chain stores differed significantly (so independent retailers thought) from the less standardized, less corporatized environments of the independent booksellers, who emphasized customer service and a dedication to bookselling as a kind of knowledge provision to a community. During the 1960s, therefore, two new kinds of sellers began to change how books were bought and read in North America: the chain stores in malls, and the independent maverick paperback sellers who were part of counterculture movements. Because each type of store appeared to serve different markets, the independent sellers did not see chain stores as a threat to their way of understanding the book business. But when the two newer streams in bookselling finally began to compete in the 1990s, the struggles between independents and chains showed traces of their very different ideologies—formed during the 1960s— about what books are, and how they should be sold to the general public.

In the 1990s, the North American book retail market began to change due to two factors: the advent of the big-box retailers[3] and the appearance of online booksellers, most notably Amazon.com and its subsidiaries worldwide. In the United States, the mall chain B. Dalton was purchased by Barnes & Noble, a bookseller that had been in business for over a century. Barnes & Noble also bought chains like Doubleday Book Shops and Scribners, making their company the biggest player in the United States. As mall construction slowed down during the 1980s, Crown Books grew its chain business by using deep discounts to attract consumers. Then, in 1990, Crown Books built the first Super Crown, a big-box retail store based on the Toys "R" Us prototype (L. Miller 2007, 50). Not be outdone, Barnes & Noble built an even larger flagship big-box store. The Borders company also entered the big-box retail market in 1990, and by 1995 it had become a publicly traded company with many big-box stores in its stable. Large chains' sales rose from 23% of the book retail market in 1993 to 50% by the end of the decade. Independent booksellers that could not survive this competition began to close, although (as we shall see) the ones that survived were able to thrive in the new environment (Thompson 2010, 31–32).

But the dominance of the large chains in the market was already under threat. Chain stores had already had to shift away from maintaining backlists and stock more frontlist titles because they could move them faster. This practice created what John Thompson has called "the hardback revolution" as mass-market paperback sales began to decline (Thompson 2010, 34–35). The result was that the backlists of publishers were not as much in demand. But this began to change in 1995, when online retailing became part of the industry. In that year, Jeff Bezos launched Amazon.com, an online book retailer that used a warehouse distribution system similar to those of the big-box retailers. Amazon proved to be a good venue for selling backlist titles and specialist books, since it did not need to maintain this stock: the company's practice of on-demand ordering from suppliers meant that it could do what chain stores could not in this area (Thompson 2010, 43). Together, online and big-box retailing began to take market share away from the mall chain stores, whose numbers had started to decline. The big players' practice of deep discounting began to negatively impact the sales of independent sellers as well, who had relied on bestsellers to pay for the less popular stock on offer. Independents in the United States and Canada complained about these deep discounting practices, and about the capacity of the large companies to buy books in large lots at higher publisher discounts, thereby eliminating the ability of independents to locate and sell popular books at competitive prices (L. Miller 2007, 168–69). Unlike the chains, big-box retail environments imitated the relaxing and highbrow environment of many independent bookshops, with their comfortable chairs, classical music on offer, wooden bookshelves, and a café nearby. Independent retailers in the United States tried to counter the rise of big-box book retailing by emphasizing their willingness to provide customer service, but they also emphasized their belief—as independent store owners—in community-building as part of their retail enterprises. The stress on community was meant to highlight a long-standing suspicion of the American public toward large corporations and their challenge to what their critics often posit as authentic American life in small towns or urban neighbourhoods. As Miller says, "maintaining that no large corporation can be truly sensitive to local needs and traditions, the [American] independent bookseller purports to stand as a bulwark against the total destruction of meaningful community life" (2007, 120). It appears, however, that Americans do enjoy shopping at big-box stores and chains, as a market-share study by *Publisher's Weekly* indicates (Milliot 2008, 8). Corporations—for better or worse—are a major part of American retail life. The lament of independent booksellers for a different kind of retailing where, like the local neighbourhood bar Cheers seemed to represent on the show of the same name, the bookstore is a place "where everybody knows your name" is a kind of retailing that "Americans at least profess to miss" (L. Miller 2007, 121). During the 1990s, American independent stores formed organizations to oppose practices like deep discounting, and they appealed to their customers to shop at independent stores for ethical reasons. The American Booksellers Association even pursued a legal suit against large retailers, although the suit was not successful (L. Miller 2007,

171–98). What is worth noting about the opposition of independent retailers to the practices of corporate booksellers is that independent stores in the United States have had to forge a "brand" for themselves to differentiate their ways of doing business from those of Barnes & Noble or Borders. The result has been that independent booksellers are much clearer than they have ever been about the "culture" of their stores, and they are very conscious about how store practices contribute to that culture, a culture connected to the culture of book appreciation they believe their customers share. As independent stores develop this idea that store culture and book appreciation are at the core of their business, new book merchants—this time large chains that do not sell books primarily, such as Walmart, Costco, K-Mart, and other wholesalers—are becoming a challenge to big-box chains, particularly in the area of frontlist selling (Thompson 2010, 46–49). Like the department stores of the 1930s and 1940s, these large chains pose a threat to specialist bookstore chains like the now-defunct Borders chain and Barnes & Noble, but perhaps not to the independent stores that have managed to survive.

In Canada, the pattern of retail development has been similar to that of the United States—the story of book retailing in Canada shows in high relief what the battle between independents and chains has created in the book industry. Chain stores, which were brightly lit like supermarkets and organized much like B. Dalton's or Waldenbooks, included the Canadian-owned Coles Books, which was mall-based, SmithBooks, a mall chain that originated in the United Kingdom, and, in Quebec, Archambault, a predominantly French-language chain. There were also smaller chains in operation that were not based in malls, including Toronto's mini-chain Book-City, Winnipeg's McNally Robinson, and Vancouver's Duthie Books and the Book Warehouse. Coles Books also owned the flagship store, World's Biggest Bookstore in Toronto.

Until 1995, the relationship between these chain stores and independents was fairly stable. In that year, the federal government of Canada prevented Borders from entering the bookselling market on the grounds that an American book superstore would endanger the independent retailing market and its championing of the Canadian culture industry (L. Miller 2007, 112–13). One result was the emergence in the same year of Chapters, a big-box retailer that was the result of a merger between SmithBooks and Coles and partly backed by American superstore Barnes & Noble. As in the United States, suddenly two of the largest chains in Canada had become a single super-chain, and that chain moved rapidly into big-box retail. Chapters used a marketing strategy identical to that of Barnes & Noble: classical music played in its large stores, each store had a Starbucks café, and the comfortable chairs and wooden bookshelves were designed to provide a highbrow retail experience for customers that would rival the atmosphere found at independent bookstores or libraries (Dixon et al. 2001). Like their American counterparts, Chapters also practised deep discounting, which undercut the sales of independent stores. Additionally, there were complaints in the media from booksellers and Canadian publishers that Chapters (initially at least) did not carry enough Canadian titles or that deep discounting was going to force Canadian-owned independents out of business (Steward 2001, 22; Eichler 2001, 17; Tedesco 2003, 2). Jack Stoddard blamed the failure of his Canadian distribution company, General Books, directly on Chapters and its policies regarding Canadian-owned publishing and distribution networks (McMurdry 2001, F3).

Like their American counterparts, Canadian independent retailers blamed the collapse of independent chains like Duthie Books or independent stores on the appearance of Chapters on the retail scene, and many customers agreed with them (Ali 2000; Fulford 2000; Jones and Doucet 1999). But Chapters, too, was vulnerable to changes in the marketplace. Although the chain was successful at first, it faced competition from Amazon.com in 2001, when the company began a Canadian website and opened a warehouse in Ontario after successfully fending off a legal challenge from Indigo—another big-box store that sold music as well as books—and from the Canadian Booksellers Association (*Gowlings Intellectual Property Report* 2004). When Chapters began to falter, Indigo facilitated a hostile takeover, and in doing so created a single big-box chain of bookstores in Canada.

But whether the enemy was Chapters or the even larger Chapters Indigo did not matter to independent retailers. As their American counterparts did, Canadian independents, under the aegis of the Canadian Booksellers Association, embarked in 1995 on an aggressive educational campaign to convince customers that independent retailers were members of the community, and that Chapters (and later Chapters Indigo) threatened book culture in Canada because it did not promote community (Lockheed 2003;). Although Chapters Indigo and Amazon.com control much of the market share of bookselling in Canada, that campaign was successful with many bookstore patrons who acted much as "citizen-consumers" and opted to shop at independents as a political stance against large corporate retailing in the book industry (L. Miller 2007, 198–200).

Years after their appearance, the existence of a big-box chain is still cited as a major reason for independent store closures.[4] Critics of the store still openly voice their dislike about Chapters Indigo's status as Canada's only big-box bookstore chain, citing its commercial feel and its lack of community involvement. Librarians also expressed opposition to Chapters (before its merger with Indigo) in a variety of professional and public forums (Dixon et al. 2001). The sense of animosity against Chapters (just before its merger) has even led to it being described as "Romulan," a reference to an enemy race in *Star Trek* that even other "evil" races like the Klingons do not like (Kingwell 2001, A14). This type of criticism took many forms in the public press (Dixon et al. 2001), but one online example is worth discussing in detail here because it focuses on genre as the crux of the "problem" of store culture at Chapters Indigo. This 2007 post on *The Torontoist* blog takes Chapters Indigo to task partly because the store does not have an "intuitive" generic classification system. Here is the explanation for the nomination of Chapters Indigo for "Villain of the Year" 2007:

> The simple task of trying to find a book [in Chapters Indigo] is complicated and made more difficult by tables, displays, and towers of "lifestyle" items that must be overcome before proceeding to an actual book section. Even then, though, the quest can become more tedious based off of the perpetually perplexing, arbitrary categorization system. Why is there a "Literature" section? It's all literature isn't it? ...
>
> Chapters/Indigo is physically and intellectually what a bookstore is not. Independent bookstores with rickety hardwood flooring; the pungent fragrance of old, dust-infested books; store owners who know their books; and those wonderfully rare gems hidden between dust and questionable food stains are a dying breed. (*Torontoist* 2007)

This post captures the suspicion that many members of the book-buying public—those who espouse "citizen consumer" principles—have about Chapters Indigo. Criticism of Chapters Indigo in this blog passage includes its status as Canada's only large chain (which is the reason for the ironic reference to all the chains it absorbed at the beginning), its gift shop, and (as a result) the perceived lack of support of the Canadian publishing community at the store. There is also nostalgia for "old" local bookstores and their non-corporate feel, although the features of the ideal store read more like those of a used bookstore than a store that sells new titles. But what is most interesting about this criticism is that it questions the *generic* choices of Chapters Indigo, and uses them to suggest that the atmosphere and sense of caring in an independent bookstore are superior. As the writer says, the classification system in a Chapters Indigo store appears to him/her to be arbitrary, and it is unclear for the writer why there is a "literature" section. The relatively disorganized, even eccentric picture of independent stores is presented as a contrast that must be preserved. Classification systems are always arbitrary and are idiosyncratic in any store environment, but the difference—which the blog author senses—is that a Chapters Indigo store does *not* have a local culture because it is part of a chain, and so its generic classifications do not appear to be naturalized because they do not refer to the values of any specific community. In other words, the writer does not trust the store because the classification system is not "organic" to his/her understanding of bookstore culture as non-corporate, supportive of local writing communities, and focused on knowledge of books as special objects. Therefore, the writer understands the generic ordering of Chapters Indigo to be alien because the store's culture is alien. Conversely, it could be said that it is the generic ordering of books and the layout of the store that produced that sense of alienation. How is the link between culture and genre produced in a bookstore environment, so that customers can "sense" a culture? In the next section, I focus on how bookstore cultures are understood at the eleven sites where I conducted interviews and did participant observations. Once we see what the culture of each store looked like, we can examine how ideas about genre were entwined with everyday work practices to create each store culture.

COMMUNITY AS IDENTITY: THE CULTURE OF BOOKSTORES

In my interviews with independent booksellers across Canada, some of the widely circulating stories about the conflict between Chapters Indigo and the independent retailers did surface, but as I asked questions about work practices such as shelving or ordering, and as I asked about the logic of store layout, the story that many staff members told was similar to what Laura J. Miller says happened in the United States. The bookstores that did survive the arrival of big-box retailing and online retailing developed a heightened awareness of the importance of store culture and the importance of presenting a bookstore as "more than just a place that houses books" (2007, 125).

Unlike the image of the dusty, haphazard—and dearly loved—bookstore in the *Torontoist* blog, the independent bookstores I visited were anything but arbitrary in their layout. Book acquisition strategies, shelving practices, and the information that publishers provide to help sell books all play major roles in the development of store culture, and, generally, the staff of the ten independent stores I visited were clear about what kind of store culture they had. Even the design of store windows contributed to store image and the culture it wishes to encourage.[5] This did not prove to be quite as true for Chapters Indigo, although as we shall see, the store manager I interviewed did try to indicate how stores might "act" as independents do whenever it was possible to make this claim. Before we can see how ideas about genre facilitate the development of store culture in these bookstores, it is instructive to see what store culture means to the owners and managers of these ten independents and one chain store.

In Halifax, Nova Scotia, two independent stores, Frog Hollow Books and Bookmark II, had markedly different cultures, although both had similar ideas about how they are not like chain stores. The Chapters Indigo store is not located in downtown Halifax, which means that neither store faced direct competition from it, and so both stores understood their role as that of community involvement. Heidi Hallett, the owner and manager of Frog Hollow Books, talked about how her store was a mall store, but she made sure to differentiate it from chain stores. In her discussion about the large size of the non-fiction section in her relatively small store, Hallett said that "people stories are what people are really interested in, in our store. We do a fair bit with history, I think, more than some of the other stores in the city.... we try to bring in different cultural studies books—we try to sort of find them from the smaller publishers, some of them you're not going to find in the mainstream stores."[6] Hallett's description of her store as a place where customers buy "people stories" is her way of understanding non-fiction as a category, but it also underlines her sense of the store as a store *for people*. It was meant to be a friendly place that encouraged literary community and emphasized customer service: the online shopping guide *The Coast* described it as "an institution among Halifax literati [that] is just as well-known for its carefully selected books" (*The Coast* 2008), and *Where Halifax* saw the store as a "friendly bookstore specializing in unique books dealing with topical and local issues, often carrying titles that you won't find elsewhere" (*Where Halifax* 2008).

The layout of Frog Hollow Books reinforced this image of the store: it was a small store with wooden shelves, which gave it a "warm" look like that of a used bookstore or library. The labels for the shelves were handwritten by the staff (fig. 1) because the staff were encouraged to make up their own categories and book recommendations. At the time, the store sponsored most of the large readings and author promotions in Halifax, and so the

Fig. 1   Handwritten rubrics on the shelving at Frog Hollow Books, Halifax.

store windows (also designed by the staff) were designed to tie into those events. The result, as the online reviews show, is that the store was seen as a place open to community in general that also contributed to the literary community in the area. Perhaps because it was located in a small mall that is not immediately visible from the street, the success of Frog Hollow Books depended on this friendly, knowledgeable, customer-oriented image and on its position as the promoter of literary events (held in larger venues) that helped to keep it in public view.

Bookmark II, which is located on Spring Garden Road not far from where Frog Hollow Books was, creates a different store culture in order to appeal to its customers. Mike Hamm, the store manager, used to work in a mall chain store. He described Bookmark II as different from that environment because unlike the "television-driven" and "family-centred" emphasis of a mall store, he sees Bookmark II as "book review-driven."[7] The look of the store emphasizes this aspect of its culture: there is no seating or play area for children. Bookmark II is clearly a store for serious adult shoppers: its wooden shelves are set into large buttresses with the names of categories on them, and there are very large category markers on plastic sheets above the shelves, unlike the hand-lettered cards and solid wooden shelves of Frog Hollow Books. But this does not mean that Bookmark II is not a community-centred store: it is one, but its community differs from that of

Frog Hollow Books. With its highly visible storefront on a major shopping street in the downtown area, the store serves "a transient population" that includes university students and staff as well as tourists coming from the cruise ships in the harbour who want to buy local interest books. Hamm says that this is why Bookmark II has a strong emphasis on selling current affairs books and political books.

Of the store culture generally, Hamm says that being a manager is "not just a job, [this is] not just a bookstore, we're part of the community." Hamm understands the store's contribution to the Halifax community to be an active one that is primarily liberal and left-wing (which is the reason for the emphasis on current affairs books), although there are attempts to stock books for diverse audiences because the store is very responsive to customer requests. All practices at Bookmark II are oriented toward community development: the store windows, for example, are the place for community-oriented displays, such as one for Gay Pride Week, while sections in the store about local history and gender issues are there to serve diverse community groups. Bookmark II has a tradition of ordering books for university courses, which is another way that it serves its local constituency, particularly at times when the local universities did not have bookstores of their own. At the time of this interview the store did not do readings or author events, because, as Hamm said, Frog Hollow Books was doing a good job in that area.

Like Frog Hollow Books, Bookmark II consciously works to serve its community and harmonize its practices with those of other retailers. The image of the store and the stock they carry work to create a culture of customer loyalty. As Laura J. Miller points out, the emphasis independent retailers now place on "community" of this nature is in fact a quite recent development that happened in response to the growth of bookstore chains in the 1970s. Unlike earlier times in the United States when "the bookseller tended to be cast in terms of the businessperson's civic responsibility" (2007, 119), booksellers began to argue that this nurturing of community is the main difference between them and corporations: "maintaining that no large corporation can be truly sensitive to local needs and traditions, the independent bookseller purports to stand as a bulwark against the total destruction of meaningful community" (119). The owners and managers of Frog Hollow Books and Bookmark II clearly understood their community role in this way.

In Montreal, Quebec, English-language independent store Paragraphe creates quite a different store culture, since it serves a different kind of community in a large urban centre. Although it is partly owned by French-language chain Archambault, Bruce Cartledge, a store manager and the book buyer for Paragraphe, said that the store has been allowed to maintain its own sense of identity.[8] Cartledge saw Paragraphe as a supplier of books for the universities McGill and Concordia, and felt that on this basis, Paragraphe could compete with Chapters Indigo because that store "might beat us [Paragraphe] in fiction as far as quantity goes because they have the space for it, but I think we punch our own weight, beat them, as far as non-fiction goes." Cartledge envisioned his store as an intellectual place specializing in academic areas like globalization studies, women's studies, and philosophy, but the store has a slicker, more corporate image than many independents: as is the custom at the chains, the display windows are bought by presses for promotional purposes, and space in "end caps," which is a term for the display areas at the ends of shelving, is often rented by small presses. There is a security scanner at the front entrance, and bookshelves are made of high-quality wood. There is an area, much as there is in Chapters Indigo stores, where customers can sit on comfortable chairs to read, and there is a café in the same building.

Like Frog Hollow Books, Paragraphe is the city leader in sponsoring author events, but there is little talk from Cartledge about belonging to a community as such. Instead, he presents Paragraphe as a city landmark: a place where well-known people who live and work downtown shop (I saw Jean Charest, then the Premier of Quebec, browsing in the biography section the day I was there, and Brian Mulroney and Lucien Bouchard are regular customers). Paragraphe is also where anglophones and francophones alike come to buy the latest books. Cartledge is proud of the university connections to Paragraphe, and often mentions them when he talks about non-fiction, a moniker that he sees as a marketing category. Unlike the staff of other independents in my study, he talks less about customer service than selection, perhaps because he is the buyer for the store. But Cartledge's confidence in the culture of Paragraphe is unmistakeable as he talks about "killing" Chapters Indigo in certain areas. Paragraphe is an important place for intellectuals in an urban environment that serves its immediate community (people who live and work downtown, university staff and students) and the city itself. Unlike Archambault, which sells gifts and music in its chain of stores that resemble well-lit supermarkets, Paragraphe serves its community with a wide book selection and the sponsorship of major author events.

In downtown Toronto, the four different independent booksellers I visited all had clearly defined store cultures and all professed to serve a specific community in the city. Although there are chain bookstores in Toronto, these independents in the city centre did not see Chapters Indigo or (in one case) Amazon.com as competitors, because of the emphasis they put on community involvement and development. Like the stores in Halifax, these stores were thriving when I conducted interviews, even though Chapters Indigo and Amazon.com between them have over 80% of the market share (A. Miller 2008, FW6). The sense of community and customer service, according to this *National Post* article, were making the difference in Toronto: "the indies still standing [after the arrival of the big companies] are beating the odds by offering unique stock, well-informed employees and a sense of community for their customers. When Canadians are looking for a bookstore that is about more than the stock on the shelves, they continue to turn to these stores" (A. Miller 2008, FW6). As we saw with the Halifax examples, community-building has come to be the hallmark of the survival of independent sellers, who are careful about the store culture they create to interface with specific communities. In Toronto, the situation is similar.

At Another Story Bookstore, for instance, owner and manager Sheila Koffman talked about how after eighteen years in business she moved her store to the Roncesvalles neighbourhood in Toronto's west end. She did this because she did not want to compete with Book City, a small local chain, and because she felt that the culture of her store matched that of the community in the area. Koffman envisioned her store as a politically left-wing business with a strong emphasis on political non-fiction books and politically progressive children's books. Her vision makes the store a good fit for Roncesvalles, which has a strong community identity and is represented by the New Democratic Party (NDP) at both the provincial and federal levels. Koffman considers community-building key to her success as a bookseller: "If we had ever decided to just be a bookstore and do business that comes off the street, we would not have survived."[9] The store stocks left-wing political books up front instead of fiction, and it has a large children's section and play area in the store's centre. Display windows are designed by the staff and relate to events like Holocaust Week and International Women's Day, or holidays such as Halloween. The community involvement of Another Story can be seen in the children's readings held in-store in the play area, and in the wholesale business the bookstore does with libraries, NDP events, community events, conferences and schools. "We do a ton of book tables so we sort of have two businesses," Koffman said, to the extent that they partner with left-wing presses such as Between the Lines to share resources at these events. Koffman admitted that her decision to do this kind of work is financially precarious at times, but it is her belief in the ethical value of her work that keeps her motivated: "I often pinch myself and say how lucky I am to be doing it, and selling the books I want ... I love when [left-wing] books sell ... I had no interest in children's books at first, and now I find myself looking [at how other stores sell these books]."

For the feminist bookstore the Toronto Women's Bookstore, service to a specific community—in this case, instructors at the University of Toronto as well as women of colour and their allies— provided an opportunity to think differently about every part of running a business, including the classification of stock. In the case of this store, its chosen mandate included encouraging and promoting the writing of women of colour and writing by people dedicated to anti-racist work. Perhaps surprisingly, this feature of the store made it, in the words of its manager of 2006, Kristen Hogan, "'possibly the most successful feminist bookstore in North America."[10] The Toronto Women's Bookstore saw reading as a political act that is central to social change. The store sign included this quotation by Alice Walker, an African-American feminist writer: "If a book doesn't make us better, then what on earth is it for?" The store's highly developed website included an extensive mission statement page.[11] It even had a Facebook group called "We Love the Toronto Women's Bookstore" that foregrounded the store mandate: "Since 1973 the Toronto Women's Bookstore has been a vibrant part of the women's community. We are the largest non-profit feminist bookstore in Canada. Our love for books, our support of communities struggling for progressive social change, and our commitment to feminist anti-oppression politics are reflected in our collection, our events, our workshops and our solidarity work."[12]

The store's organization reflected this commitment to alternative business practices: it was a non-profit business governed by a board of directors. The store made money from selling books used for University of Toronto courses, and this revenue allowed the staff to stock progressive titles and to run writing workshops and events for writers who are women of colour. The store's location near the University of Toronto helped it to sell course texts, but otherwise, Hogan said, the location did not suit the store: the building was too small and it was not fully wheelchair accessible. Rather than depending on street traffic for sales, the Toronto Women's Bookstore maintained access to its community through word-of-mouth, its courses and workshops for writers, and its online presence. The store itself sold non-book items, like t-shirts, handmade silk scarves, and children's toys, but only those that were in line with the store's mandate. The simple wooden shelves were full of books. The classification of books is the main way in which the store attempted to impart its culture and even to teach its customers to think differently about identity categories, but I will discuss that more fully in the next section.

The website of Pages Books, a Queen Street West independent seller, had as its banner a monochrome cartoon of the storefront, with street performers outside and young urbanites looking at the window displays. The banner encapsulated the store image: Pages Books had been at the centre of what it called "the hub of Toronto's dynamic cultural industries" since 1979, when the store opened near the Art Gallery of Ontario and the Ontario College of Art and Design. In keeping with this location, it was a street-focused store specializing in art books and magazines, cultural theory books, and literature by small presses.

Pages therefore presented itself as community-focused and serving a community of young cultural producers rather than as mall- or family-focused, much like Bookmark II does. As its "About Pages" section described, the store engaged actively in community-building: "Pages operates in the tradition of bookselling that goes beyond selecting, stocking and offering books for sale. The tradition extends to being a gathering place where ideas are exchanged and communities developed." On its "History" page, there was information about the store's historic integration with the alternative culture of the Queen Street West area, and about a landmark censorship trial where the owner, Marc Glassman, successfully fought for the right to have a feminist display in one of the windows, supported by major writers and intellectuals, including Margaret Atwood, June Callwood, and Ken Danby. Pages clearly presented itself not only as a purveyor of new writing and design but as a voice for public expression, rooted in a specific notion of urban community.[13]

The store layout supported this image of Pages. Like Bookmark II, there was no seating, and no children's area. There were almost no books for children. The centre of the store was dominated by a large cash and order desk; around this, there were large magazine racks, book tables piled high with new offerings, and shelves crammed with book stock. The lighting was florescent and harsh, and the floor had a brightly coloured block design. The image of Pages, then, was that of a cool, urban store where serious book and magazine buyers did not need to be encouraged to linger because they were there for the books and magazines anyway. The large order desk emphasized the importance of book ordering and customer service in this environment. Gregory King, a bookstore manager who did the backlist ordering for Pages, underscored the importance of the store image to the culture of Pages: "our [Pages'] presentation is a lot different from other stores. People come in and they are looking for another idea of an independent bookstore ... like somehow cleaner ... carpet, hardwood floors, quieter."[14] Pages' goal to serve its chosen community (and not those who want an independent store that is less "urban" in feel) meant that customer reactions like this were a badge of pride for King. For him, customer surprise was part of the resistance Pages was trying to make to the ongoing gentrification of the Queen Street West area that started in the early 1990s. To underscore his point about Pages as a community bookstore, King said that Pages was known for its support of small presses (it sold some items on consignment) and for its art book selection. Pages was also known for its customer service, so much so that King saw Pages as a worthy competitor for Chapters Indigo: "we [at Pages] do books that Chapters won't order. My understanding is that they don't order books that aren't in their warehouse. Anything not in their warehouse, they won't order it. But Pages can get it." King added that Chapters Indigo was not located on Queen Street West itself, and so it did not affect foot-traffic sales very much either.

Why did Pages have such a defined cultural sense? According to King, the atmosphere at Pages was a direct result of the vision of the owner and his decision to locate the store on Queen Street West. Marc Glassman controlled new book ordering personally, and the store stock was a reflection of his interests as well as what sells: "he [Glassman] has this idea about cultural theory and what we want to represent, about architecture and what we want to represent," but King added that as the area gentrified, walk-in traffic was changing both orders and sales. This created a tension for Pages, which historically had defined itself as a store that served students, avant-garde cultural producers: "early on [in the history of the store], the writers, artists and OCA (Ontario College of Arts, now OCAD) students discovered the shop's unique selection of small-press literature, belles lettres, radical politics and books on art."[15] Online publicity on the "History" page also reported that its success depended on serving this core market: "while other bookshops closed down in the late 90s, Pages defied the onslaught of corporate retailers and expanded again." Window displays were not sold to publishers for advertising. They were used to showcase new books and the events Pages ran called "This Is Not a Reading Series." King admitted however, that as the Queen Street West area gentrified, Pages was beginning (albeit with reluctance) to alter some aspects of its store culture in order to serve these new customers.

Fig. 2   Memoir is shelved with History at Type Books, Toronto.

To some extent, the culture of Pages in 1979 can be found in a newer Toronto bookstore that is also located on Queen Street West, but in the considerably less gentrified area of Trinity-Bellwoods. Type Books had been open just seven months before I interviewed its manager and book buyer, Mika Bareket.[16] The store was started by Joanne Saul and Samara Walbohm, who wanted the store from the beginning to be a community-centred place where it was possible to find unusual books and books about design. The title of the store has the double meaning of "type" as another term for "kind" or "genre," and as a reference to typography and text design. Type was featured on *The Hour* on CBC (hosted by George Stroumboulopoulos) as a "cool" or edgy bookstore, because the physical environment of Type is markedly different from that of most bookstores. Bareket even tries to order finer editions of classic books to fit the store's appearance, "because the look of the store is so unusual; it's like a boutique in a way, our walls have fancy toile wallpaper, we have interesting furniture." In keeping with the store's image, there are black metal library shelves—having them was a money-saving decision, says Bareket, but the owners also wanted to pay homage to the look of university library shelving. In the front of the store, opposite the cash counter, there is a rack of design magazines, and there is a separate children's book and activity area at the back. There is also a basement area that functions as an art gallery, an activity space for readings and a literacy program for neighbourhood children called Word Play, run by two retired teachers.

The focus on children's books and community-development programs for children partly comes from Bareket's previous experience as a children's book buyer, but it also comes from the community focus of the bookstore itself. Like other independents, Type sees its store culture as community-focused and the store as a potential centre for community development. In the art gallery space, Type has hosted small-press book launches, readings, and a talk for children about the difference between an independent bookstore and a bookselling chain. The clientele includes people who live in lofts, young families, and neighbourhood cultural producers, which leads Type to feature books by local authors and small presses when they can. In the tradition of Pages, Another Story, and Bookmark II, Type is a community-fostering place with a well-defined sense of its image and store culture.

In Edmonton, Alberta, Sharon Budnarchuk, the owner of Audreys Books and the president in 2007 of the Canadian Booksellers Association, considers customer service and employee participation as key to the survival of her store.[17] "Bookstores are all about relationships" said Budnarchuk, who gives staff responsibility for ordering in key areas of the store and lets employees borrow any book they want to read. Then, she explained, when customers ask for a book, that employee will be able to provide expert assistance due to their familiarity with the stock, and can build a trust relationship with customers who want help finding the right books. The staff, in turn, feel that they help to shape the work of the bookstore.

This attitude to bookselling staff is one way to deal with what Laura J. Miller refers to as the "deskilling" of the bookselling workforce. Deskilling resulted when chain bookstores began to grow. The chains required more staff and a centralized structure. The rationalizing of bookselling at chain stores also led to a division of labour between manager/owners and staff at large chains. This led to employee unrest at stores like Borders, which did try to hire skilled staff, but then faced an attempt to unionize the stores in the chain. Even Amazon.com saw an unsuccessful attempt by employees to unionize in order to get better wages, benefits, and respect (2007, 202–207). Finally, the computerization of bookstore ordering and inventory at chain stores and independent stores alike made it "much less necessary than it was in the past to find staff who are knowledgeable about books. Rather than knowing who George Eliot is, an employee merely has to get the spelling right to look the author up in the database" (2007, 203).

Budnarchuk's approach, which is to let staff have major input into the running of day-to-day operations, is a solution that is (so far) unique to independent retailers because the store is small enough to allow for a more collective organizational model. This approach is reflected in the layout of the store, which features employee "favourites" up front near the cash register, and a second order desk where staff can easily help customers with selection and ordering. A second level at Audreys has a large children's book section, non-fiction books about hobbies, genre fiction, and the managerial offices where Budnarchuk works. This is also where Audreys hosts its author readings, for which it is widely known. Like other stores in the interview sample, Audreys sponsors author readings and major events (such as a costume event to celebrate the release of the last Harry Potter book in the series) in order to boost its community profile.

As Budnarchuk also points out, running an independent store in Edmonton's downtown core has its challenges. Before more condominiums were built in the downtown area in the late 1990s when Edmonton's population began to grow quickly, most of Audreys' customers were government workers who came to the store on their lunch breaks, or students and staff from the nearby University of Alberta. The customer base of government workers is the reason why Audreys has a large section of books about globalization, because "[Audreys is] probably one of the few stores that carries a large amount of political books. Nobody else does." Although Budnarchuk says that Calgary, the other major urban centre in Alberta, has more businesspeople working in its downtown than Edmonton does, she added that government workers in Edmonton are more interested in Canadian issues than Calgarians are, and Audreys carries books about Canadian history, politics, and culture as a result.

Audreys' dependence on business from government workers and the University of Alberta population meant that the store suffered from provincial funding cuts in 1993 and 1994. Government workers and university staff were laid off in large numbers. At the same time, Chapters opened a large store on Whyte Avenue, a major shopping area in the city near the University of Alberta. The ability of Chapters (and now Chapters Indigo) to order books in large lots meant that the company could (and did) undercut Audreys' pricing of bestsellers. Like Pages Books or Bookmark 11, Audreys' survival in the wake of Chapters Indigo's entrance into its marketplace depends on its ability to provide high-quality customer service and book selection, its downtown location (the late 1990s saw a boom that created an increase in condominium dwellers, government workers, and university staff and students), and on its reading series, which draws customers to its store.

The Book Warehouse chain in Vancouver, British Columbia, had an entirely different strategy from stand-alone independent stores like Audreys when it came to competing with Chapters Indigo. It has been estimated that the presence of Chapters, and then of Chapters Indigo, drove 40% of independent bookstores in Vancouver out of business. Their presence in Vancouver has been identified as a major factor contributing to the bankruptcy of the Duthie Books chain in 1999 and, along with the earlier mall store trade at Coles and W.H. Smith (later SmithBooks), a factor contributing to the demise of Black Sheep Books, another well-known Vancouver independent bookstore. Another chain, Blackberry Books, reduced its size to a single store in 2001, and because of the presence of Chapters decided to concentrate on customer service rather than expand its stores (Moore 2001, H24). In this environment, it may seem surprising that a small Vancouver-based chain like Book Warehouse survived, and even thrived, as long as it did with precisely the areas of strength that Chapters Indigo has in its ability to discount. But Book Warehouse was no ordinary chain. Its website related that the chain was founded in 1980 by well-known local musicians, who placed seven outlets in vibrant downtown neighbourhoods, including Kitsilano and Yaletown, that were undergoing a process of renewal. Unlike other independent stores in my interview sample, Book Warehouse began as a remainder and bargain book chain. In 1985 Book Warehouse began to sell bestsellers at a 20% discount, which the company still does today.[18] Gary Crompton, the book buyer and vice-president of the West Broadway Book Warehouse location, said that the discounting of bestsellers aimed "to give good value to customers: the remainders balance the margin out."[19] Crompton's focus on discounting and profit margins as central to the identity of Book Warehouse is what made them a different kind of independent seller. The Book Warehouse chain did emphasize the importance of customer service in light of the presence of Chapters Indigo in downtown Vancouver, but Crompton said that the solid neighbourhood presence of Book Warehouse, the special relationship the chain had with a book wholesaler to get orders filled quickly, and their in-store inventory system that tracked sales in each section of each store meant that Book Warehouse competed with Chapters Indigo and Amazon.com, and he did not feel that the former in particular was a major threat.

The practice of Book Warehouse was unusual because discounting has long been a problem for independent sellers and has been seen by them as a flashpoint in the struggle against mall chains, department stores, and big-box stores. As Laura J. Miller points out, book discounting in department stores has been seen as a threat to traditional bookselling since the turn of the last century. Department stores fought publishers in the American court system about the right of publishers to fix prices until the 1950s (2007, 153–54). Even after this period, when discounting began to be seen as normal practice in other areas of business, booksellers still saw discounting as immoral: "For [independent booksellers], the undiscounted prices at which they sell books to the public represent all those extras—the personalized relations, the commitment to diversity, the sensitivity to local needs—that they believe cannot be reduced to market valuation, and that they insist that no chain can provide. In this view, the chains' discounts destroy the possibility of offering these extras and reduce books to just another interchangeable commodity. For independents, pricing remains very much an issue of morality" (L. Miller 2007, 156).

In Canada, Chapters' practice of discounting caused similar kinds of friction among booksellers. When Chapters was formed from the merger of SmithBooks and Coles in 1995, the federal government of Canada placed the company on a three-year probation period that incorporated restrictions on business practices to prevent Chapters from dominating the book market. This included preventing Chapters from trying to control book pricing. But when Chapters emerged from probation in 1998, it created a wholesale company called Pegasus, and industry personnel feared that through that company it would force publishers to accept deep discounting practices (Lorinc 2000, C06). This practice is seen as discriminatory by independent booksellers, including Sharon Budnarchuk of Audreys, who in her interview with me voiced that Chapters could now undercut the sales of bestselling books, forcing independents to do the same. Canadian independents, like those in the United States, viewed this not as competition but as unfair competition and a disruption of book culture at its core. *Quill and Quire* reported on the ensuing culture shock at the time: "'People are actually shopping for price on a book!' cries an astonished Hamilton [Ontario] bookseller, Bryan Prince, who says he's recently been fielding comparison-shopping phone calls" (Lahey 1999, 27). Prince's surprise shows the clash between the older belief that publishers, sellers, and consumers see books as more than commodities, and the retailing approach to books that sees them as commodities like any other.

There were more surprises to come. Through its wholesale company, Chapters began to order books from Ontario, not from local distributors in British Columbia. The fears of what this would do to the distribution of local books, plus the fear that Chapters could force publishers in Canada to publish only what it would order, prompted the Canadian Booksellers Association to make enquiries about Chapters' deep discounting practices, specifically of textbooks. Chapters, in turn, claimed that it did not discount many books, although it is clear that the industry did not believe this claim (Sellers 1999, 36–37). Discounting books is no longer such a problem for independents, for instance when there is a nationalist issue at stake. In 2007, independent stores like the McNally Robinson bookselling chain in Winnipeg, Manitoba, or Audreys books in Edmonton, Alberta, reduced their cover prices of American-produced books to protest the higher prices publishers were still placing on books despite the parity between American and Canadian currencies (Weeks 2007, C1; Shultz 2007, H9).

But at Book Warehouse, discount pricing was the norm and always has been, even though in other respects the chain operated like an independent store focused on community presence and service. The culture of Book Warehouse, then, was founded on pricing and value and not on the provision of high culture: the stores all featured discounted items in the windows and the stores displayed discount signs advertising new stock, with bestsellers located at the front of the store. At the same time, however, Gary Crompton emphasized that each store in the chain had a different feel in tune with the neighbourhood in which it was located, because Book Warehouse was well known for its high level of neighbourhood-centred customer service. The West Broadway store, for instance, sold more bestsellers than the other stores, while the Yaletown store, which catered to loft-dwellers and condominium owners nearby, carried and sold the most books about dogs of all the stores. New Age spirituality books were favoured at the Bayview and Kitsilano stores, in keeping with the alternative cultures in these neighbourhoods. The stores themselves featured wooden bookshelves in the classic independent style. The store fronts had distinctive awnings or, in the case of the Yaletown store, a neon sign with a "cool" art deco feel. The image of the stores, therefore, was not like that of a brightly lit mall store, but of an urban store like Pages in Toronto, a serious store for book buyers who like a bargain but who also like the bookstore "experience" that associates knowledge about books with store environments. The Book Warehouse entry on the West End Community Network web site sums up this dual philosophy: "On entering a Book Warehouse store, our customers find literally thousands of interesting and irresistibly priced titles in a pleasantly relaxing environment. We pride ourselves on our comfortable in-store environment with excellent music played over high-quality sound systems and places to sit, read, converse and drink coffee. All of Book Warehouse's standard bookstore titles are discounted at least 20 per cent from the list price."[20]

Here, traditional highbrow book culture and the bookstore as community place were emphasized (the store had "excellent" music and there was a place to drink coffee), but the store emphasized its identity as a discount retailer at the same time. Gary Crompton saw this philosophy as key to success in competition with big-box retailers: many customers in the last decade had told him they would rather shop in Book Warehouse than in Chapters Indigo. This is why Crompton believed that it was possible to compete with Chapters, not "by going head to head" with the company, as Duthie Books tried to do, but by having a clear identity and a commitment to customer service. Although Book Warehouse's discounting image made it different from other independent stores in this interview sample, it shared the belief with other independents that community service and store culture were key to its success.

In the conflicts between independent booksellers and Chapters Indigo, the Duthie family book chain in Vancouver has been cited often as a major casualty. Duthie Books is credited with developing book culture in Vancouver, particularly because of the work of Bill Duthie, who started the original store. Celia Duthie took over the Duthie chain from her father and expanded Duthie Books to nine stores in an effort to compete with Chapters, but in 1999 the chain went bankrupt and was reduced to a single store. Across Canada, the fate of Duthie's was held up as a sign of what big-box retailing would mean to the Canadian independent book industry (Nickson 2004, A18; Keyes 2000, 16; Toller and Hewett 2000, 5; Burgess 1999, F9). However, Duthie's was down but not out. Only a few years later, Celia Duthie said that the closures were good for Duthie's, and that the remaining store was doing very well financially before it closed in 2010. Duthie Books became a symbol of how independent retailers could survive and even thrive in the wake of big-box stores like Chapters Indigo, or online sellers like Amazon. com (Perry 2002, A15; *Niagara Falls Review* 2001, A9; Harris 2000, E8).

Ria Bleumer, the manager and buyer at Duthie Books, agreed that "the last straw" in the difficulties of the Duthie's chain was the opening of Chapters in Vancouver.[21] She saw the arrival of Chapters as positive, however, in that the presence of the chain improved the commitment to customer service at Duthie Books: "If we weren't already doing a good job with customer service, the push from box stores has made us better. I know that we have improved with that." The store refuses to do publisher-sponsored display windows and is committed to handselling books. If Bleumer saw a book come into the store that she knew a regular customer would like, she would call the customer to tell him or her about the new book. Practices like these, Bleumer maintained, signify cultural differences from Chapters Indigo: "it's a different culture [here at Duthie Books] from Chapters. The priority in this store is customer service and knowledgeable staff." At Duthie Books, this priority translated into having a large and eclectic backlist so that relationships with customers could be formed when they found books they like: "they [customers] have been looking everywhere, literally ... and [here] they find that book on the shelf which then makes them customers for life, basically." Duthie Books also took special orders, which Bleumer said were very popular with customers. She tried to order books that she thought that her customers would like, taking what she called "a calculated risk" with some titles. Customer service at this level meant that unlike Gary Crompton at Book Warehouse, Bleumer did not talk much about pricing or discounting, but more about customer relationships, the knowledge she and other staff had about specific sections and about the role of book prizes, such as the Giller Prize or the Governor General's Literary Awards, in what sold at the store. The store image supported Bleumer's discussion of the store culture: it was large, with glass doors, a wooden dropped ceiling with contemporary lighting, a curving wooden cashier desk, a large set of racks for magazines, and classic oak shelves for the books. The modern feel of the store was offset by the wooden decor: Duthie Books was for book shoppers who were there for the book selection (Duthie Books did not have a café, and there were no chairs in the store), but the use of wood gave the store a warm atmosphere that was in keeping with its commitment to another kind of "warmth": customer service. Unlike Book Warehouse, there were no sale signs, although there were advertisements for Giller Prize books while I was visiting, and unlike Pages Books, the lighting was not harsh and the floor was not brightly coloured. Clearly, the culture of Duthie Books was meant to be alternative to that of Chapters Indigo in that it aimed to be a people-centred bookstore where traditional ideas about booksellers as knowledgeable and community-oriented were prevalent.

What of Chapters Indigo, the only big-box store I visited? Does Chapters Indigo *have* a store culture? The answer is that it does, but in keeping with its position as a national chain, its stores do not have local cultures. As the *Torontoist* blogger points out, the culture of Chapters Indigo is centrally managed from its Toronto office, and so the store environment is rarely related to the culture of its neighbourhood or street: this means that Chapters Indigo simply cannot be a "community" store as independent booksellers understand that term. And, in fact, Chapters Indigo stores have features that most independent stores do not have. Most branches of the chain have a Starbucks, another corporate chain, a music listening and purchase area (in Indigo stores, this area is much larger), and a gift and card area on the ground floor. The ground floor near the cash register always has a "New and Hot" section, which is filled with books that the central office thinks will sell. There is a large magazine rack on the first floor. The second floor, which at the store I visited was accessed via escalator, has all other book sections and a children's book and play area. The store is very brightly lit, and there are armchairs and wooden shelves. The escalator, café, and lighting all make Chapters Indigo look like Ikea (furniture), another big-box store. The large selection of books organized in endless racks, the large signs advertising bargains or new books, and even the gift shop make it look like other big-box stores that sell electronics or even carpet.

I have been in many branches of Chapters Indigo, and although I visited a store in Edmonton on Whyte Avenue, an area known for its independent shops, clubs, and restaurants, this branch of the store seemed like other stores in the chain that are found in big-box super malls in the suburban areas of cities. These are constructed, as Laura J. Miller points out, for the entertainment of consumers. The store has various places where customers can relax and be entertained as well as ways to shop for goods other than books, because this was how big-box stores sought to compete with independents. They too began to emphasize "community," but in the context of the big-box stores, community meant "creating an atmosphere that puts customers at ease and encourages them to stay awhile" (2007, 125). Big-box stores have also installed WiFi in their cafés and run events such as poetry slams, readings, and music nights as a way to bring more book buyers into stores (2007, 126–28). The interpretation of community as "relaxation," however, does mean that instead of creating an identity for itself that varies from store to store, Chapters Indigo, like other chains, creates a feeling of familiarity with its brand that is maintained by repeating what is familiar to customers nationwide. Chapters Indigo has this familiar feel because much of the store is centrally managed. Therefore, I always know when I enter a Chapters Indigo store that I will see the same gift shop, the same halogen lighting and wooden bookshelf design, the same coffee shop, and presumably the same book sections as I see in any other branch of the store. And what I will see is not a "discount" superstore or a store that looks like a warehouse. At Chapters Indigo, customers are meant to have a middlebrow shopping experience that will look like an experience at other chains. As Laura J. Miller points out, this attitude to bookstore customers was developed by mall chains during the 1960s in order to attract new shoppers for books who would have been afraid to go into the intimidating environment of independent stores. Many of those new shoppers in the mall stores of the American suburbs were women (2007, 90–91). In Chapters Indigo, therefore, I will be comfortable, but I will also be made aware of possible book bargains. The environment may seem to be highbrow in that I will hear classical or jazz music playing in Starbucks, but I can look up books on the store computer myself, similar to Ikea. If I find a customer service representative and ask him or her for help (as I have done on numerous occasions at a Chapters Indigo store), he or she will use the computer system to look up a book for me. That is how employees know if product is in stock, similar to employees at Future Shop. I do not expect the kind of customer service and handselling of books that I would receive at an independent bookstore. But I will be able to browse, and to read in an available chair if I wish. Before I go into a new branch of the chain, I already know what the experience will be like.

This is not necessarily how the staff at the store want you to see Chapters Indigo. During my interview with Katherine Connaught, the assistant manager of the store on Whyte Avenue in Edmonton, she was careful to point out that there is some difference in the ways stores carry books.[22] The Whyte Avenue area, Connaught said, is "artsy" and so there are more art books in the store than in a west-end store, which has more tourists and so stocks more travel books. The Chapters Indigo in the location I visited also does not generally sell what it calls "specialty" books (by which it means books by smaller presses) because it does not see itself competing with the independent retailers in the area such as Wee Book Inn, Audreys, and Greenwoods. Connaught said, in fact, that they often recommended that customers go to those stores "because they have a different clientele." Connaught's recognition of "difference" is a recognition of store culture, although she did not elaborate on this.

Presumably because she was aware of some criticism of the chain's approach to customer service, Connaught also said that different Chapters Indigo stores do try to respond to customer requests and do make new book sections based on what customers want. She mentioned that even at a big-box store like Chapters Indigo, staff members work there because of their love for books, not because books are retail items. As she says, "I don't find bookselling to be retail. I'm actually a hairdresser by trade [so I know what retail is]. I think it's different because retail-wide, people say they want to work in retail. But in bookstores, you're there because you want to sell books.... I think people get into it because they love reading, they love books." This attitude to books and bookselling does not differ from the views expressed by managers like Michael Hamm, Sheila Koffman, or Kristen Hogan about why they love working in the book industry. Laura J. Miller's descriptions of the struggles to unionize labour at Borders locations in the United States show a similar commitment to the book industry by its workers who wish to be treated as knowledgeable professionals (2007, 203–208). This kind of commitment is at odds with the stereotype of chain staff as drones who do not care about books, an image that has been perpetuated by independent booksellers who want to appear different from the chains in this way (2007, 201). But as we shall see, the treatment of genre at Chapters Indigo, and how that treatment surfaces in book buying and shelving, shows how genre plays a role in delineating the difference between big-box stores and independents.

GENRE PRACTICES IN THE WEB OF CLASSIFICATION: BUYING AND SHELVING NON-FICTION

Independent stores use a loose set of tactics in order to continue to do business in the wake of the arrival of big-box bookstores. Classifying and shelving books could be seen as a tactic in Michel de Certeau's sense (1984, 34), an everyday response to the globalized book trade's attempt to standardize generic practices and ignore cultural specificity in the bookselling environment. A cluster of these tactics encompasses the approach of booksellers to the buying and shelving of non-fiction books. Unlike fiction, which is usually understood to mean novels and short stories that are not generically identifiable (as, for example, mystery or science fiction), non-fiction is not a catchall rubric. On the backs of their books, publishers like Random House or HarperCollins will list a book as "non-fiction," but rubrics can also include an array of smaller categories, such as "self-help," "cookbook," "biography," or "history." As a result, non-fiction cannot be understood to be a term for a genre, but a discursive term that itself sets the stage for other genres. Generally, "non-fiction" is understood to be about something that exists or existed in the real world, and which can be subject to verification.

But that is where similarities end between different genres of non-fiction. It is no wonder that most bookstore workers I interviewed said that they did not think much about non-fiction as a category, and it is also unsurprising that they almost immediately discussed non-fiction in detail in terms of the categories that were meaningful at their bookstores. Genre, then, operates within the discourse of non-fiction in a local sense. Unlike fiction, which all stores carry, non-fiction genres are closely related *as genres* to store cultures. What kind of non-fiction a store carries, how it is displayed and shelved, and how it is divided into sections provide information about store culture and the values of its staff and customers.

How do store managers, owners, and staff acquire non-fiction books, and how do they classify them? Is this process different from or similar to the practices of a big-box chain like Chapters Indigo? From my interviews, I concluded that most independent store owners use a tactic that I call "the web of classification" to help them buy and sell non-fiction books. Some book-buying practices are common to all stores whether they are independent or not: someone—the buyer, a manager, or the owner—sits down with representatives from publishing houses and examines catalogues that the publishers have sent. The buyer selects books for the "frontlist," which is the list of newly published books and for the "backlist," which are the books that the store has decided to keep stocking. The publishers ship books to the store either directly or via a wholesaler who ships them from a warehouse that ideally is located near the bookstore. The books are received either in a warehouse (for chains) or into the store itself (for independents), are catalogued in a computer system, and are placed on the shelves. This is where comparisons end, however. The process of book buying responsibility and decision making is not consistent, and within that process, it is possible to see ideas about genre at work. The shape of this process is not that of a structured diagram, where one process follows another, but a web, in which there are many inputs into the selection and classification of a book. Although large publishers clearly expect sellers to use the rubrics on the backs of their books, only two independent booksellers I interviewed said that they used these, and both sellers (at Book Warehouse and Duthie Books) said they used them only when they worked within their own systems. Instead, most sellers rely on their own readings of publishing catalogues (Bruce Cartledge of Paragraphe only uses catalogues, for instance), the opinions of trusted publishing representatives who point out which books will sell to the constituency of a particular bookstore, the opinions of staff members about which books should be shelved where in a store (sometimes these are determined collectively in meetings), their own feelings about what kind of book

Fig. 3   Monument to generic ordering. Bookmark II, Halifax.

should be sold in their store, and their own ideas about where it should be sold. In the case of difficult-to-categorize books, or books that seem to fit into many genres, staff will "'cross-shelve'" more than one copy of a book in different sections, or will create new categories—such as "Armchair Travel" or "Graphic Novel"—to handle new kinds of books.

Michael Hamm of Bookmark II, for example, sees ordering as a dynamic process. Staff and customers have input in terms of what he orders. He understands non-fiction at his store to mean "political books" about current affairs, and biography, and his understanding of his store's culture is that it supplies books about current events to its customers. Bookmark II is also responsive to reviews of a book, any prizes it has won, and to the opinions of publisher's representatives who understand Bookmark II's store culture. Therefore Hamm takes this constellation of factors into consideration and tries to order books that are in line with the store's emphasis on left-wing politics, but he also stocks opposing viewpoints on a subject "because readers want all sides of a question." Bookmark II also emphasizes community development, and so Hamm is not only responsive to what customers ask for, he also anticipates what they might think about an issue or question and orders accordingly.

When a book is either hard to classify as biography or when it also is about a current event, staff at all independent stores resolved possible

Fig. 4   More evidence of labelling. Bookmark II, Halifax.

generic problems by cross-shelving the book—that is, another copy of the book was placed in a different section. The layout of Bookmark II is what I would consider to be a monument to generic ordering: when I visited not only were the store pillars labelled generically, but there were additional signs over each section, and over the middle aisle sections as well. Sections are placed near each other, Hamm says, to enhance the "flow" of customers through the long, narrow space. "Current Affairs" and "Political Science" are up front, rather than "Current Fiction," to signify their importance to the store's culture and the customers. "Science Fiction" and "Detective" books, which belong to genres of books with dedicated fan cultures, are located at the back of the store, far away from the front desk, because those customers never need help from staff and will go only to those sections, ignoring all others. They are impervious to sales techniques.

The centre aisles of the store tell a different story, however. Here is where books that are more difficult to classify are placed, near to the front desk so that staff can help customers more easily. "Non-Fiction," far from being generic in an academic sense, is seen as the left-wing equivalent of "True Crime." That section, for instance, is where readers can find the story of Reena Virk, a teenaged girl who was murdered in Vancouver, British Columbia, during the 1990s by other teenaged girls in a race-motivated crime. The section is also "double-faced" or shelved with "Biography."

Fig. 5   Non-fiction is double-faced with True Crime. Bookmark II, Halifax.

Hamm finds Biography hard to stock as a section and refers to it as a catch-all. It is located near the cashier desk because customers do not always understand how to find books there. Although the field of biography studies sees biography as clearly generic and separate from autobiography, it is significant that in the environment of this bookstore, "biography" competes with "political memoir" and functions as a way to shelve life writing that is not about current events. According to Hamm, the store staff try to resolve dilemmas about where to put a book by cross-shelving biographies in the current events sections and then helping customers to make connections between events and lives. This is a popular, and even spatial, way that biography is understood, and an understanding of the genre of life writing that is different from how it is seen in an academic context, where the connection between events and lives is often interpreted as poetic.

The politics of genre also factors into the creation of new genres in the context of the community-based store culture. In an interesting community-service move, Bookmark II created a separate section called Queer Studies in response to a GLBT (gay, lesbian, bisexual, transgendered) reading group that came in and asked for one. After some debate about whether it was a good idea to not "'mainstream'" books for this group of readers, Bookmark II created this classification and placed it in the store where

Fig. 6   A children's non-fiction section filled with toys.
Toronto Women's Bookstore, Toronto.

these readers would feel, as Hamm says, "comfortable" even though he would rather shelve gay mysteries in the mystery section. Disregarding the generic labels on the back of books, Bookmark II includes segments of the store's community in generic decision-making and helps it participate in the web of classification.

Hamm's experience is similar to that of other independent bookstore staff who wish to order books within a strong store culture. Sheila Koffman of Another Story, for example, understands non-fiction as biography and left-wing political books (she does not try to stock opposing viewpoints about an issue). She is so convinced of her mission to carry these kinds of books that she stocks political books at the front of her store, even though some customers complain about this, and wonder why she does not shelve fiction near the front. A complaint like this signifies the presence of conflict between the generic expectations of some customers and the store culture Koffman wishes to promote. Koffman also said that she carries children's non-fiction (she even has a section devoted to non-fiction for young adults) because it often contains progressive political ideas.

In the case of the Toronto Women's Bookstore, the web of classification extended to a critique of classification itself as gendered. Even the physical organization of the store reflected its mandate and principles. Book sections

Fig. 7   Labelling by identity politcs, not by genre.
Toronto Women's Bookstore, Toronto.

at the Toronto Women's Bookstore were not divided into fiction and non-fiction, The exceptions were the children's section, which had a non-fiction area filled mostly with toys, and the Canadian non-fiction section, although the latter section did not contain solely non-fiction books. This is because, as Kristen Hogan said to me, women's experiences have often been treated as if they were fictional and as a result, the store philosophy is that fiction has just as much power to change lives as non-fiction does. Accordingly, the sections were organized along the lines of identity politics, and fiction and non-fiction were shelved together. According to Hogan, this shelving practice also offset the problem found in feminism itself when the experiences and writing of women of colour are treated as a supplement to white women's experiences. Classification still produces some problems, as in the dilemma of shelving Cherrie Moraga's writing: it is hard to know whether her work goes in the Chicana/Hispanic section or into the lesbian section. Hogan said that problems like this are most often solved by cross-shelving books, as Bookmark II does. At this store, shelving and classification worked as a tactic not only to get readers for books but to educate readers about the politics of generic classification by shifting its boundaries. Here we can see genre clearly operating as social action at the level of the store organization itself.

At Type, Mika Bareket said that she sees the book-buying process as an "algorithm, a big complicated equation" involving many factors. For example, in an interesting twist on the usual view of Amazon.com, Bareket sees their catalogue as complementary to her own database, and makes daily use of the covers and ordering information to assist her when she orders. Type has made unusual generic choices in its refusal to separate mysteries out from other kinds of "fiction," a complicating of the assumed divide between generic books and "literature" that she says customers appreciate. There is a separate memoir section that is shelved next to history because it is easy to "slide the marker over" from one section to the other, which represents a connection for Bareket between people and events. Since part of the store culture involves catering to children, Bareket also has an extensive memoir section for children because "reluctant readers often prefer real stories." There is no biography section, but there is a section called Artists and Photographers so that it is easy to find the lives of cultural producers near their work.

The strong store culture of Pages Books, with its commitment to avant-garde art production, cultural theory, and small presses, led to idiosyncratic, playful section titles such as "Really Really Small Presses" or "Belles Lettres." Gregory King saw non-fiction as a category at the front of the store, where new books are placed before they move to other categories at the back. Frontlist ordering was controlled by the owner of the store, who, King said, ordered books in harmony with the store culture or "what we want to represent." As with other long-standing independent stores, publishing representatives worked with the store culture and did not try to push Pages into standardized ordering practices. As King said: "We [at Pages] have a good relationship with all our publishers, they trust us, we've been around long enough. They are okay with us."

Unlike stores like Bookmark II, Another Story, or Pages, which reported that biography was not an easy section to manage, Ria Bleumer of Duthie Books indicated that the biography section was central to her store's image and that biographies always sold well. The section itself was in a centre aisle of the store—a placement that indicates its central status in the store's culture, but it was still close to the order desk so that browsers could easily receive assistance, a tactic in line with Duthie's commitment to knowing what their customers wanted. Why was biography so popular in the store? Bleumer also mentioned that her store had twenty-five sections, and that fiction was only one of these. The single classification for fiction indicates that unlike Chapters Indigo but like Type, Duthie Books did not distinguish between fiction and genre fiction, but it also shows that in a store committed to customer service and handselling, much attention was paid to the categories for non-fiction so that customers could find exactly what they wanted in each section. In the web of classification at Duthie Books, Bleumer did sometimes use publisher's rubrics, but, like Heidi Hallett of Frog Hollow or Gregory King at Pages, she placed more emphasis on the importance of relationships with publishing representatives who understood her store culture and knew from experience what she would be interested in.

Since it was a chain, Book Warehouse had a different approach to ordering than the single stores did, but shared some of the ways in which independent stores acquire and classify non-fiction books. Gary Crompton saw non-fiction "very definitely" as a category that had purchase for him, but only in terms of the SKU (stock-keeping unit) Book Warehouse used, which organized books into thirty-two categories and then determined how each category sells. Travel writing was a SKU, for example, and remaindered travel writing a different SKU. Compton watched each SKU to see how it sold, and reordered or priced on sale books according the figures about SKUs that he received from each store. The SKU did not always match publisher rubrics for a book, and Book Warehouse employees could, at each store, modify the SKU to reflect aspects of their respective store cultures. The web of classification for Book Warehouse included a cycle of acquisition in which Crompton met with publisher representatives, but then he held a four-day meeting with the store managers to discuss what books would be appropriate for each store. According to Crompton, store managers could convince him to take a chance on a book at those meetings. At the level of book acquisition and classification, Book Warehouse was clearly a hybrid store where it mattered how books sold but also where it is possible to stock books that are part of a store culture on the chance that they might be of interest.

Returning to the irate *Torontoist* writer, the generic organization of Chapters Indigo seems foreign to him or her because, as we have seen in the case of independent stores, classifications are connected to store cultures and therefore do not seem idiosyncratic. In the case of chains, as Laura J. Miller has observed, store culture has been created to be non-threatening and like that of other stores that do not sell books: this has been done to encourage a new type of reader to visit the store without intimidating him or her (2007, 88). There could be differences in the ways customers use independent stores and the way that customers see Chapters Indigo: one study of Chapters before its merger with Indigo showed that most people who shop in Chapters make use of the coffee shop and read or do school-work there, with another significant number browsing in its fiction section, but in both cases relatively few customers actually bought books from the store (Dixon et al. 2001). The result is that there is no clear store culture in Chapters Indigo related to its physical location other than its general com-mitment to provide relaxation (in the coffee shop and the reading chairs) and book-shopping entertainment. Moreover, without a specific store cul-ture in each store that can affect how books are ordered, Chapters is more seamlessly connected to the classification systems of large publishers than most of the independent sellers in my study. For example, Katherine Con-naught of the Whyte Avenue Chapters Indigo confirmed that non-fiction is what publishers say it is on the backs of books. Classification and book ordering take place in the central Toronto offices of the company, a strategy that moves the web of classification away from the local management of the store. It is possible for individual stores like Connaught's to ask the central office for a new section of books if there is customer demand, and she can "just order" books whenever she wishes, but books only stay in the store if they can sell, even if the volume of sales is low for the item. Chapters Indigo does not retain them for the enhancement of store culture, as would be the case at Paragraphe, which keeps philosophy books even when they do not sell, or Pages, which did the same for expensive art and design books. Moreover, Chapters Indigo does not differentiate between books that are mass-market paperbacks and books that are trade paperbacks and hard-covers, with one exception. The section "fiction and literature," Connaught explained, was formerly called "classics," and it included books that were *not* generically identifiable as science fiction, fantasy, horror, true crime, or mystery. This was the only time at Chapters Indigo that I saw evidence of generic decision-making that did not simply adopt the categories publish-ers printed on the backs of books.

There are other differences too. As I mentioned previously, every Chap-ters Indigo store has a "New and Hot" section near the cash desk. That sec-tion is always laid out "as per head office." Throughout the rest of the store, non-fiction books are classified—Connaught used the phrase "'broken up'"—into dozens of subcategories, each with a "New and Hot" section of its own. These sections consist of books that major publishers have told Chap-ters Indigo will sell. Unlike the discussion at independent stores about the importance of handselling books and customer service, there is a "Chapters Recommends" section that also includes new releases and top sellers for the store. But until 2008, Chapters Indigo did include a plan for non-fiction that was aimed to approximate the expertise of independent booksellers: the Indigo Trusted Advisor program. Indigo Trusted Advisors were well-known experts for non-fiction book sections, who made recommendations for books in that section. The Trusted Advisors for Health Issues, for example, included representatives from The Arthritis Society, Toronto's Mount Sinai Hospital, and the Canadian Paediatric Society.[23] David Suzuki was the Indigo Trusted Expert on environmental books. According to Connaught: "we [at Chapters Indigo] want to give our customers the best information. If we don't read our sections, I don't know what is best, so we get people to do that for us." On the one hand, the Trusted Advisor program can be seen as a way to compete with the emphasis on customer service that independents say is their strength. Trusted Advisors presumably chose books that major publishers might not choose, particularly in the areas of non-fiction where there are widely divergent opinions. On the other, the Trusted Advisor program, along with the online "Heather Recommends" section, where Chapters Indigo president Heather Reisman provides a list of her favourite books, can be seen as an admission that Chapters Indigo cannot provide the same type of personal service and a commitment to community service that an independent bookstore can. The Trusted Advisors are experts in certain fields, but (with the possible exception of Heather Reisman), they did not advise the customers of Chapters Indigo because of their professed love of books or knowledge of their customers. They were not there to guide potential readers to a book he or she would like, but to say what books a potential reader of non-fiction *should* read. In a sense, the Indigo Trusted Advisor program represented a return to what Laura J. Miller says is an older model for bookselling, when booksellers were expected to guide customers to the "right," morally improving books to read. In the area of consumer choice, when thousands of books are published each year, "the control of choice now occurs less through personal interactions with paternalistic elites" (2007, 68) and more through offering books that sellers think consumers might like. The Indigo Trusted Advisor program in this sense worked against the other efforts at Chapters Indigo to create an environment where consumer choice is sovereign. Since the program was discontinued in 2008, Heather's Picks and a Twitter feed on the Chapters Indigo home page with "real time, personalized suggestions" are the ways in which the sense of the bookseller as a personal guide survives at Indigo stores in particular.[24]

In general, Chapters Indigo performs the social work of global classification, and participates fully in the type of standardization that critics of globalization warn about, since with few exceptions, non-fiction books at Chapters Indigo are classified and shelved according to the generic markers on the back covers of each book. Although Connaught's comments about the dedication of the staff, her recognition that "books are different," and her statement that Chapters Indigo is not just another retail store are similar to the expressions of dedication I heard independent booksellers make, the lack of local store culture at Chapters Indigo works against what the staff feel about working there. The layout of the store and its centrally controlled book-buying structure mean that the store does not participate in community life, and does not subscribe to the ideals of the book trade that the independent stores owners and managers espouse in order to stay competitive. In the end, Chapters Indigo treats books as retail items that are not different from other commodities found at big-box stores and in so doing, is forced to compete with Amazon.com's ability to provide discount books directly to consumers without providing any bookstore culture to readers. Its treatment of genre as a transparent practice that usually does not require tactical management is clearly successful for many of those who shop at the store, but the hostility that supporters of independent bookstores have toward the chain shows that this form of generic classification actually works at the level of a *techne*[25] that excludes groups of people who expect a different type of knowledge management at a bookstore.

CONCLUSION

What does the theory of genre as communicative action have to say about the acts of classification in each of these bookstores? First, it is clear that genre *does* matter to the environment of a bookstore. In the case of Bookmark II, the act of classifying non-fiction books and then placing them strategically within the store fits with an understanding of the store's clientele and culture. Here we see how something as "invisible" as the placement of books contributes to ideas about culture. Genre in bookstores structures everyday communicative life between people: it structures how books are ordered, displayed, and even sold and in this way, it shows (especially in the instance of non-fiction) how to "know" one's place socially and how to act inside or outside a system. Moreover, often in an unnoticed way, genres set the rules for interaction, including who is allowed to be legitimately in a group, and who is not allowed to belong. The request made by the GLBT reading group to the manager of Bookmark II for a separate GLBT section indicates that the group itself experienced the terms of exclusion because of generic choices, and its members decided to intervene at the level of systemic ordering, rather than simply asking for more books that they wanted to read. And Michael Hamm, even when he did not want to do this, listened to that group and created a space for that group and its way of seeing classification.

But how does the genre structure the terms of ordering? In other words, do classification systems work in ideologically neutral ways? Kristen Hogan's comments about the Toronto Women's Bookstore indicate that generic choices—for instance, the decision made by the store to *not* organize their store generically—are political and are deeply related to the culture of the store itself. Anne Freadman describes genres working in this way as "ceremonials," that is, as "games that situate other games" that determine how any symbolic interaction between different parties is to be carried out (1994, 46–47). Genres, therefore, have much to tell us about discursive communities, including "what sorts of communication ... a genre encourage[s]" and "who can—and who cannot—use this genre" (Coe et al. 2001, 6). At the Toronto Women's Bookstore, the belief that women's lives have been treated as if they were fictional, and the belief that the politics of generic ordering more commonly found in stores can be racist, directly affected how books are categorized and shelved. Here, we can see that genres not only structure what we know and how we know it, but they also work to exclude certain kinds of knowledge because, in the terms of the system, that knowledge cannot even be transmitted or admitted.

Like Louis Althusser's good subjects, genres seem to "work all right by themselves" without us having to think much about them (1990, 135). However, the tendency of Amy Devitt and other genre theorists to see genres as powerful, but also as value neutral, must be counterbalanced by Michel Foucault's picture of the episteme as the quiet organizing of power/knowledge itself (1980). The difference between the ways that independent stores classify books without reference to what publishers' categories say, and Chapters Indigo's close adherence to mainstream publishing classification systems shows how Canadian independent booksellers decide what *kinds* of books to order in keeping with their store culture, while Chapters Indigo, as a chain retailer, cannot do this. And, clearly, the independent stores I visited managed, in the wake of the competition from big-box stores such as Chapters Indigo, to survive, and even thrive, by using classification as one tactic among many to create a counter-practice to big-box retailing and retain the community-centred culture that many customers seem to enjoy. Since I interviewed the independent booksellers for this chapter— Frog Hollow Books in Halifax, the Toronto Women's Bookstore, Pages in Toronto and Duthie Books in Vancouver—have closed, and the Book Warehouse has the chain Black Bond Books as an owner. Do the closures work against this argument for survival? I would argue that they do not. In the case of Pages, high rents in the now-trendy area of Queen West in Toronto forced the store to close in 2009 (Terefenko 2009, A1). However, the store closed only the brick-and-mortar side of its operation. The store now runs a website called *Pages Beyond Bricks and Mortar* that promotes books by independent presses, publicizes artistic and cultural events, and makes it possible to special-order some titles.[26] Duthie Books also closed in January 2010 because of increasing rents (Nelson 2009), but the manager I interviewed, Ria Bleumer, used the closure as an opportunity to start her own (lower-rent) bookstore, called Sitka Books and Art (Elien 2009). Bleumer has said that "the three key words in our mission statement are Independent, Local, and Culture," a clear endorsement of contemporary book retailing philosophy for the stores that survive in the current retailing climate (Arsenelia 2010).

The two very different strategies adopted by Pages and one staff member from Duthie Books show that independents are capable of being successful by creating different store cultures than those of the big-box and chain retailers. Unlike other culture industries, bookselling attracts customers who often do *not* endorse big-box retailing and who actively wish to oppose the forces of globalization, even as they participate in what I would call everyday capitalism. In some localities at least, genre as a social practice is used to bring books to readers, readers to books and—these entrepreneurs hope—new and useful ideas to the people who need them.

Chapter 3

GOING PUBLIC: SELECTED MEMOIRS PRODUCED BY RANDOM HOUSE AND HARPERCOLLINS

In the previous chapters I constructed a picture of the industry that makes memoir possible and helps it to circulate in specific conditions. Now I turn my attention to three outcomes of the production of memoir. First, I examine how memoir is categorized by larger mainstream publishers and I analyze some characteristics of memoirs produced by these publishers. I follow this with a more detailed look at what the paratextual elements and content of some lesser-known memoirs can tell us about memoir as a process and a product of identity at the beginning of the twenty-first century. Why do I choose lesser-known examples? It is a common practice to discuss memoir by listing its better-known or most notorious titles. Ben Yagoda uses such an approach in *Memoir: A History*, where he lists hundreds of memoirs in the first chapter with better-known examples first, summarizes many of what he calls their imitators, and classifies the titles for nine pages because "the American memoir is so capacious that it cannot be contained in just one category; this is the time of a million little subgenres" (2009, 10). But Yagoda's list turns genre into mere taxonomy because it simply is not possible or even advisable to classify the thousands of memoirs, biographies, and autobiographies in print. The categories Yagoda uses—like "schtick lit" or "dad memoir"—feel provisional. The lists of books and authors tell us little other than their titles. Since, as I discussed in the introduction, it is one of the properties of genre to generate the conditions for the rediscovery of similarity and familiarity, Yagoda's typologies simply confirm the properties of generic writing while damning most of it with faint praise.

My focus here is different. Since memoirs for mass audiences most often are produced by large publishing houses, I provide some history of two of the largest English-language publishers in the world—Random House and HarperCollins—to see how the development of these companies affects how they understand memoir as a category of writing. Then I turn my attention to the sample of memoirs published or reprinted on or around the year 2003 to identify some of the broader features of memoirs, without referring to well-known examples that may (or may not) characterize the genre. In this way, the reader of this book is spared endless lists and typological designations but it also becomes possible to see whether some of the myths about memoirs circulated in the popular press are true. As I discussed in the introduction, this approach comes from the result of a survey I conducted of all the titles produced in 2003 so that I could identify some of the salient trends in the production of memoir. The books I discuss in this chapter represent different aspects of the trends I identified in the sample. All four of these books approach their subjects differently, but they share a feature worthy of note: they all are by relatively unknown authors who "go public" within the memoir genre and share their stories of marginalization with their readers. Two of these were published under the auspices of Random House imprints: Toby Cecchini's *Cosmopolitan: A Bartender's Life* and Patricia Volk's *Stuffed: Growing Up in a Restaurant Family*, and two were published by HarperCollins: *Hacker Cracker*, the story of former computer hacker Ejovi Nuwere (written in collaboration with David Chanoff), and Jack Sacco's *Where the Birds Never Sing*, his writing of his father's account of World War II and the liberation of Dachau. These titles provide examples of how each publishing house categorizes memoir in to try and reach a certain audience, and they indicate trends that remain important to the memoir boom. Cecchini's book is written in the tradition of Anthony Bourdain's bestselling memoir of restaurant work, *Kitchen Confidential*, and is supported by the appeal of reality television shows of restaurant life. Volk's is a memoir of Jewish identity and of the development of New York City that is reminiscent of *London: The Biography* (2001). Nuwere's book, with its description of the fall of the World Trade Center towers and its tale of how an African-American boy raised in a ghetto could become a security specialist, is both a story in the tradition of Horatio Alger and an early witness narrative of the 9/11 disaster and an account of the effects of seeing the tragedy unfold. Jack Sacco's story is both a document that adds to materials about the Holocaust and World War II and a war memoir, a well-established and popular way for relatively unknown people to record their encounters with major historical events and evaluate their emotional impact.

Before I examine the categorization and content of these memoirs, I would like to set the scene for their production with an account of the respective histories and development of the two largest English-language publishers in the world: Random House and HarperCollins. The stories of these two publishers provide a snapshot of the larger developments in the publishing industry that I detail in chapter 1. But they also show how the development of the *culture* of these two publishing houses has resulted in different ways to think about memoir as a genre, and has produced different types of titles as a result.

EXPANSION: THE STORY OF RANDOM HOUSE

The history of the founding and development of Random House encapsulates the larger story of American publishing since World War I in its movement from New York-based family firms to multinational corporations. Random House was co-founded by iconoclastic publisher Bennett Cerf and his partner Donald Klopfer in 1925 when they bought the Modern Library line from the Boni & Liveright firm, where Cerf had been the series editor. The Modern Library was an American version of the British Everyman's Library, which was a series of affordable hardcover reissues of classic titles. The focus of the Modern Library was reissues of European modernist works with some works by contemporary American authors.[1] Cerf and Klopfer began to produce the series with cheaper cloth bindings instead of the original lambskin, created the famous torchbearer logo that appears on the spine of every Modern Library book, and added more American authors to the series. They recouped their original investment of $215,000 in two years. Cerf and Klopfer changed the name of their company to Random House to reflect their desire to publish fiction and non-fiction without limitations, literally at "random." In a clever move, Bennett Cerf secured the foreign publishing rights to James Joyce's *Ulysses*, and then arranged for a copy of the book to be stopped at U.S. customs because it was deemed to be obscene. Cerf won the right to publish an uncensored edition of the text in a highly publicized court case, and from then on Random House was a well-known publishing house. During the 1930s, Cerf signed some of the best-known contemporary authors in the United States and worldwide, and Random House acquired a number of major authors—including William

Faulkner and Isak Dinesen—when it made its first acquisition: the publisher Smith & Haas.[2]

From the 1930s until the 1950s, Random House and the Modern Library became known for producing editions meant for the developing American mass readership and for publishing the work of some of the best-known American writers, including Truman Capote, Gertrude Stein, and Sinclair Lewis. In his memoir of the publishing business *At Random*, Bennett Cerf detailed his hands-on personal style of management at the time, which featured an loose and informal company culture and described himself—a public figure who among other things was a judge of the Miss America beauty pageant and a radio show host—as a freewheeling public advocate of books, writing, and ideas (Cerf 1977). As at other publishing houses, editors who worked for Random House were loyal to the company and were given significant control over what they published. Jason Epstein in his memoir about the publishing business remembers this era at Random House with fondness — when authors and editors had close friendships, and work and play went on in the elegant Villard Mansion on Madison Avenue (Epstein 2002).

Although the company culture stayed much the same, Random House had already begun to expand internationally by creating Random House Canada in 1944. It started a college books division to make textbooks and other student editions.[3] By the late 1950s, Cerf and Klopfer were in the same position that other houses were facing: they were close to retirement age and were not sure how company succession could be managed if one of them died and the other could not afford to buy out the other half of the company (Cerf 1977, 276). They arranged in 1959 to sell 30% of their stock in the company to the public. This was a major change for a publisher and resulted in a shift in the values of Random House away from the ideals about publishing held by the owners to the management of the company as a business with responsibility to shareholders (Cerf 1977, 278). In 1960, with the capital from the stock issue, Cerf and Klopfer bought the highly respected family firm Alfred A. Knopf, and its fabled backlist, from owners who also faced succession issues. In a precedent that continues to mark the structure of the company, Cerf agreed that Knopf would remain a fully independent publisher under the Random House banner. A year later, Random House bought Pantheon, another important New York trade publisher with an impressive backlist of European authors, and Andre Schiffrin became its editor-in-chief. As they had with Knopf, Random House allowed Pantheon to operate much as it had when it was an independent company (Schiffrin 2001).

Random House's decision to grow the company through acquisitions served it well during the 1960s, but as its profits increased, other companies in the process of building multimedia empires began to be interested in acquiring it. Random House fended off several offers before it accepted a deal from RCA in 1965, and Bennett Cerf stepped down as president. His successor, Robert L. (Bob) Bernstein, increased revenues during the 1970s, although editors who had worked for Random House began to complain that the company under Bernstein was more interested in profit generation than in publishing good books (Schiffrin 2001, 2–7). RCA sold Random House when it realized that the book business was not able to generate profits in the way that other media industries could, and because—as I discuss in chapter 1—the idea of synergy between publishing, film, computers, and education turned out to be an illusion (Thompson 2010, 106). Si Newhouse, a businessman who owned several media conglomerates, bought Random House and added more publishing companies to its stable, including British publishers Jonathan Cape, Chatto, and the Crown Publishing Group ("About us").[4] Finally, he sold the entire operation to the German media conglomerate Bertelsmann in 1998.

Like other foreign-owned multinationals, Bertelsmann wanted to be a major player in the American publishing industry. The company had already bought the paperback mass-market publisher Dell in 1976, Bantam Books in 1980, and the major trade house Doubleday in 1986. Now it merged these companies, called Bantam Doubleday Dell, into Random House, a move that made Bertelsmann the largest trade publishing group in the world. Today, Random House has dozens of publishers and imprints under its banner, including Broadway, Crown, Anchor, Vintage, and Ballantine Books (J. Thompson 2010, 112). In 2009 with its international subsidiaries, Random House made approximately $1.70 billion, a decrease from 2008 (Bertelsmann 2009). But in 2010, the U.S. division of Random House saw a significant increase in sales and placed 138 titles on the *New York Times* Bestseller list. The increase in revenues plus a 300% increase in e-book sales over the first six months of 2010 means that Random House still dominates the publishing market worldwide and remains the leading publisher in the United States even in an economic downturn (Bertelsmann 2010). Random House publishes approximately eleven thousand new books per year, and it keeps 500 million of its books in print, in paper, audio, and electronic formats. Three of its books won the Pulitzer Prizes for fiction, non-fiction, and biography in 2009 (Bertelsmann 2009, 43). In 2012, Bertelsmann and Pearson combined their publishing operations to create a single unit, Random House and Penguin. This merger created an even larger publisher in theory, but the two operations have remained separate.

Its position as the largest publishing group in the world, owned by an even larger multinational media corporation, indicates that it is not possible to pinpoint what Random House's policies about memoir as a genre might be. Random House runs its many imprints and subsidiaries in what Thompson calls a "federal" system where imprints are allowed to maintain separate editorial teams and—sometimes—separate sales and marketing forces, although Random House constantly balances the need for imprints to have creative autonomy with the need for the larger corporation to control profits (J. Thompson 2010, 128–29). The new corporate headquarters of Random House at 1745 Broadway in New York is an impressive skyscraper that "may look to the casual observer like the house of a well-ordered bureaucracy where all procedures have been formalized and standardized, but in reality it is more like a conservatory that houses a plurality of microenvironments, each of which is allowed to grow its own exotic varieties of vegetation provided that it meets certain conditions" (Thompson 2010, 129).

An example of this "conservatory" approach to publishing is the treatment of imprint. Many Random House imprints were once well-known publishers in their own right. Some of these retain autonomy in the area of purchasing books as long as they create cultural capital for the larger corporation and meet financial targets. Others experience a change in corporate culture when they are bought and as a result become more market-driven than they had been.[5] Since different imprints have different relationships to the parent company, Random House's marketing strategy for different imprints varies widely. For example, the Crown Trade group was previously Crown Publishing, a mass-market paperback company that has produced celebrity memoirs and mass-market genre fiction. Within Random House, Crown "is known today for the broad scope of its publishing program and its singular market responsiveness, qualities that are reflected in its savvy selection of authors and books and in its aggressive efforts to market them."[6] Words like "market-responsiveness" and "aggressive efforts" show that the historic culture of Crown is retained within Random House. Crown publishes bestselling memoirs by politicians, with notable titles including George Bush's memoir *Decision Point* and Barack Obama's *The Audacity of Hope,* as well as mass-market non-fiction like *No Ordinary Joes,* an account of four American submarines in World War II, or *Miracle Ball,* a story of one man's quest to find out what happened to famous home-run baseballs.

The Knopf Doubleday Publishing Group, by contrast, exists as the result of the acquisition of some of the most respected trade publishers in New York. It represents the cultural capital Random House needs in order to maintain its image as a quality publisher, and so Knopf Doubleday is introduced on its website in this way: "Alfred A. Knopf was founded in 1915 and has long been known as a publisher of distinguished hardcover fiction and nonfiction."[7] This statement is followed by a list of major writers who have been published by Knopf, with names such as Thomas Mann, Toni Morrison, Alice Munro, and Cormac McCarthy. Knopf still exists as a "publisher" with a distinct identity, and so its non-fiction offerings largely consist of trade books. At the time of this writing, the current list for non-fiction on the Knopf website included well-known non-fiction authors such as Oliver Sacks and the late Christopher Hitchens and Nora Ephron.[8] Pantheon, another venerable and respected publisher owned by Random House, also publishes trade memoirs that are more literary in nature: in December 2010, its website featured a memoir by Michele Norris, a National Public Radio host. The publicity banner includes an enthusiastic endorsement by Toni Morrison, who calls it "an insightful, elegant rendering of how the history of an American family illuminates the history of our country."[9]

Random House's strategy is to encourage at least the appearance of diversity in the marketplace, particularly since—as John B. Thompson points out—publishers cannot mass-produce books without maintaining cultural capital. Cultural capital in the book business usually stems from maintaining the semi-independence of a former house as a type of brand so that it appears that traditional publishers are still in operation. The result is a delicate balancing act between the historic specialization of a specific publishing house and the need for the whole corporation to make a profit (2010, 140–45). Random House is a corporation with a profit agenda, to be sure, but its success rests on not appearing to be that way. Arguably, Random House's history has changed the American publishing industry more than any other single company, and yet it maintains the illusion that little has changed in the way that its imprints do business.

ADAPTATION: THE STORY OF HARPERCOLLINS

HarperCollins, the third-largest publisher in the United States, has been owned by Australian Rupert Murdoch's multinational News Corporation (News Corp) since 1989. HarperCollins' history reflects the waves of mergers that changed the publishing industry as a whole and shows how some parts of the publishing industry over time have retained something of their histories as they adapted to the values of the mass media corporations that bought them out. Founded as J. and J. Harper in 1817 by two American brothers, Harper was known for publishing the popular magazines *Harper's Bazaar* and *Harper's Weekly*, and for publishing popular authors like Edgar Allan Poe, the Brontë sisters, Charles Dickens, and Mark Twain. In 1962, now called Harper Brothers, the company merged with Row, Pearson & Company to form Harper & Row (Preuss 2009).

Collins began as a one-man printing operation in 1819 in Glasgow, Scotland. In 1868 Collins became William Collins Sons & Co. Ltd. The company published bibles, atlases, dictionaries, and reprinted classics. They also published important authors of popular genre fiction such as Agatha Christie, C.S. Lewis, J.R.R. Tolkien, and H.G. Wells. During the 1940s, Collins Sons & Co. also became known as a major children's literature publisher (Pruess 2009). In 1981, acquired a 30% stake in Collins Son & Co. through one of its subsidiaries, and in 1989, they bought out Collins Sons & Co. and acquired Harper & Row, merging these companies to form publishing giant HarperCollins. The company's revenues in trade and mass-market publishing in 2007 were $1.29 billion globally, with 70% resulting from American revenue. (J. Thompson 2010, 113). Similar figures were reported by News Corp in 2009 (News Corporation 2009, 20). Publishing is not a major part of News Corp's business. Revenues generated by HarperCollins form only 4% of News Corp's total profit, because the company's main revenue comes from television and cable network programming and film production. But News Corp sees HarperCollins as an important part of its cultural capital. It calls HarperCollins "one of the world's pre-eminent English-language book publishers, headquartered in New York City" as a way to show that it is a legitimate player in the capital of English-language publishing,[10] and the company has reported with pride that HarperCollins placed 168 titles on the *New York Times* Bestseller List (News Corporation 2009, 28).

HarperCollins has retained its reputation as a major publisher of children's literature and mass-market titles and has expanded to publish major trade titles. The history of HarperCollins as a publisher of popular books for children and adults means that it is a good fit with the style of News Corporation, which sees its role as a provider of film, television, and journalism as entertainment (News Corporation 2009). Its separate spiritual books division and imprint Zondervan is the publisher of one of the biggest blockbuster non-fiction titles in the United States, Rick Warren's *The Purpose Driven Life* (J. Thompson 2010, 113). Unlike Random House,

HarperCollins did not preserve the separate identities of its merged companies, except in the case of Zondervan, the largest publisher of religious books in the United States, William Morrow, a respected trade publisher, and Avon, an imprint for romances. Under News Corp, HarperCollins is divided into separate divisions such as Children's Books, Harper One (spiritual and religious materials), Harper Perennial (trade and mass market), and Harper Paperbacks. The structure of HarperCollins is less federal than at Random House, with a more centralized structure and more control over aspects of the acquisitions and marketing processes (J. Thompson 2010, 128–29). As a result, HarperCollins does appear to have a more easily recognizable identity than Random House as a publisher of blockbuster trade fiction and non-fiction, and of mass-market paperback genre fiction and non-fiction. In 2010, it published Sarah Palin's next memoir, *America by Heart: Reflections on Family, Faith and Flag* and prominently promoted it on its website.[11] Other popular memoirs are featured too, many of them by well-known public figures, including television producer Kelly Cutrone's bestselling memoir and compendium of advice for women who want to succeed in business, *If You Have to Cry, Go Outside*, Agathe Von Trapp's *Memories Before and After the Sound of Music*, and "legendary American artist" Patti Smith's memoir of her relationship with Robert Mapplethorpe during the 1960s and 1970s, *Just Kids*. Memoirs by more "ordinary" people are often tied to extraordinary events, such as *Strong of Heart*, the memoir by fire fighter Thomas Von Essen about the 9/11 bombings. Although it does have the William Morrow imprint to bolster its image as a publisher of quality trade books, HarperCollins is firmly committed to publishing mass-market books and the more splashy non-fiction titles that contribute to the continuing visibility of the memoir boom.

A SNAPSHOT VIEW: RANDOM HOUSE, HARPERCOLLINS, AND GENRE

The histories of Random House and HarperCollins show that the changes in the publishing industry have resulted in some differences between the ways in which two of the biggest players present their corporate identities. Those changes do result in some differences between the ways that each publisher classifies its personal non-fiction books. But my study of a random sample of books published under the auspices of Random House and HarperCollins in or around the year 2003 also shows that the politics of representation with respect to authors does not differ substantially between the two companies. And my analysis suggests that some of the myths of the memoir boom perpetrated by its critics are in fact true, while others remain mythical. The following analysis of these trends can only be a snapshot, capturing a brief point in a production cycle rather like the way a camera captures a moment in place and time, and it freezes that moment for analysis. Like a camera shot, too, my picture of what the industry thinks about memoir and how it attempts to classify it reveals significant things about what genre means to this cultural industry. But it also obscures other factors at work in the work of classification, factors that I address by looking at how the race, class, gender, and public persona of the authors and subjects in these books appears in these publishing genres.

My random sample of the total 163 books published by Random House and HarperCollins around the year 2003 that were labelled biography, autobiography, or memoir somewhere on their back covers yielded 64 titles, 35 published by HarperCollins and 29 by Random House or its imprints.[12] The classification systems each publisher uses differ considerably, and they sometimes do not reflect what the book cover says about the genre of the book. They do, however, show what each publisher thinks about the genre of memoir and how to classify it. HarperCollins most often uses the word "biography" to indicate biography as the story of one person's life told by another and it uses the word "memoir" to signify a life story told by the author in the first person. *Where the Birds Never Sing*, however, the story of Joe Sacco and his World War II regiment, is classified as a "memoir," when it is in fact by his son Jack, who wrote Joe's "voice" in the first person. I will return to the specific case of *Where the Birds Never Sing* in more detail, but for now it illustrates how the categories HarperCollins uses do not always match the narratives they describe. The most popular category is "Biography: More," with fourteen entries. "Biography: Memoirs" appears six times as a way to designate autobiographical and biographical narratives. There are more specific terms added to these terms—such as "women's studies" or "sports" or "computers/African American." The aim here could be to help bookstores to cross-shelve books by area of interest, or to create categories that help users of Amazon.com to find books, because Amazon.com has a separate category for memoirs, but the categories biography and autobiography yield the same number and type of hits. HarperCollins published a slightly higher ratio of life stories by or about famous people than by ordinary people (1.5 to 1), so the lower use of "memoir" as a category could reflect that, for this publisher, these non-fiction genres are meant to signify the "truth" or veracity of a story, and not the type of narration. Biography, memoirs, and autobiography appear as interchangeable terms, which could reflect (as some booksellers say in chapter 2) how some readers look for books about or by a specific person or event and do not look specifically for the genres of biography or memoir.

Random House has a slightly different strategy of classification. Unlike HarperCollins, which uses the word "memoir" as another word for autobiography, only three Random House books in the sample were labeled "memoir." All of these were by people who were not in the American public eye, including Marjane Satrapi. More books were either called biography (five titles) and autobiography (six titles) than at HarperCollins. But the most-used term was biography & autobiography at nine entries with limiters after this term, such as "true crime," "Presidents," "eulogy and tribute," or, in one case, "literary." Many of the books in these classifications were by or about famous people. Random House uses the terms autobiography and biography more as critics would, to designate different types of narration. But much as HarperCollins does, it creates a dual term, biography & autobiography, to deal with books that might be either or both of these genres, and then limiters are added, presumably to help with cross-shelving in brick-and-mortar bookstores and libraries, and to assist customers searching online vendors such as Amazon.com. Unlike HarperCollins, however, Random House does use the term "memoir" to signify books that contain personal narratives by relatively unknown people. In that sense, Random House uses "memoir" much as its supporters do in the popular press—rather than using the older definition of memoir as either an unknown person's response to historical events or the life of a famous public person, these writers think of memoir as an emerging form of writing by relatively unknown people about their own lives.

These observations cannot entirely explain how memoirs circulate because, as I have shown, the work of genre is dynamic in the book industries. Bookstores do sometimes cross-shelve biographies and memoirs by other categories, such as music or politics, because potential readers sometimes read memoir as a way to learn about a person, a period, or a topic. But some bookstores do not follow the rubrics provided by publishers. And, as we have seen, the categories themselves sometimes seem arbitrary. But this feature of the categories shows how genre reflects to some extent the culture of each publisher: Random House, a publisher that portrays its imprints as its mark of traditional quality, uses autobiography and memoir as expressions of stylistic difference, while the more populist trade and mass-market publisher HarperCollins uses memoir more loosely as a way to designate any personal narrative by any person, in a tacit (and probably unexamined) assumption that *any* personal story is a public story. This latter way to view memoir contains populist assumptions about personal non-fiction that do not differentiate between stories by (or about) celebrities, ghostwritten or told-to narratives, or accounts by people who are not famous. In classification systems at HarperCollins, it is the story that matters, not the method of telling it.

The breakdown of these books by the author's or primary subject's gender, race, and class confirms some of the general observations about the memoir boom, but in some cases, the figures show that common assumptions about the politics of memoirs are not accurate. In the most general sense, most memoir and biography produced by both publishers is written by men, and most authors who get their work into print are white. One in four authors in the HarperCollins sample were female, while the statistic for Random House was one in three. Only six authors in the HarperCollins sample were identified as a race other than white. Three authors in the Random House sample were identified as non-white. Some authors, such as Isabel Allende or Marjane Satrapi, do not speak English as their first language and their works have been translated, but they are few in number and they appear due to what can be termed extraordinary circumstances (Allende is a major author, and Satrapi—as I discuss in chapter 4—was published in 2003 because she is from the Middle East). The image of the memoir boom as a democratic phenomenon that allows for the emergence of new and different voices does not, according to this sample, automatically signify that members of oppressed groups gain access to the public sphere through mainstream publishing. When they do, as Gillian Whitlock has said, they appear under unusual circumstances in the "transit lane" of liberal democratic empathy, activism, and Orientalist interest in the East (2007, 12–13) and—I would add—in the idea of Central and South America as well.

A more specific look at how other factors interact with these writers' gender and race tells a more complex story about genre in this sample.[13] Roughly half of the books published by HarperCollins are by or about famous figures. Random House published slightly fewer books by famous people, but the ratio of famous figures to ordinary authors at 1.4 to 1 does not differ significantly from HarperCollins. From this, I suggest that the widely circulated belief that celebrity memoirs and biographies glut the book market does not appear to be the case. High-profile memoirs by political figures like George Bush and Sarah Palin, or celebrity "tell-alls" like HarperCollins' ghostwritten memoir about soccer star David Beckham appear—through publisher marketing schemes and media uptake—to be more significant than they are, because the stories and their authors have high-profiles and exhibit what publishers call "platform" in the public sphere, which allows them to be easily marketed.

At the same time, memoirs and autobiographies in the sample by women who are not celebrities outnumber biographies about ordinary women's lives by nine to one, while the numbers of memoirs and biographies by or about men are equal. Women who are celebrities or public figures have biographies written about them (there are six in the sample), but fewer public women write memoirs (there were two in the sample). Famous men publish memoirs and have biographies written about them in far greater numbers, but the ratio between these types of genres was roughly equal at fifteen apiece. What these figures suggest is that personal narratives by women are becoming central to the growing sense that memoir by non-celebrities is becoming much more important (and more popular) and that the terms for memoir are shifting. Women with a story to tell but no public identity are, it appears, going public to some extent in mainstream publishing and joining men who are already engaging in this practice. Some of the backlash against personal narratives by non-celebrities as the product of narcissism or self-indulgence could be seen as part of a larger backlash against the entrance of women as serious writers about their lives into the marketplace and the public eye.

Women who are beginning to get their narratives into the public eye are most often white, however, and they are middle class or elite. Stories of working-class women of colour seldom appear in my sample and when they do, it is due to extraordinary circumstances: the single book in the sample by or about women of colour (published by HarperCollins) was a collection of prison narratives by women, commissioned and edited by well-known author Wally Lamb, who is white. Personal accounts in the sample by men of colour confirm the importance of class position for writing and being published: only two of the eight books by or about men of colour were about the experiences of working class men, while the remaining six were about upper-middle-class or elite men. Of the two working class accounts, one—*Hacker Cracker*—was about the journey of a working-class (or below) African American and his rise to a position of considerable power and authority, a story to which I will return.

The books in my sample show that the category of memoir is in considerable flux in the categorization systems of these two publishers, and that what publishers think a memoir is about may not match how it appears in public discourse, or how it is found by readers. In fact, for at least one publisher, the categories of biography and autobiography appear interchangeable, possibly in reference to an idea that readers look for non-fiction not by author or genre, but by topic or area of interest. Genre here is not about social action, but is a system of classification that purports to put books in their places, a guide to help others in the industry get books to those who might want to read them. But the categories of class, gender, and race to which the writers and subjects of memoir, autobiography, and biography belong reinstate the role of genre as a deeply social force that determines to some extent who is able to go public, and under what circumstances. It is this last aspect of genre and its work within the rhetoric of memoir that deserves more in-depth analysis, and therefore it is to specific memoirs— and their paratextual elements—that I now turn.

Hacker Cracker: A Journey from the Mean Streets of Brooklyn to the Frontiers of Cyberspace

Hacker Cracker was first published in hardcover in 2002 by William Morrow, the trade imprint for HarperCollins. In 2003 the book was published as a paperback by HarperCollins' Perennial imprint. The paratextual elements of this memoir mark it—uncomfortably, as I will show—as a sensationalist tell-all about computer hacking and an account of how Ejovi Nuwere escaped a life of poverty and violence to become a successful businessman. *Hacker Cracker* is the story of Nuwere, an African American who grew up in the rough neighbourhood of Bedford-Stuyvesant in New York City and who through a combination of intense personal drive, the backing of a strong family headed by his grandmother, and some luck becomes first an early computer hacker and later a systems security specialist who is now an entrepreneur. The memoir is not meant to be a literary treatment of the subject. Nuwere is not the author of the book: David Chanoff is listed on the cover as the author "with" Nuwere and opposite the title page, a list of Chanoff's other books "with" other authors appears in an open acknowledgment of his skill as a ghostwriter. The book's slightly clichéd subtitle doubles as a plot summary and an endorsement of American adventurism: readers are meant to follow Nuwere "from the mean streets of Brooklyn to the frontiers of cyberspace." This journey could be compared to the life of Malcolm X and his own journey from a life in petty crime in inner-city Boston to his role in the Nation of Islam and his status as a major figure in the struggle for justice for African Americans. But it is not. An endorsement from a review in *The Boston Globe* compares Nuwere's memoir not to Malcolm X's autobiography but to a Horatio Alger narrative, the classic rags-to-riches tales Alger wrote in the nineteenth century that came to symbolize the American dream's promise of material success for any person by means of hard work: "Horatio never accomplished so much," the review reads. The subtitle on the front and the endorsements on the back that call Nuwere's memoir a story of "survival and success," or "a rare and inspirational story" position *Hacker Cracker* within this tradition of success through American capitalism because Nuwere's story is meant to inspire others. But one review and part of the blurb on the back cover announce the presence of another narrative thread: the confession of illegality and the promise to reveal a hidden subculture. *Kirkus Reviews* calls *Hacker Cracker* "a testimonial to the power of positive, if sometimes illegal, thinking" as an attempt to reconcile this message through a humorous reference to Norman Vincent Peale's bestselling self-help book. The blurb shows that this memoir is not about self-help, but about a potentially uncomfortable clash of American values: "*Hacker Cracker* is at once the most candid revelation to date of the dark secrets of cyberspace and the simple, unaffected story of an inner-city child's triumph over shattering odds to achieve unparalleled success."

The familiar story of a child overcoming oppression and poverty through his or her own efforts supports the liberal democratic ideology of much American memoir and fiction, with hints of Benjamin Franklin's ideas of self-improvement added to this. It makes sense that HarperCollins would try to relate this book and its unlikely protagonist to these ideals as a way to sell this book to readers who do not share Nuwere's cultural or class background. However, some parts of the American dream do not materialize quite this way in *Hacker Cracker*. Nuwere does not achieve success by leaving his old life behind and simply working hard to succeed, and the narrative is not about survival or overcoming impossible odds. It is not even about "leaving" the ghetto for a better life, itself a familiar trope for American readers and film and television viewers. *Hacker Cracker* is actually about a different kind of social movement: the memoir illustrates how useful Nuwere's upbringing in Bedford-Stuyvesant was to him, how the underground world of early 1990s computer hacking operated as a type of counter-public, and how the 9/11 attacks on the World Trade Center—which Nuwere personally witnessed because he worked for a company in Tower One—showed him that hacking was not a way *out* of community but a way into it and its promise of affective belonging.

In *Hacker Cracker*, hacking becomes Nuwere's way of educating himself. By the end of the memoir, hacking also becomes a way for him to theorize social mobility. The development of hacking as a social practice in the memoir is what enables Nuwere's story not to take the form of a conversion narrative that would move him completely from the world of the ghetto into a version of a white middle-class idyll as the solution to the problems of inner city poverty, violence, and institutional breakdown. *Hacker Cracker* is about a different way to move through publics rather than a way to move away from them. The book opens with an expression of cyclical movement between incommensurable states of being. In a prologue we see Nuwere as a security professional shutting down a rogue employee's computer just as he is about to be fired. Nuwere is able to do this because, as a hacker himself, he knows what the employee is thinking. He expresses this state in frontier terms: "during the day I wore my white hat. At night after work, I put my black hat on and went into the underground" (2002, 2). Nuwere defeats his adversary because he knows all about him, and he is able to understand what he would try to do in the same situation: in essence, he *is* his own adversary because he knows "all the things a good hacker knows, tricks of the trade" (4). The scene establishes Nuwere's skill at fighting that he learned in Bed-Stuy's toughest neighbourhoods. But it also establishes that Nuwere is still "street" and still engaged in illegal acts. He has not moved from one state to the other: he exists between them and must devise an ethics for hacking in order to balance his life.

To illustrate this point, the plot moves to a literal description of life out of balance. With his uncle Osie, Nuwere visits a hospital where his mother—a drug addict—is dying of AIDS-related causes. The visit ends in violence when Osie provokes gang members at the hospital, and they both have to fight them off. Nuwere is despondent: "I felt like I'd been sucked right back in … you can be in any state you want and the streets will suck you back in regardless," leaving him feeling helpless to save his mother or himself from the violence and poverty in his life (2002, 19). With this movement from Nuwere as the hacker/not-hacker who has the power to control his adversaries to Nuwere as powerless to help his mother, his uncle, or himself, *Hacker Cracker* sets up the dimensions of the problem Nuwere must solve. He must stop being a fighter, and become a hacker—someone who understands how systems work. He must hack America itself by using the system's own terms against itself so that he can move between the world of the ghetto (where his mother is) and the rest of the world. Hacking is what enables Nuwere to go public because it creates the terms for his mobility.

In his early years, Nuwere survives the random violence and gang wars of Bed-Stuy through a combination of family support, street smarts, his group of friends, and—most importantly of all—his ability to pretend to be someone else. At school, he becomes known as an imitator of civil rights speeches, and he even speaks out on behalf of education for the state of New York in this style. The reception he receives changes his life: "that was the moment when I knew that I had to be in the public eye. I just had to" (73). At first Nuwere thinks that this means that he should train to become an actor, but he does not succeed at this because the school he attends is too rough: Nuwere ends up having to join the Zulu Nation, a relatively non-violent gang "whose main purpose was unity" (96). Zulu Nation worked as a counter-public, with hip hop and music chapters, knowledge chapters, and a fighting chapter in order to create a sense of culture, tradition, community, and protection for its members. But Nuwere leaves when he discovers an even more dynamic counter-public: the underground world of computer and phone hacking, credit card fraud, and software trading. Nuwere borrows his uncle's computer and, as he says, stumbles upon an important phase in the development of the Internet during the early 1990s, when security systems were in their infancy.

The ethics of this counter-public now form some of the underlying ideas of the open-code, open-access Internet: "you were *supposed* to trade software. There was *supposed* to be this free interchange of ideas" (114). Nuwere discovered through software trading and then hacking that this ethic was anti-capitalist and egalitarian: "people valued other people according to how intelligent they were, not for anything else" (116). Disadvantages did not exist. It no longer mattered what Nuwere's race was, how much money he had, how educated he was, or where he lived. The hackers he knew wanted to exchange information, ideas, and skills. In short, they wanted to learn from each other: "I was in my school," Nuwere comments, "my real school" (188) as opposed to the underfunded, unsafe inner-city school he attended each day and where he learned very little. Nuwere proves to be a good "student" of hacking when he hacks into the University of Pennsylvania mainframe and—because he cannot be a university student any other way—hacks into a student identity and lifestyle as well. As Nuwere says, the goal of hacking is to adapt to a system in order to exploit its weaknesses. As he had when he was acting, he becomes someone else: "If I break into your machine," he says, "all of a sudden I'm you. I'm seeing the same things you're seeing…. I feel this personal intimacy with you, because I'm in this special place I would never have access to otherwise" (151).

From this hack onward, Nuwere realizes that hacking provides him with the chance to be socially mobile in ways that were not possible for him in the offline world, to literally "be" someone else for a period of time. But hackers do not just want to crack systems. They want respect from their community. They want to go public within their counter-public. One of the goals of Nuwere's hacker group—Digital Yakuza—was to become publicly known: "to be famous, to get that recognition and respect" (138) from other hackers and have his exploits publicized in *2600*, a hackers' magazine (177–78). When hackers go into a site, they often change webpages or other aspects of programming in order to leave a digital signature or tag so that other hackers know that the site has been hacked. News of this circulates quickly through informal networks. In order to become known as a hacker, Nuwere and another member of Digital Yazuka hacked into a system so powerful that Nuwere's discussion of the hack in *Hacker Cracker* is crudely censored, presumably to avoid a lawsuit. The title of chapter 12 and much of the content of chapters 12 and 13 are blacked out, as are any references to the highly secure system Nuwere penetrated. The text could have been rewritten instead of censored. Why, then, call attention to censorship at all? On the copyright page, a warning appears: "Various names, places, and occasional details have been changed or censored for reasons that will be apparent to every attentive reader." This warning is unusual in that it includes a reference to censorship and it says that attentive readers will understand why this is the case. In effect, Nuwere is asking his readers to "crack" the code of censorship in the text and to figure out from the details that are provided what the name of the "high tech organization" (194) is.

Cracking and hacking, then, become rhetorical strategies for Nuwere and the readers of *Hacker Cracker*—just as readers must take an active role and "guess" who the hacked organization was, so Nuwere becomes a subject with agency through hacking. Hacking is a social-marginal activity and even, Nuwere suggests, an addiction. But in the end, it becomes Nuwere's way to make a living, because Nuwere's hacking results in a series of legitimate jobs in the computer security industry when his talents are recognized. In this way, hacking becomes a way for Nuwere to access a different way to live without giving up the survival skills he learned in Bed-Stuy. As he says when he debates whether to move to Japan, "I feel like I've been hacking foreign cultures most of my life" (230). Nuwere maintains his sense of identity as an identity of *movement* when he refers to himself as a gray hat, someone who can still be a hacker and a security specialist at the same time: "What is very difficult is to wear two hats—to be one guy in the day, another guy at night. Some people, though, can be gray hats. They play both sides of the fence. I consider myself to be a gray hat" (233).

As a gray hat, Nuwere is able to move between social and economic silos in the offline world, much as he moves through cyberspace. But near the end of the book, the 9/11 attacks change his sense that he is autonomous and free to control his destiny when the United States is subject to what could be termed the most significant hack in its contemporary history. On September 11, 2001, Nuwere is late for work at his job in the World Trade Center, and he is only a few blocks from it when it starts to burn, and then collapse. With others, he is caught in the dust cloud. When it clears, he goes to ground zero and sees the devastation first-hand. For the first time, Nuwere sees the results of this unwanted intrusion as a violation: "they [the attackers] had stolen something from us. Our sense of security. Our sense of freedom. In the middle of a bright morning they had robbed us" (241). Nuwere's rise as a hacker had never included a sense that he too was an American because, as he observes, poor Americans of colour do not get treated as full citizens. But the crisis causes him to change his mind. As he helps his company rebuild its computer systems the next day, he realizes that he is part of a community: "It struck me that we [the members of the company] were partners, teammates—words I never would have used before, that probably would have embarrassed me even to think.... Does tragedy on this scale do something permanent to your feelings about others, about your dependence on them, and theirs on you" (246)?

The feeling of belonging that Nuwere experiences stays with him, and it changes his ideas about hacking: "my greatest hack in life was simply to get to where I was now [rebuilding the computers] to where I was part of something much larger than myself and my own private dreams" (246). The experiences in the aftermath of 9/11 were a final movement from Nuwere's private dreams to his sense that he was part of a public, and that he belonged to others and they to him. This realization does not make Nuwere into an American patriot; rather, it causes him to move in a different way. Nuwere went on to realize his dream of moving to Tokyo, starting his own securities companies, and establishing a non-profit organization that supports technology in education for students .[14] By the end of *Hacker Cracker*, the activities of hacking and cracking systems have become the key for Ejovi Nuwere not to compromise a system or "become" someone else to escape his life but to forge a mobile identity that can move between systems, and have a sense of citizenship as an expression of affective belonging to a community.

Stuffed: Growing Up in a Restaurant Family

This family memoir by Patricia Volk first appeared as a hardcover in 2001 with Knopf, Random House's flagship trade imprint with a reputation for producing high quality books. Volk is a well-known writer of fiction and has also published non-fiction for the *New York Times Magazine*, *The New Yorker*, *Playboy*, and GQ, making her a good fit for the publishing culture of Knopf and for Vintage, another Random House trade imprint, which published the paperback version in 2002. Reviews of the book published on the front and back covers include glowing reviews from the *Guardian*, the *Los Angeles Times*, the *Daily Mail* and *The Washington Post*, indicating that the book and Volk have a high enough profile to merit reviews from major newspapers. The production of *Stuffed* therefore positions it clearly as a high-quality trade book about ethnic minority experience that is meant to be read for its style rather than for sensationalist elements.

This turns out to be the case. Patricia Volk's memoir is not about restaurants (a problem that some reviewers had with the book because they thought it would be about what running a restaurant is like) but about the identity of her family as a "restaurant family," four generations of Jewish-Americans in New York who ran a series of restaurants and delicatessens. If the dominant metaphor of *Hacker Cracker* is hacking as a practice to secure social mobility, the dominant metaphor of *Stuffed* is also found in its title and its description of a lack of mobility. To be "stuffed" is to be the recipient of too much food, too much love, and too much care. It is about not being able to move without help, a condition that can be painful but also a source of humour and wit as a way to ease the pain: "You weren't considered fed unless you were in pain. The more somebody loved you, the more they wanted you to eat. In a restaurant family, you're never hungry, you're starving. And you're never full, you're stuffed. When anyone rose from the table without a two-handed boost, my grandmother wailed, 'Please, God, don't let him have gall-bladder!'" (2003, 4).

In this memoir, stuffing is also a writing practice. Volk's own account of her family's love for each other (and their capacity to irritate and alienate each other) is stuffed with anecdotes about her unusual relatives. Her great-grandfather is Sussman Volk, "the man who brought pastrami to the new world" and started a delicatessen. One of her grandfathers won the land for his house in a card game with the mayor of New York, then went on to invent the wrecking ball and run one of New York's best-known demolition companies. Her other grandfather was the first man to carve meat in a store window. Her father ran one of the restaurants his father had founded: Morgen's Grill in the garment district. Volk's father also opened the first frozen-food store in Greenwich Village and invented the first See-Thru wristwatch. But these are just the public achievements of her male family members. Volk's memoir is also about unusual female members of her family, all of whom are memorable for the roles they played in private life. These include her sister JoAnn, who delights and amuses her by turns, her Aunt Lil, who had a pillow with this message in needlepoint: I've Never Forgotten a Rotten Thing That Anyone Has Done to Me, and her Aunt Ruthie and her capacity to be sweet and then insult her family members when they least expect it. The anecdotal approach of *Stuffed* allows Volk to mix public and private achievements in a celebration of her family and the role they played in building (and rebuilding) modern New York.

The response of reviewers to Volk's accumulation of intimate details in *Stuffed* is varied. Reviews range from irritation and dismissal on the book-cataloguing website *Goodreads* of the approach as a valorization of trivial family detail, to admiration in print reviews for Volk's enthusiasm for her family (Bethel, 2001; Veale 2002; J. Larson 2003). One of the more interesting endorsements of the book is by Nancy Pearl, a well-known advocate of reading programs and libraries in the United States. In a program for National Public Radio on December 3, 2010, Pearl listed *Stuffed* as one of her favourite memoirs because—unlike many memoirs that emphasize pain and suffering, memoirs that she says she will not read—she enjoyed Volk's love for her family, even for her "weirdest" relatives (2010a). In the written version of her reviews for the program, Pearl adds these observations: "Volk's family is sufficiently odd enough to keep anyone's attention, while her writing (she's also the author of a novel and two collections of stories) is both witty and tender. I pored over the all-too-few family photographs, wished that there was a family tree that I could refer back to, and most of all wished that I, too, could be part of the whole Volk/Morgen clan" (Pearl 2010b). Pearl's reaction to *Stuffed* emphasizes Volk's reputation as a writer and her ability to deftly characterize the members of her family, aspects of the book that trump—for Pearl—a plot structure that would depend on conflict.

The opening of the book clearly positions *Stuffed* as a memoir about a family's relationship to food and to each other. Food is immediately a metaphor for family culture. The family's private life is literally the food they serve in Morgen's restaurant in a humorous collapse of the products of their labour into a domestic space: "Our hallway was the color of ballpark mustard. The living room was cocoa, my mother's wall-to-wall, iceberg green. The floor of the lobby was maroon-and-white terrazzo, like Genoa salami. When our elevator went self-service, the wood was replaced by enameled walls that looked like Russian dressing, the lumpy pink kind our house-keeper, Mattie, made by lightly folding Hellmann's mayonnaise into Heinz ketchup with a fork ... we were a restaurant family, four generations in a six-block radius. When you opened our fridge, food fell on your feet" (2003, 3).

Volk "stuffs" her descriptions of food into the house, just as her family is stuffed into time (four generations) and space (a six-block radius). There is too much food, and food literally surrounds them in the decor of the fam-ily home. The type of food is important too: most of it is American ("ice-berg" lettuce, "ballpark mustard," "Heinz ketchup," "Hellmann's mayon-naise") and all of it could be served at a delicatessen or sandwich shop run by Volk's family. The colours represent American food that is not regional or culturally specific. Working-class and middle-class people alike would recognize it. But the only producer of food mentioned is Mattie, the Volk family's African-American cook and housekeeper who lives with them for more than thirty years and who, as Volk points out, inevitably had a com-plex relationship with her Jewish middle-class employers. Therefore, the opening establishes that *Stuffed* is about a jumble of private and public ideas about food. The home is literally built from delicatessen food because that is her family's livelihood, but the only domestic cook is Mattie. Although this family is—as Volk often shows—exuberantly and proudly Jewish, most of the food the family makes and eats is not Jewish or Yiddish but American. And it is not hybrid, because Morgen's restaurant did not make fusion food: "the trend in fusion cooking today combines two cuisines. Santos [chef of Morgen's] kept his cultures pure. He cooked what was called a continental menu. Each foreign dish was made strictly the way it was made in its coun-try of origin" (165).

This insistence on purity and the importance of correct behaviour is part of the family culture. It is also gendered. The women in the family place a premium on beauty because "everyone in our family was gorgeous" (141). She concludes that "gorgeous" is a family word for love and affection (153). But when Volk was growing up, she experienced beauty as tyrannical. In a family where eating food was tantamount to accepting love, she and her sister constantly dieted, terrified that they would become fat (109–11). Her father called her "lardass" (11) as a term of affection. Her mother constantly tries to improve Volk's life and appearance because as Volk says, "what she wants from me is an even cleaner, thinner, happier life than she has. Mom made me, and now she can make me better" (61). Her Aunt Ruthie loves her, and then criticizes her as she gives Volk a piece of halvah to take home: "I am adored, adored. But then there it is—the Aunt Ruthie zinger....*This is for your husband ... You don't need it ...* Zing! Does she think I'm fat" (136)?

Mattie, the housekeeper, is not only the focus of correctness and purity but also of the problem her family had with acknowledging class and race differences that contribute to this domestic discourse of purity. Mattie "was a perfectionist" (69) as a cook and a cleaner, and she took pride in her work. Most of the recipes repeated in *Stuffed* are hers, including recipes for steak with Morgen's seasoning salt and for chocolate cake. Volk says of her: "she was so meticulous, she could train raisins" (67). But she also slept in a room smaller than Volk's and made a low wage because women in Volk's neighbourhood engaged in informal "salary fixing" (71). To make up for these injustices, the family pretended that race did not exist: "It was a bizarre Jewish New York sensibility that we could somehow protect Mattie from prejudice by never acknowledging that there was such a thing as color in the first place. We pretended to be color-blind, and yet my mother rang for Mattie with a crystal bell ... Mattie did not appear to mind. But I did" (74).

Years later, when Mattie died and Volk is given a quilt she had made, Volk understands how Mattie dealt with the life she lived. She takes the quilt to a quilt restorer for repairs and is told that there is a deliberate error in the quilt called "make it fit." Volk says that she is surprised because "the woman who made this was a perfectionist" but the restorer replies, "For pleasure, we do what we would not do in our front parlor" (77). Volk learns to restore the quilt herself, and writes that "it feels like spending time with Mattie again" (78). Unlike her relationship to Mattie in which Mattie worked and she is the passive (and guilty) recipient of love that cannot be openly acknowledged, Volk finally works with Mattie's handiwork that she did for herself, not for Volk's family. In doing so, she understands what kind of person she was apart from her relationship to her job. "When in doubt, follow Mattie," the restorer tells her when Volk asks how to repair the quilt. In her writing, Volk does this as well: when a national magazine asks her to censor references to Mattie's race because the "readers don't want to know she's black" (74), Volk breaks with her family tradition and does not perpetuate this silence. She does not say if she withdraws the piece, but her relating of this incident in *Stuffed* suggests that she did. Her tribute to Mattie in *Stuffed* is Volk's own way of "make it fit" for Mattie's memory that finally makes visible the politics of race, class, and affect that bound Volk and Mattie together, and that also kept them apart.

Unlike the women in her family, whose eccentricities, wit, and work are all part of domestic life, Volk's male relatives have almost aggressively successful public lives, and—with some notable exceptions—negative private lives. Her Uncle Al, the family's only professional (he was a dentist), is respected as a "genius," even though he openly cheated on his wife (34). Her grandfather Herman Morgen became a successful restaurant owner in New York, but he once violently beat her up when she was a child because she would not brush her teeth (123). Her grandfather Jacob Volk ran New York's most successful wrecking company (he was the relative who invented the wrecking ball) but he beat Volk's father with a cat o' nine tails, "an instrument of torture outlawed before he was born" (91). The only man who is able to successfully navigate the public sphere and the private world of the family in *Stuffed* is Volk's father, and the memoir could be read as a tribute to him. Near the beginning, Volk's father is introduced as a renaissance man who can do almost anything, and who teaches Volk what he knows. Her father's talents include teaching her "how to swim, speak French, drive, eat using the utensils American-style (which nobody in America seems to do), spot weld, solder, emboss, ride English, ride western, make meringue, sing pop songs ... deglaze a pan, suck meat off a lobster a lobster doesn't know it has, blind a mugger, kill a rapist with a rabbit punch, remove stains," and so on (11). Her father's skills are both domestic and public, traditionally male and traditionally female. Because his own father died when he was still a boy and his childhood was unhappy, Volk decides to devote herself to her father: "The idea was, if I could make him happy, I could somehow make it up to him that he'd grown up fatherless, shipped away, shot" (15). This proves to be difficult, since Volk's attempts to teach her end in often comic failure because, "what I was good at wasn't what he taught" (14). At the end of the memoir, Volk's dad reappears, dying of cancer but still wanting to live because—in characteristic fashion— he has computed how many minutes he has left on earth and he does not want to waste any of them (212). After she describes his death, Volk ends the narrative with a description of the last trip she makes with him to his restaurant, and of her last motorcycle ride with him: "I feel the way I always feel with my father: safe" (239). But the closing of the store is also a closing of her family's history: "Mom and Dad fed the people that clothed the country when MADE IN AMERICA was the label of choice ... for one hundred years our family fed New York" (237). Volk links the closing of Morgen's with the closing of other New York institutions, with the end of close-knit families and the end of a type of American economy dependent on a rootedness in one place: "one generation ago, four generations met weekly for dinner. Now those people live in Honolulu, Scottsdale, and Boca Raton" (237). The last text in *Stuffed* is in some ways its most eloquent testimony to this change: it is a compilation of selected New York City directories from 1887 to 2001 that list the names and addresses of Volk's relatives and their businesses. In 1887 there is only one: "LIEBEN Louis furs." The names and businesses proliferate throughout the early part of the twentieth century until the 1950s. Then there is a blank until the last entry, 2001. Only the names of Volk, her parents and sister, and a few other relatives appear. There are no businesses. Only Patricia Volk lives in New York.

Stuffed is a celebration of family life that ends with this simple statement of the loss of work, place, and even family. The figure of Volk's father, a man who could be at home in a domestic space and in the space of the workplace unifies both worlds, and strengthens her sense that "in a family you don't come from nowhere. You enter the world already part of something" (230). But when her father dies, this sense of family as stuffed into each other, into New York, and even of New York as a place stuffed with personal history, begins to disappear. *Stuffed* is dependent on reading the space of family and of Jewishness literally as the space of New York and by extension, of America itself. But because it memorialized a way of life that by the end of the memoir is beginning to disappear, it is an intensely nostalgic view of family and American identity. *Stuffed* ends without concluding that it is possible to maintain—except through memory—what this identity could mean. Like the family apartment that takes on the look of what the restaurant produces, New York itself takes on the flavour of Volk's family in this memoir, until her father's his own death removes this intense identification of family, community and city.

Cosmopolitan: A Bartender's Life

Unlike *Stuffed: Growing Up in a Restaurant Family*, Toby Cecchini's memoir is primarily about what it is like to labour in New York's food and beverage industries from the 1980s to the present. It is about *serving* the public and what it costs him personally to do this. And unlike *Stuffed*, it eschews nostalgia and idealization of labour in the food industry. Here, service is foregrounded, and family life is placed in the background.

This memoir is a description of a day and a night in Passerby, the bar that Cecchini co-owned and ran, accompanied by other observations Cecchini makes about what bartending involves. *Cosmopolitan* was published in

2003 by Broadway books, an imprint of Crown owned by Random House. Like Volk, Cecchini was already a published writer of magazine articles, having written about bartending for GQ and *Slate*. His success in these venues is probably the reason why the publisher took a chance on publishing this first book. Broadway itself is known as publisher of popular memoirs that often become bestsellers. It is the publisher of the runaway bestseller *Tuesdays with Morrie* and well-known travel writer Bill Bryson's *The Life and Times of the Thunderbolt Kid*, and it has published memoirs by George Bush, Barack Obama, and Carol Burnett. The description of Broadway on the Crown/Random House website states that the company "publishes a variety of nonfiction books across several categories including memoir, health & fitness, inspiration & spirituality, history, current affairs & politics, marriage & relationships, animals, travel & adventure narrative, pop culture, humor, and personal finance."[15] The length of this description shows that Broadway publishes non-fiction books with popular appeal, but, significantly, memoir heads the list. *Cosmopolitan* was therefore a good risk for a company known for publishing memoir and popular non-fiction, but it also was considered a good risk because of the success of *Kitchen Confidential*, chef Anthony Bourdain's professional memoir that is also an exposé of restaurant kitchens, published by Harper Perennial in 2000.

Bourdain's *Kitchen Confidential* was a bestseller about the difficulties of restaurant work. It was released when celebrity chefs and reality TV shows featuring cooking and restaurants were becoming popular, and the book became a critical and material success because it sought to defuse—in a humorous way—the glamour of restaurant work. Bourdain went on to write other bestselling books that combined personal confessions and accounts of his experiences in the food industry, including *The Nasty Bits* (2006), *No Reservations* (2007), and *Medium Raw* (2010). *Kitchen Confidential* was made into a short-lived fictional television series by the Fox Network. It is unsurprising, therefore, that Bourdain would have imitators, since as I discussed in chapter 1, new and unknown non-fiction authors often find publishers based on the generic comparability of their books (30–31). On the front cover of *Cosmopolitan*, the following blurb by Anthony Bourdain underscores its comparability. Bourdain calls *Cosmopolitan* "marvelous.... a hard, funny, sad and unflinching look at the world from the other side of the bar." There are no other reviews of *Cosmopolitan* in its paratext, and so comparability is the main way that readers are to be attracted to this book. Results for this strategy have been mixed. Informal comments about *Cosmopolitan* on Amazon.com's website range from appreciate reviews from readers who are also bartenders and who appreciate Cecchini's industry-insider approach, to readers who dislike the book because they romanticize bartending and thought that Bourdain's own book was better.[16]

The title of *Cosmopolitan* also reflects the role of the agent in determining the look and feel of a non-fiction book. Cecchini is often cited as one of the inventors of the popular Cosmopolitan cocktail, although Cecchini himself has said that he adapted an existing drink and gave it that name (Cecchini 2003, 58–59). But the drink has still been attributed to him despite his protestations, and so his agent suggested that Cecchini should title the book to reflect the problem. Cecchini said in a recent interview, "it was actually my agent's idea to name the book *Cosmopolitan*.... He's like, 'It's the thing that has haunted you forever. You have to address it'" (Schott 2008). Cecchini does address the conditions for his invention of the Cosmopolitan at length in the memoir as a result, but the title also serves to focus other aspects of the narrative. Cecchini grew up in Wisconsin, but he came to New York after living in Paris and learning about food and wine in the southern regions of France. In New York he became a waiter at the Odeon, one of Manhattan's top restaurants in the 1980s, there learning his bartending skills. He went on to run another bar before he opened Passerby. If to be cosmopolitan is to be free of local attachments and to be able to move between environments and even nations, Cecchini is cosmopolitan in his appreciation of professionalism regardless of the circumstances and his training in many locations. He is also cosmopolitan in his desire to create in a bar space a place for people to be public in the city. To him, a bar "is in fact an important catalyst in creating the bonds of a community at its simplest: a place for people to talk with those they like and learn to live with those they don't" (2) because "people have to go out to meet other people" (3). The bar is therefore a place where many people meet and learn to be a community, but is also the stage for the professionalism of the bartender, a place for the bartender to be artistic in a way that few people recognize. *Cosmopolitan* is both an appreciation of the bartender's art (the drink) and an analysis of the environment through which the bartender moves (city life in a communal space).

Cecchini regards bars as public places because, as he says, "drinking, as a pastime, is relatively democratic" (78). When he stumbles upon an ornate old hotel bar in the Upper East side that serves him professionally he is elated, because his class differences from other patrons are—in the environment of the bar—erased. He begins to explore other similar hotel bars in the area, "seemingly exclusive but in fact open to the discerning or intrepid public" (78) and in the process discovers the history of New York's elite from the 1950s. Even as he himself worked at the Odeon, symbolic of the star-studded venues of the 1980s, he discovered in the older bars the possibility of change for himself, from a poverty-stricken waiter and bartender to someone who regarded his work as an art form: "To say that my discovery of these history-drenched, old guard East Coast haunts changed the way I think about people and altered my perception of the possibilities open to me in this world is not as vast an overstatement as it sounds ... at the time that they were built, these hotels were the apotheosis of luxury, and their creators were clearly looking to make impressive spaces that suited the types of worldly wise travelers passing through New York" (81–82).

As he sits in these spaces that had turned into "time capsules" because they were insulated from the hectic bar scene that he worked in himself, Cecchini begins to see how a bar itself could be more than a workplace, but a cultural record for a city. When he is invited to open Passerby, his small bar located in the meatpacking district of Chelsea that stayed open until 2008 (Schott 2008), he seeks to create a space that is an extension of the art gallery next door, and that hides itself away, much as the grand bars did. Passerby had no sign, and so it had to be either discovered or introduced to new clientele by the artists who did shows in the gallery next door. Inside it was "scruffy" but also "knowingly urbane," an environment where artists and hipsters felt equally at home with working-class locals from Chelsea (22–23). In a sense Passerby became a manifestation of New York City's cosmopolitans, just as the older hotel bars were created as a distillation of New York for cosmopolitan travellers who themselves were just "passersby" in the city.

The focus of *Cosmopolitan* is the figure of the bartender as a working-class servant, even though Cecchini owns his own workplace. But the bartender's position in a bar as a mixer of complex drinks means that, like cooks and chefs, bartenders are both professional and servile at the same time. According to Cecchini, the bartender's labour for an often-ungrateful public is a performance fraught with difficulty. It is a balance between the realities of working in a dehumanizing environment and the mixture of pride and shame with which good bartenders regard their work. Cecchini's description of bartending during a rush hour is the "dirty submarine ballet" (158). The phrase is a description of the filth and grime associated with the job, a reference to the lack of space in which to work and the term "ballet," used by bartenders, to indicate to each other where they are and how to move around. The first two terms signify the often-degrading work conditions. But the third term is about professionalism, because "ballet" is about the way that they move their bodies through space so that everyone can do the job. As Cecchini says, good bartending is very much like a performance: "making a drink can be a poetic exercise, a choreographed set of practiced reflex motions every bit as moving and pure in its efficiency as Chinese opera" (55). In a rush, the difficulty of ballet has a certain beauty for those who are watching, but Cecchini quickly qualifies it:

> There's a kind of sickly beauty to these screeching, urgent moments [of the rush] for me, if only because they strip away all the niceties and solicitation of careful bartending and pare what I do down to a simple, brute contest of endurance and production ... it's hard [for customers] not to watch the crazy, tight spasms of this trained animal churning out refreshments at a hundred miles an hour. In the way that athletes speak of being in "the zone," I can now feel my muscle memory take over and, as though a spectator myself of my own actions, even I am fascinated. (172)

Cecchini shows how difficult the job of bartending is in many moments like these, but even he qualifies the beauty of doing the job right with words like "sickly," or "brute," or "animal." The bartender remains an object in the eyes of a customer, a machine whose purpose is to deliver drinks in the moment of the rush.

At other times Cecchini writes about interacting with customers both good and bad and about manipulating elements of the bar such as the music, the glassware, or the quality of the drinks so that the experience of customers is affected. In addition to the low pay and long hours, it is the physical aspect of the job that is the source of shame for Cecchini, since being regarded as little more than an animal—although a fascinating one— creates a split within himself. Even he is alienated from his labour. Customers who witness this physicality sometimes see themselves as subjects and the bartender as an object for their pleasure. Bartenders, Cecchini writes, often fend off unwanted sexual advances because "it is as though, once on display, you are the assumed plaything" (122). They are offered drinks and drugs (142). Cecchini takes pride in the performative aspect of his job, but then says that it is also shameful: "I wish that I could be this good, this masterful and assured, at something other than bartending" (173). Like other bartenders, he is afraid of becoming "entrenched in this profession" (193), an admission of fear that bartending is a menial job, and not an art.

Cosmopolitan represents an attempt to turn the bartender from fantasy object into a subject so that readers can see what the conditions of production are for the drinks they order. The stories about the difficulties of running a bar are meant to be a corrective for the idea that anyone who pours a drink knows how to be a bartender. However, once these stories are told, Cecchini provides recipes to show his readers how a drink can be a work of art. Significantly, the first recipe is not by a professional bartender but by Cecchini's own father, an artist and inventor whose recipe for a gin and tonic is described by Cecchini in loving detail (9–11). When Cecchini orders a gin and tonic in a bar, he is shocked at its low quality. Ironically, it is his father's desire to innovate, and not Cecchini's professionalism, that makes this drink "simple as a Quaker prayer and written in stone" (9). Cecchini's own approach to bartending as an art stems from his father's attitude, and it is what keeps him dedicated to quality even in the difficult atmosphere of the bar. *Cosmopolitan* ends with a selection of recipes—an indirect homage to his father—called "Five Classic Cocktails and an Interloper." Cecchini includes the instructions for classic drinks such as the Sidecar, the Manhattan, the Martini, and the Negroni. He also includes the Margarita, a drink hated by bartenders because of its complexity, and finally—inevitably—his own recipe for the Cosmopolitan. Just as the reader of *Hacker Cracker* is asked to crack the system of censorship in the book, so the recipes in *Cosmopolitan* are there to provide the active reader with their own experience of making a drink into—as Cecchini often says—a work of art. Like Cecchini, the readers of *Cosmopolitan* are asked to become actors, subjects who can perform and who have agency, now that they have experienced for themselves the art—and life—of a bartender in the reading of this memoir.

Where the Birds Never Sing: The True Story of the 92nd Signal Battalion and the Liberation of Dachau

Where the Birds Never Sing was published by HarperCollins in 2003 as a hardcover, and reissued as a paperback by Harper Perennial one year later. As a book produced by HarperCollins' main division, it is meant to be seen as a populist memoir about war, and it is aimed at an audience that reads war materials. Reviews on the book's back cover, for example, are not from major newspapers or magazines but from *Publishers Weekly*, a publishing industry journal, by a columnist for the television program *Fox News*, and by an author of military biographies. The book's high production values (first in hardcover and then lavishly produced paperback) mark it as a trade book. But it is also part of one of the most significant subgenres of memoir by nonprofessional writers: the war memoir. More than most other types of self-narrative, war memoirs have enabled nonprofessional writers—and particularly working-class men—to become writers of the stories that result from being caught up in major and dramatic historical events. In this particular case, however, the structure of the story is highly unusual, and several paratextual devices mediate the eyewitness account. As I discussed earlier, *Where the Birds Never Sing* is labelled a memoir by HarperCollins, but technically it is not. It is the story of Joe Sacco and some of his friends who served in the 92nd Signal Battalion, a group of American soldiers that were among the first 250 liberators of Dachau concentration camp. The book was written by Jack Sacco, Joe Sacco's son, which should makes it a biography, but Jack Sacco wrote the accounts given to him by Joe and other surviving members of the battalion in the first person so that the story appears to be told by Joe Sacco himself. The story reads as if it were a memoir, although Jack Sacco openly relates the process of writing the book in an introduction, and his name appears on the cover.

It would seem that Philippe Lejeune's autobiographical pact is violated here and that readers would not trust such a story. But other paratextual elements establish the narrative as trustworthy, despite its unusual technique. For example, the subtitle on the front cover says that it is "the true story of the 92nd Signal Battalion," a small unit within the 42nd Rainbow Division, part of General Patton's army that landed in France on D-Day and fought across Europe. The story is stated as "true" in part because of controversy about the liberation of Dachau. The official account of the liberation of Dachau (M.W. Perry 2000) was compiled from hastily written reports soon after the war had ended, and it contained some errors. In addition, as another compilation of reports, *Dachau 29 April 1945: The Rainbow Liberation*, points out, "many reports are interpreted and distilled. The basic facts are present but are just secondhand recitals. They are devoid of subtext and emotion" (Dann 1998, 1). There are few published eyewitness accounts of the liberation of Dachau from the perspective of rank-and-file soldiers. Therefore, it is important to establish that this story is true and that the reports of the related atrocities at Dachau are accurate, but it is also important to have an account that recounts what these men saw and felt when they came to Dachau. Here, the genre of memoir is made to accommodate an urgent demand for this kind of witnessing that helps to restore not just what happened, but how it felt to be there in that place, at that time.

Another important paratextual device works as a guarantor of truth for the narrative. The book's foreword is written by Bob Dole. Dole is a former Republican senator who ran for the vice-presidency and the presidency. His involvement is meant to link Joe Sacco's story with that of a public figure.

Dole is also a veteran of World War II who published *One Soldier's Story: A Memoir* in 2005 as a way to foreground his experience as a soldier. Dole's foreword positions *Where the Birds Never Sing* as a heroic story of soldiers from World War II, but it also contains an injunction to remember the heroism of ordinary men. Dole calls Joe Sacco a "hero" and says that "there are principles worth defending and evils that must be stopped" (xiii), but he also says that "our ranks are thinning… our stories are worth remembering" (xiii). The foreword ends with honouring in this way: "thanks to men like Jack Sacco, Americans will never lack for stories of heroes" (xiii). Significantly, Dole says nothing about the liberation of Dachau or about atrocities, although he does say that "this book does not glorify war" (xiii). But Dole's foreword also glosses this book as a narrative about American patriotism in its naming of Joe Sacco as a hero, and Jack Sacco, the author of the book, as a heroic chronicler. "Thanks to men like Jack Sacco," Dole writes, "Americans will never lack for stories of heroes. And thanks to men like his father, Joe, we'll never forget how heroes are made" (xiii). When Dole wrote this foreword, as I will discuss in more detail in chapter 4, the United States was preparing for another war, this time with Iraq, and the people of the United States were still recovering from the first attack on its shores since Pearl Harbor. Therefore, Dole's references to the heroism of ordinary soldiers in the past can be attached to the truth of this narrative (Dole would be seen as trustworthy) and to the actions of American soldiers in the immediate future.

Finally, Jack Sacco's introduction serves as a witness to the veracity of his own father's account. Like the children of many Holocaust survivors whose parents cannot bring themselves to tell them what happened, Joe Sacco only tells his son part of the story of his battalion, until Jack is twelve years old: "One day, just after I turned twelve, he called me into the family den and asked me to sit with him and my mother. He pulled out a small photo album…. 'I didn't want you to see these until you were old enough,' he continued. 'My buddies and I took them they day we liberated the concentration camp at Dachau.'" (xv).

Joe proceeds to show these photographs to his son, and Jack is overwhelmed by the images he sees. His father tells him that "the unspeakable horrors caught on film … were only a glimpse of what he had witnessed when he entered the camp" (xv). Later, Jack showed his friends these photos and found that the story of the men who had taken them was also powerful. He concludes that the story should be more widely shared, because he thought that it was important to show what it *felt* like to be a young soldier, far from home "and, more often than not, unsure of their true mission" (xvi). The final picture here is of Joe's desire to share the photographs and the story with his family as a breaking of his own silence:

> He [Joe] told me that for several years after the war, he would not speak about the atrocities he'd seen. He didn't think anyone would be able to understand the magnitude and significance of what he and his buddies had experienced. His eventual decision to show me and my siblings the photographs of Dachau, therefore, was not made lightly.... but he thought it would be important for his children to see what he'd witnessed first-hand ... and he wanted us, through his witness, to stand vigilant against such inhumanity ever being allowed to happen again.
>
> And now as his story is told, I share that responsibility with you. (xvii)

Jack Sacco's introduction establishes the story of his father as a story of testimony and witness told through photographs. His own version of the story is based on his father's version of events, but the idea of witnessing as an ethical response to atrocity is preserved, and passed to other readers because his father approved his son as a transmitter of the story. This is probably why the only review of *Where the Birds Never Sing* calls the book an "odd duck" (Gold et al. 2003) but there are no other criticisms available.[17] In the older sense of memoir as the story of one person told in tandem with another, this book also furnishes the "hidden" story of Jack Sacco as a witness to his own father's story and the effect it had on him. It is, in this sense, about secondary trauma and the response to atrocity. The status of the book not just as biography but as a "hidden" memoir about the story told to and through Jack Sacco may explain why Jack Sacco writes the story of his father in such an immediate way.

The tone of the book and most of its subject matter are not given the moral imperative of witnessing, however, until the final chapter about Dachau. Jack Sacco is a writer and film director living in Los Angeles, which is perhaps why the style of narration is hard-boiled, as if the soldiers are speaking in an old film. But unlike old films, these soldiers are not heroic. They are comic. They swear, drink, look forward to liberating French towns so that they can meet women, and often get into comic situations, such as this one:

"Chandler?" I whispered.

"Huh?"

"What's the code word?"

"What?"

"What the hell's the code word?"

"Hell, I don't know ... I remember he [Captain] told us not to forget it, but I don't remember what it was."

"Well, that's just great, Chandler," I said. "That's just great. Shit." (162)

In another example, one of the soldiers manages to introduce them to Bing Crosby, who is scheduled to perform in a USO review. Crosby tells the soldiers from Sacco's battalion some dirty jokes while showgirls in "revealing costumes" listen in (212). The purpose of these anecdotes is to establish that the soldiers were in fact not heroic, but ordinary young men. Most military situations, unless one of their number is injured or dies, are seen in a humorous light.

This light tone ends with the soldier Chicago's joke at Dachau. When Averitt, another soldier, asks what the smell is, Chicago replies, "That's what Nazis smell like when they're scared shitless" (276), a typical snappy comeback. But other soldiers say "welcome to hell" (276) as a response, and then Sacco is "nauseated, dizzy, and confused" (276) as he looks at the dead and dying. He and his friends discover railway cars filled with dead bodies and piles of prisoners who had been killed by Nazis for target practice. When Sacco sees a dead mother with her baby in her arms, he begins to cry: "I wasn't alone. Many of the other men were crying. Some were enraged, angry, belligerent, stunned. Others were silently walking around with dazed looks on their faces as the overwhelming stench of death shrouded the camp" (279).

Finally, Sacco begins taking pictures of the atrocities he sees. These are the pictures that he showed his son Jack, and they are reproduced (in miniature) throughout this part of the narrative. Sacco also relates the shooting of ss troops by Americans and how he and his friends handed over an ss guard to the prisoners and watched them beat him to death (283). Later, they see tortured prisoners in the medical building (287) and stacks of bodies in the crematorium. They vent their anger by helping to march the townspeople of Dachau through the camp (288).

These atrocities (and others) these men saw are now well known and are part of the record of the Holocaust. The pictures Sacco took are shocking, but many of the images resemble those that already circulate in the public realm. What is important about this part of the testimony is that how the soldiers feel when they see the death and suffering at Dachau is recorded. This is a witness narrative in which ordinary people are witness to atrocities. In this way, *Where the Birds Never Sing* contains the physical record of what it felt like to be a witness, and relates how this feeling was not, in fact, heroic in any way. The chapter ends with an affirmation that is given without jokes or invented dialogue: "each of us finally and forever understood why destiny had called us to travel so far from the land of our birth and fight for people we did not know. And so it was here, in this place abandoned by God and accursed by men, that we came to discover the meaning of our mission" (289). The mission was to save the living at Dachau, but it was also to bear witness to the suffering of the prisoners and to fully see the dead. It was also to bring rough justice to Dachau by forcing the townspeople to see the camp, and by allowing or causing the death of ss guards, an atrocity that was overlooked because the suffering at Dachau was so great.

Where the Birds Never Sing is a war memoir with a difference. Although most of its focus is not on the liberation of Dachau and the book is in fact an almost jarring cinematic and humorous treatment of the work of the 92nd Signal Battalion, the arc of the narrative ends at Dachau in a denial of the very heroism and patriotism that Bob Dole in his foreword had said was a characteristic of this story. It is told through a double narrative of sharing photographs with his son, and then letting his son tell his own story for the public to read. Like other memoirs of witnessing, *Where the Birds Never Sing* works against more official stories about America's role in the Second World War (and, by extension, patriotic versions of America's future roles in Afghanistan and Iraq) in order to communicate, in an approximation of an unmediated way, what it was like to discover, experience, and chronicle one of the worst examples of genocide in the modern world. It is a story that goes public in order to bear witness, not just to an event but to the work of affect on those who witness it.

READING FOR CITIZENSHIP

Each of these four memoirs is about a different type of public belonging, and in that sense, each can be read for what they say about citizenship as a lived experience rather than as a formal system of obligations and rights. Although the majority of memoirs published by major companies do not reflect differences of race, class, gender, and religious/cultural differences in great numbers, the ones that do also become ways for the authors to negotiate what citizenship means to them. In *Hacker Cracker*, Ejovi Nuwere literally moves from a condition of statelessness, where he does not belong to the nation because he is poor and African American, to an understanding of belonging that moves between the twilight world of hacking and the "white hat" world of business. Patricia Volk's idea of citizenship is based on her membership in her Jewish family and its work in the restaurant business of New York: much of *Stuffed: Growing Up in a Restaurant Family* is about exploring the boundaries of this type of citizenship of the family and of the public spaces of New York until her father dies, at which point the threads tying the family to New York, to their culture, and to each other begin to break. *Cosmopolitan* is also about belonging, but this time the space of belonging is the chaotic space of a New York bar, where the activity of drinking holds strangers together, and the figure of the bartender and his/her labour becomes the idea of the *publican*, the person who serves drinks but who also makes a *public* come into being through that labour. Finally, Jack Sacco's *Where the Birds Never Sing* is a chronicle in the tradition of the war memoir that seeks to construct a witness position for his father and for the other soldiers who saw Dachau, unmediated. It is at once the most overtly patriotic narrative of the four, but it is also the most critical of the idea of patriotism and of formal citizenship. In the end, Joe Sacco is changed by what he sees, but the result does not make him a better citizen of the United States, or even a better soldier. His recognition of his destiny lies in bearing witness, through this book by his son, to the pain that the recognition of belonging can bring, a recognition born when he beholds the dead and knows that their last stories must be carried by him to share with others. This recognition of what is carried and this ability to transmit what citizenship and belonging can mean for an individual is one of the sources of memoir's power and attraction for readers who were not at Dachau, or in a New York delicatessen, or at the World Trade Center towers, or mixing drinks for a noisy clientele and who want to know what these experiences are like, and what they can mean if what they *felt like* is communicated to another. Memoir is one means of sharing such experiences and reflecting on them as their authors—who have no previous public presence—go public with these stories. In the next chapter, memoir's capacity for making such connections in light of world events will be explored in the response of readers to Marjane Satrapi's *Persepolis: The Story of a Childhood* and James Frey's *A Million Little Pieces*.

Chapter 4

EXCEPTIONALLY PUBLIC: MARJANE SATRAPI'S *PERSEPOLIS I: THE STORY OF A CHILDHOOD* AND JAMES FREY'S *A MILLION LITTLE PIECES*

In 2003, more than one hundred and sixty books labelled by their press as memoir, biography, or autobiography were published by Random House and HarperCollins. Some of these books sold relatively well and were re-released as paperbacks. As is the case with the majority of books published in any given year, some titles were not successful and probably few people bought or read them. Two titles published that year stand out as exceptional in a way that leads me to reconceptualize the logic of the exception as it has been developed in auto/biography studies since the late 1980s. These two books were the English translation of the first two volumes of Marjane Satrapi's *Persepolis* and James Frey's memoir about addiction and recovery, *A Million Little Pieces*. At first glance, *Persepolis: The Story of a Childhood* and *A Million Little Pieces* seem to have little to do with each other. Satrapi's story of her childhood and teen years in Iran during the rise of fundamentalism in the 1970s is in the form of a graphic memoir—also called a graphic novel or an example of "commix"[1] and has often been compared to *Maus I* and *Maus II* by Art Spiegelman (Foroohar et al. 2005; Hoashi 2007). *A Million Little Pieces* sold moderately well at first, but became a national bestseller when it was chosen for Oprah's Book Club in 2005. Subsequently, James Frey was found to have exaggerated and fabricated elements of his life story, and after a series of nasty public confrontations he was humiliated and his publisher, Random House, issued an offer to refund the purchase amount if any reader was dissatisfied by the truthfulness of the story (Rich 2006).

The popularity of both books at an important point in the recent history of the United States does in fact tie them together in ways that work against the idea in auto/biography studies that marginal texts matter more than mainstream or popular ones. Until very recently, popular or mainstream texts have been regarded with suspicion in much of the scholarly work of auto/biography studies. This wariness has taken two forms: on the one hand, auto/biography scholars who have been trained in the techniques of literary analysis have sometimes equated mainstream texts with a kind of commodification that for them signals a lack of literary quality. Early autobiography critics interested in canon-building saw "memoir," for instance, as a non-literary genre belonging to the market and subject to market forces, as opposed to autobiography, which is literary. Later critics constructed a poetics for autobiography based on aesthetic criteria similar to that applied to other literary works such as the novel or poetry, resulting in the exclusion or marginalization of works that did not meet the implicit demands of the criteria.[2] On the other hand, auto/biography scholars who have critiqued these kinds of positions because they worked to exclude texts by marginalized authors have championed texts that are marginal *politically* but not in other ways. Arguments for the poetics of these texts are usually about bringing these texts into academic purview or the classroom because they are worth reading for ideological reasons and because they seem to exceed the generic terms of autobiography itself. This approach is evident in studies of non-canonical texts by women, Aboriginal people, or working-class people, for instance (Kaplan 1992; Goldman 1996; Wong 1992; Stanley 2000) It is particularly pronounced in Leigh Gilmore's use of the term "limit texts" to identify texts that challenge the limits of a genre but have a level of complexity that makes them worth reading. They are what she calls experimental texts, and she says that these kinds of texts are central to the development of autobiography itself. With this, Gilmore implies that avant-garde writing that is neither popular nor populist is what has shaped autobiography as a discourse, even when market forces are taken into account. And so, it is what she chooses to study in *The Limits of Autobiography* (2001, 16–17). In auto/biography studies, this kind of logic of the exceptional autobiographical text tends to govern the tendency for scholars to examine texts that are avowedly unpopular with many readers or that many readers, particularly those who read books produced by mainstream presses, would not have heard about. This kind of study is valuable, since politically aware scholarship derives part of its energy and ethics from calling attention to texts and ideas that are not mainstream. But such an approach cannot admit to the presence of and popularity of a range of texts that are not experimental, and it does not account for how they are received. In this chapter, I wish to refocus scholarly attention on texts that do not conform to Gilmore's idea of the limit as formally experimental, but that are nevertheless "exceptional" in other terms. Although Gilmore would not anticipate my use of her term, it is the reception of these two books that makes them "limit texts" in the case of my sample. If we remake the term "limit texts" to mean texts that challenge the limits of a genre in cultural terms, *Persepolis: The Story of a Childhood* and *A Million Little Pieces* do fall into this category.

The reasons some books become popular enough to be part of public debate and even invite controversy include the need (which is a name for what is generated by the author and/or publishers, booksellers and readers) for a story to be told. The need in this case is related to American ideas about citizenship and the public sphere during a time of intense political change. I could have chosen other texts that do this kind of work, and there were a number of them published at almost the same time. In this way, these texts represent a wider tendency in the American book publishing industry at the time.[3] The social context in which they appeared, the attractiveness of their stories to an industry open to identity production, and the media convergence of two different types are what made the books take on "exceptional" qualities unrelated to questions of aesthetics. They looked as if they would "sell," and they did. And they appeared at an important time for many American readers and they struck a chord with many of them for social and political reasons.

The year in which both of these books appeared ties them together in what might be unanticipated ways. 2003 is an important date in the recent history of the United States because in March of that year, the United States and some of its allies began the invasion of Iraq and the subsequent occupation of that country. In 2002, Vice-President Dick Cheney had already linked al Qaeda, the organization that carried out the attacks of September 11, 2001, to Iraq. He claimed that Iraq harboured terrorists. His statements to this effect had an emotional impact on the American public, and helped to convince Britain to join in a war effort (Metz 2008, 113). Bush also claimed that Iraq had weapons of mass destruction (called WMDs) and that Saddam had used gas against Kurdish opposition forces in 2003, using these reasons to support his belief that war with Iraq was necessary. Subsequently it has been shown that in fact Iraq did not have the means to make WMDs and Saddam Hussein did not actively support terrorist activities. The links the Bush administration claimed existed between al Qaeda, the terrorist group response for the 9/11 attacks, and Iraq were later shown to be untrue (Fawn 2006).

But in 2003, despite the lack of enthusiasm shown by most other countries who refused to join Bush's "coalition of the willing," Americans did support Bush and his claims. The new, more aggressive approach advocated by George W. Bush in that year included dismissing the opposition of other nations that did not accept Bush's version of the truth. He threatened military action against any unfriendly nations, including Iraq and what Bush called "the Axis of Evil," which included Iraq, Iran, and North Korea (Hooglund 2006). The 9/11 attacks on the United States had made Americans ready to agree with an aggressive policy in the Persian Gulf region: in December 2001 according to Gallup, 74% of Americans wanted military intervention in Iraq. By September 2002, 57% of Americans surveyed thought that war with Iraq was an extension of the war on terrorism (Newport and Saad 2002). In March 2003 just before the invasion was announced, a poll by *The Washington Post* and ABC News found that 64% of Americans approved of Bush's handing of the Iraq situation (ProCon .org 2009). Although the American public initially thought that a war with Iraq should take place with the support of the United Nations, Gallup polls showed that the majority of Americans (83%) believed by mid-March 2003 that Saddam Hussein supported terrorist activities and the United States should take action against him for this reason (Jones 2003). Later in 2003 the Pew Foundation polls report that 72% of Americans said military force in Iraq was the right decision, and 83% said that they thought the war in Iraq was going well (Pew Research 2008). In April 2003, a Gallup Poll commissioned by CNN and USA *Today* showed that 79% of Americans thought that the war in Iraq was justified, even if there was no conclusive evidence of WMDs in existence (Milbank and VandeHei 2003). Why did so many Americans approve of Bush's actions? The public reaction to the 9/11 attacks on the United States a short time before and the initial approval of the invasion of Iraq as a response to these attacks indicate that many Americans were prepared to accept what the Bush administration told them. Between 2003 and 2005, the level of public trust in what the leaders of the United States said about WMDs and the Iraq invasion indicates how acceptable truth claims were in light of recent events. By the 2008 election campaigns for president, American support for the war in Iraq had markedly declined and the enthusiasm for the Bush administration's version of events had waned. But five years before in the wake of the first attacks on American soil in over a century, Americans had a different attitude to what their president said and what their media reported. For this reason, the year 2003 is key to understanding what Americans thought about truth-telling in the public sphere, and how the discourse of memoir forms part of that attitude to public statements for much of the decade.

At the time that Americans were being asked to accept a major change in their foreign policy and go to war against another country, the memoir boom already existed in the United States. There are, as I have discussed in my introduction, many reasons why the boom has been so successful. Sidonie Smith and Julia Watson in *Reading Autobiography* (2001) have argued, for instance, that confessional discourse is central to American popular culture and that confession had become both commercialized and part of political life (51). Another take on the development of the memoir boom links changes in the American political climate to changes in how Americans imagined citizenship and intimacy. Lauren Berlant wrote in *The Queen of America Goes to Washington City* that during the 1980s and 1990s the United States had seen the development of an intimate public sphere, a place where personal stories and the emotive dimension of experience had, during the presidencies of Ronald Reagan, George H.W. Bush, and even Bill Clinton, made the public sphere a place where rational debate about issues such as abortion or gay rights could not take place. In Berlant's conceptualization of the public sphere, the intimate sphere is the outgrowth of conservative attempts to make citizenship private: "The intimate public sphere of the U.S. present tense renders citizenship as a condition of social membership produced by personal acts and values, especially acts originating in or directed toward the family sphere. No longer valuing personhood as something directed toward public life, contemporary nationalist ideology recognizes a public good only in a particularly constructed nation of simultaneously lived private worlds" (1997, 5).

The combined effects of the election of George W. Bush and the 9/11 crisis in 2001 helped to intensify the intimate public sphere in the early years of the twenty-first century. Therefore, when American foreign policy began to change, it is unsurprising that Americans reacted as citizens to these events by looking to the intimate public sphere as the place where political issues could be worked out on a personal level. They looked to talk shows with some political content like that of Oprah Winfrey, to news programs on CNN or Fox, and finally to the publishing industry to learn about these events through personal stories or at least to encounter other kinds of truth-telling to help them deal with difficulties in the changing world where truth claims about Iraq and evidence for WMDs were being discussed every day in their mainstream news media. The American satirist Stephen Colbert even coined the term "truthiness" to express this quality in American politics after 9/11. In the discourse of "truthiness," truth is based on gut feelings rather than on facts. The speaker is trusted because of who he or she is, and not because s/he is correct. In Colbert's opinion, the trust Americans placed in George W. Bush and the distrust many right-wing Americans had whenever anyone disputed Bush's version of the facts about WMDS is an example of truthiness. Like Berlant, Colbert links this desire for emotional authenticity to a belief in public authenticity: "truthiness is 'What I say is right, and [nothing] anyone else says could possibly be true.' It's not only that I *feel* it to be true, but that *I* feel it to be true. There's not only an emotional quality, but there's a selfish quality" (Colbert 2006). What Colbert calls "selfish" is part of the link in American public life between personal authority and political authority in the intimate public sphere. The popularity of memoirs and other kinds of personal accounts is part of this appeal to the intimate public sphere and to "truthiness" as a political discourse. Nancy K. Miller points this out when she discusses how *A Million Little Pieces* is connected to the political climate in the United States in 2005 (N. Miller 2007a, 538). In 2003 and in the years to follow, that popularity shows how many American readers could use personal stories to work out what citizenship was going to mean in the new world order.

I would not claim that memoir reading or writing was a direct response to the invasion of Iraq at the time, but the interest in a book like *A Million Little Pieces* in which the author claims that only through his own self-belief could he recover from addictions, and interest in a memoir like *Persepolis: The Story of a Childhood* where the author escapes from a country in the area where the United States was beginning to attack can be broadly understood as ways in which some American readers learned about models of selfhood as a kind of citizenship. In both narratives, independence, freedom, critical thinking, and self-reliance in the face of dehumanizing institutional structures—all hallmarks of American citizenship—could be read as marks of what Gilmore in The *Limits of Autobiography* has called "representativeness," in which a liberal model of subjectivity, one person's life can "stand in" for the experience of another in a didactic way. Examples of representativeness include the autobiography of Benjamin Franklin (19). It is possible, then, that as the United States began to be reorganized around issues of security at home and aggression abroad that one way for American readers to deal with these changes was to engage in forms of representativeness. They read about self-help and self-reliance on the one hand, and on the other read about what they saw as a personal experience of oppression that justified American intervention and aggression. Until both stories were revealed to be more complicated than their initial readers imagined, this was one way that Americans in 2003 could act as citizens: by reading about and learning from the bestselling lives of others, and by benefitting from the knowledge that both stories they were being told were true. *A Million Little Pieces* and *Persepolis: The Story of a Childhood* provided, at least initially, very different and yet linked ways for Americans to enter the affective domain of citizenship. The reception of both and the subsequent rejection of one of these narratives throws into high relief how important truth-telling and "true stories" have become to segments of the American public, and how memoir has become central to thinking about intimacy in public, particularly since Americans read stories about trauma empathically, and understand stories about "the East" as ways to exercise empathy, rather than receiving them in some other register.

PERSEPOLIS: THE STORY OF A MEMOIR

Like Satrapi's narrative itself, the story of the journey of *Persepolis* from France to the United States is complex and intimately connected with the ways in which its texts (and most recently, the award-winning motion picture based on them) have been received. Satrapi published *Persepolis* first through the French publisher L'Association as four volumes: *Persépolis 1* appeared in 2000, *Persépolis 2* in 2001, *Persépolis 3* in 2002, and *Persépolis 4* in 2003 (Davis 2005, n.2). L'Association began in 1990 as an artist-run collective dedicated to producing black and white *bandes desinées* (the French language term for comic books) featuring serious themes drawn in an avant-garde style. From the beginning, L'Association positioned itself as a corrective to the mainstream comics industry in France, but it also sought to have comic books taken seriously as an artistic form their own right (Beaty 2007, 30). The covers of *Persépolis 1–4* show this seriousness of purpose on their covers. Each cover, drawn by Satrapi herself, features a military leader from Persia's past on horseback with the words "l'Association" below until *Persépolis 4*, which shows Marji—the protagonist—on horseback but not striking a heroic pose. The simplicity of these covers identifies Satrapi's work with the L'Association style because other covers from the same period look similar to them, and they could appeal to a French audience that approves of revolutionary figures (Constantino 2008). But they also position *Persépolis* as an attempt to educate Europeans about a specific version of the history of Iran. In *Persépolis 1*, Satrapi's narrative is preceded by an introduction signed by "David B."[4] that tells the story of Persia from

642 CE, discusses the formation of modern Iran, and mentions a series of coups sponsored by foreign nations—including the United States. The history ends with the Islamic revolution of 1979. The text is illustrated by eight drawings by Satrapi. Some are of the same military commanders on horseback that appear on the covers, and some are of military commanders in armoured cars.

Taken with the narrative, the illustrations show the succession of invasions and coups that have formed Iran as a nation but have also robbed the country of its independence (Gentile 2007). They are meant to show French readers something about the history of Iran, but they also serve to comment on the experience of military domination that Persians and then Iranians have had to endure, and they set up the way in which the text is to be interpreted. With the gloss of the introduction in volume 1 and its illustrations, *Persépolis* 1–4 clearly is an indictment of the Iranian revolution, but also historically another chapter in the history of Persia as a conquered (and renamed) nation. This is reminiscent of the reason for the title of the series, Persepolis, because the choice of title also reflects Satrapi's desire to remind her readers of the history of Persia: Persepolis was the capital of the first empire of Persia, founded by Cyrus the Great in the sixth century BCE.

Like the title of the series itself, the introduction also situates *Persépolis* not as a coming-of-age story about a young girl, but as the latest chapter in the history of Iran as a conquered nation, narrated by someone who experienced the political events as an invasion. This is why *Persépolis 4* has a cover that features Marji as the last "hero" in the series. She looks unsure of her role, since she is a witness to atrocity rather than an instigator, and she is a young girl rather than a man with an army to command. Along with the introduction, this places Marji at the centre of an entreaty to learn and remember the real history of Iran as a place that experienced foreign domination, including by Europe. The opening chapter of *Persépolis*, *"le Voile"* [The Veil] is therefore to be understood as the latest experience of conquest, this time of Iran by religious fundamentalists. But the subsequent tale of Marji's attempt to escape fundamentalism in Iran in Europe is also marked by foreign domination as again and again Marji is unable to become part of European life or make herself (and her country) understood in its own terms. The whole story of *Persépolis*, therefore, is about the problem of conquest and domination within Iran and in the experiences of expatriate Iranians like Marji. Marji becomes emblematic of her own national history.

The reaction of the French reading public and the press to *Persépolis* was overwhelmingly positive, and the series became bestselling almost immediately. Satrapi's work was discussed seriously by reviewers and readers who were not part of the traditional comic reading public (Beaty 147). The French daily *Libération* called her the "Persian comics star," and the third volume of the series was preprinted by them in 2002, "giving the work the same kind of national media exposure that a famous novelist or essayist might expect" (Beaty 146). *Persépolis* was even made into assigned reading in schools when veils were banned in the French school system in 2003. This was done in the hope that Marji's negative experiences of fundamentalism would convince Muslim girls not to wear veils. But many Moslem teenagers identified with Marji as a schoolgirl who could be rebellious even in a veil and—as Satrapi says herself with some approval of this practice—ended up wearing veils in imitation of Marji and her fighting spirit (Constantino 2008, 434–35). These examples show that *Persépolis* was read in France as a political narrative in a number of different ways, and that the paratextual elements of its production by an avant-garde press were geared to help readers do this.

The production of *Persepolis* for the American market in 2003 was very different. An excerpt from *Persepolis* in English translation appeared first in the March 2003 of *Ms.*, an American feminist magazine, presumably because the feminist content of Satrapi's narrative and its story of the oppression of women in Iran would, it was assumed, appeal to the publication's liberal feminist readership (Satrapi 2003a). Then Satrapi published a version of *Persepolis* through Pantheon Books, a division of publishing giant Random House, the same press that had published both volumes of Art Spiegelman's *Maus* (2003b). The use of this press shows that Satrapi was no longer regarded as an unknown artist, and that Random House thought her work would appeal to an American audience. This choice meant Satrapi was no longer "avant-garde" because her work was not going to appear in English via a small press. Satrapi's transition to a mainstream American market meant that some changes were made to the paratext of the series in order to make the story appeal to this new audience. *Persépolis 1* and *2* were published together as *Persepolis: The Story of a Childhood*. This is an important detail, because the change of title means that readers of the 2003 English-language version of *Persepolis* were not made aware that the book was part of a longer series. English-speaking readers would not know, and did not seem to know at the time because reviewers did not remark on it, that Satrapi's story does not in fact end with Marji escaping Iran and travelling to Europe. Instead it was possible for readers of *Persepolis* to imagine Europe, and western cultures, as part of the "happy ending" for Satrapi as she leaves her war-torn, intolerant, fundamentalist country of origin. As we shall see, that is what reviewers of the book did conclude.

The subtitle of the book also signals an important change: "The Story of a Childhood" creates an interpretive frame for the story that lifts it out of its political context and focuses attention on the child herself, while it simultaneously forecloses the possibility that there is more to the story. Moreover, the story is not about "a childhood in Iran" but is simply "a childhood." The effect of this is to create a possible "universal" frame of interpretation, since American readers would be familiar with other stories of childhood and would understand that genre of writing. The new cover of the book also supports this reading in interesting ways. The book was issued first in hardcover with an expensive jacket. The cartoons of military men in horseback are not there; in fact, they do not appear anywhere in this version of *Persepolis*. The cover shows an unsmiling Marji as a small child in a veil with her arms crossed in front of her. The jacket has an elaborately decorated "window" that has elements of Persian design, including the tulip, a symbol of spring and also of martyrdom (Naghibi & O'Malley 2005). We see Marji through this window. As Naghibi and O'Malley point out, the cover has the effect of creating a juxtaposition between the "strange"—the veil—and the familiar—the child and even the idea of a cartooned child figure. Naghibi, O'Malley, and Gillian Whitlock have all read this moment of encounter as "an opening, a distinctive mediation of cultural difference, and an interpolation of Western readers.... into a frame of dissonance, association, and juxtaposition that troubles a sense of self and the norms that frame ways of seeing the self and other" (Whitlock 2006, 977) because there is no stable identification of Marjane/Marji offered on the cover or the back flaps of the book, where Marjane appears in Western clothes, smoking a cigarette. These commentators see a slippage between Persian, Iranian, and Western signifiers here that mediates any attempt at a consistent reading and that opens the way to understand Satrapi's story as more than exotic, or "other" to their own. But this mediation may not trouble Western, and specifically American, readings as much as sustain them. If American readers were, as Naghibi and O'Malley also note, unable to decode the Persian symbols of the tulip or even of the veil, why place them on the cover? Why not reuse the French covers?

The answer is found on the cover itself and in the context for the appearance of *Persepolis* in the English-speaking book market. On the cover, the child appears not in the estranging costume of the veil, but in a version of it *already familiar* to American readers from other books on the Middle East.

The child is both framed by Persian design and is placed in a window that hides her away. The cover of *Persepolis*, then, creates a partially hidden and veiled child who must be, who needs to be, "revealed" by the reader. This is central to a symbolic vocabulary that has characterized the fascination of Americans with Iran and other countries in the Middle East: the image of the region is condensed into the figure of a veiled or hooded woman who represents the seductiveness of Arabian nights, the estrangement of these cultural practices, and the assumption that women wear this kind of covering because they have been forced to in fundamentalist regimes. All of these readings place the reader or interpreter in the role of one who can reveal the "true" self of the woman, the country, even the region, and who can help to save these women from the veil itself. This last reading becomes particularly important in light of American conflicts in Afghanistan, Iran, and Iraq, all Middle Eastern countries where Muslim people live.

In her study of memoirs by Afghan women, Gillian Whitlock has argued that English-language books about women in Afghanistan produced during the most recent war there invariably highlight the practice of wearing the burqa as a practice of hiding the true selves of these women. Western readers are encouraged to "look behind" or "lift the veil" as part of a long-standing western fascination with veils as signifiers of difference and as part of a western fantasy where the west "liberates" the east. Whitlock asks of these book covers when she sees them all assembled in a bookstore: "How can one resist interpellation as a liberal Western consumer who desires nothing more than to liberate and humanize 'Latifa' by lifting the burqa and bringing her alongside us, barefaced in the West? How does one begin to learn a more nuanced language that makes the veil a vehicle for a reflective and ethical practice of cross-cultural engagement? These are questions that are immediately raised by the production and carefully targeted marketing of these life narratives in the West, and they raise intractable problems about the practice of communicative ethics between women" (2005, 55).

Whitlock's point about the marketing of Afghan women's narratives holds true for the cover of *Persepolis* as well. Although it is possible to see that *Persepolis: The Story of a Childhood* contains more nuanced imagery that could produce other readings, Naghibi's and O'Malley's point that these readings would not be made available to American readers means that the preferred reading would be of Marji as a child caught up in fundamentalist politics, a child who needs to have her true nature revealed in the memoir in order to "rescue" her for Western consumption, particularly in a time when interest in Iran, Iraq, and other countries of the Middle East—

due to the change in American foreign policy—was on the increase. The cover is designed to animate this type of Western desire to know, to rescue, and to possess in order to educate American readers about Iran. It appears like another bestselling book published in the same year about women, fundamentalism, and Iran: Azar Nafisi's *Reading Lolita in Tehran*, with its image of two young Iranian women, heads covered, presumably looking at a book.[5] It also looks like the cover of *Lipstick Jihad*, Azadeh Moaveni's 2005 memoir of growing up in Iran and the United States, which has on its cover a photograph of a young women in a veil and wearing sunglasses, talking on a cellphone in front of a heavily decorated Iranian building. All of these covers create the juxtaposition between the familiar unfamiliarity of the veil (and sometimes of Persian decoration) and something that Americans would know about (cellphones, reading books, childhood) as a way to animate the dialectic between the unknown and the known to sell books, rather than a way to destabilize the symbolic vocabulary of the veil itself.

It appears that Satrapi knows about this kind of dialectic, and so this is probably why she includes a new paratext in *Persepolis* to tell her American readers as directly as possible how she wants to reimagine the story of Iran in light of American stereotypes. The introduction to this version of *Persepolis* reflects that Satrapi is aware of the American image of Iran as a nation of extremists, and so *Persepolis* is presented as a corrective to that point of view. This version of the introduction is not written by "David B." but by Satrapi herself, who signs it and includes the place and year, Paris 2002, below. Like the other introduction it begins with a short history of Iran and its invaders, with specific mention of the CIA's role in the overthrow of Mohammed Mossadeq and the American backing of the Shah of Iran until 1979. But then there is an alteration. This introduction does not have illustrations to underscore its political point about history. Instead, Satrapi includes a final paragraph that is meant to connect her own experience as an Iranian with the need to remember that Iran is not an extremist nation: "Since then [1979], this old and great civilization has been discussed mostly in connection with fundamentalism, fanaticism, and terrorism. As an Iranian who has lived more than half of my life in Iran, I know that this image is far from the truth. This is why writing *Persepolis* was so important to me. I believe that an entire nation should not be judged by the wrongdoings of a few extremists" (2003b).

Satrapi's placing of herself in the text of the introduction and her writing of it (rather than reusing the introduction of David B.) indicates that she has the authority (and the motivation) to tell the story of Iran. This gesture fits her into the discourse of representativeness that Leigh Gilmore says is a lynchpin of American identity and the basis for the production and consumption of life stories in the United States. Satrapi focuses on Iran's image in the west, and specifically in the United States, as a fundamentalist nation of fanatics, but her way of creating this corrective is to fit her personal story into these events. In other words, this version of *Persepolis* is not presented as a history lesson that fits Iran into a French revolutionary tradition, but as a testimony, a story of personal witness that creates an "insider" view of a country Americans have often regarded as an enemy, and as unknowable (particularly since the 1979 Islamic revolution). Satrapi herself has said in interviews that this was her intention: "I wanted people to read this book and say, 'Oh, it could have been me.' ... In today's world it is necessary that people read something like this, so they understand that this other that is so scary, this other that belongs to the 'axis of evil,' these people have a normal life" (qtd. in Malek 2006, 373).

Here, Satrapi presents *Persepolis* as a memoir that constructs the terms of familiarity for western readers. Instead of teaching them about difference or estrangement on the "other's" terms, or shocking them into an space of abjection as a trauma narrative would aim to do (Rak 2003), the purpose of *Persepolis* for Satrapi is to create paths of empathy and through identification of the other as the same, an identification that is not designed to destabilize the cultural position of the western reader. Western readers are meant to see themselves in Marji's place because much of what she says and does is meant to be familiar, even if the context is not. This strategy is meant to disrupt the circuit of estrangement and othering that has caused, in the memorable words of William O. Beeman, Iran and the United States to "demonize" each other for decades in symbolic discourse as either "the Great Satan" (an Iranian catchphrase for the United States) or as a nation of "mad mullahs" (a popular American description of the Islamic leadership of Iran) (2005). To make identification possible for American readers, Satrapi chose to emphasize the elements of the story that have universal appeal, particularly in the packaging of *Persepolis* for the American market. The result is that although the story of Marji would seem to contain much content (violence, anti-Americanism, feminism, Iranian national history) and style (comic-strip) that might cause some American readers to dis-identify with the text, the reception of *Persepolis* has been almost universally positive.

It is a good idea at this point to look at the character of that reception, since as Whitlock has observed, it is vital to look at the conditions of intelligibility of memoirs as they enter the American book market: "the issue of how life narratives appear and gain legitimacy is critical, and this will return us time and again to the ways that readers in the mass markets for life narrative take up autobiographical stories empathetically, identifying in and through trauma and in terms of human rights; campaigns for social justice that play to Western traditions of benevolence. This is the transit lane that allows life narratives to move from East to West rapidly and to become highly valued commodities for a 'primed' readership" (2007, 12–13).

Whitlock's observation that empathy is one of the key factors that undergirds western responses to trauma and human rights abuses in autobiography can be seen reviews of *Persepolis: The Story of a Childhood*. The narrative was viewed as a coming-of-age story of a young girl rather than as a memoir about historic events or even as a story situated in a graphic memoir tradition (Tensuan 2006). There are more than seventy glowing reviews of the book published internationally: most of them praised the "universal appeal" of *Persepolis* (Malek 2006). As she herself has mentioned in interviews with some bemusement, the only criticism Satrapi received was for the naïveté of her style, although some reviewers even saw the drawing as a "false naive style" wholly appropriate to the subject matter (Root 2007).

The reviews show that Satrapi's goal of creating a story to which western readers could relate was fully realized, although the result was that the political ideas in the book did not receive much attention in the mainstream media. For example, the endorsements printed on the back of *Persepolis: The Story of a Childhood* are by well-known graphic artists, writers, or intellectuals (including American feminist and public intellectual Gloria Steinem and Lebanese author Hanan al-Shaykh), presumably because mainstream publications had not yet reviewed *Persepolis*. They do not, with the exception of the noted children's author Philip Pullman, make any reference to *Persepolis* as a coming-of-age story: they tend to emphasize the political dimensions of the memoir and its detailing of revolution through the eyes of a young girl. But almost all the reviews of the first volume reprinted on the back of *Persepolis: The Story of a Return* with the heading "National Bestseller" indicate that there has been a change in the character of the responses to the book. The reviews in American mainstream newspapers and magazines reproduced on the back cover do not emphasize the political content and message of *Persepolis*. They focus on it as a coming-of-age story, a heartwarming tale or a children's book. For example, the first volume is characterized as "a letter from a friend" (*New York Times Book Review*), "the most original coming-of-age story from the Middle East yet" (*People*), a story "of growth, loneliness and homecoming" (*Washing-*

ton Post), and "a welcome look behind the headlines and into the heart and mind of one very wise, wicked, and winning young woman" (*Elle*). *Persepolis* is even described as a story "as deeply satisfying as a good, old-fashioned prose novel and as visually delightful as old picture books from childhood" (*Cleveland Plain Dealer*). These reviews appear on the back of the second volume of *Persepolis* presumably because they come from well-known publications and because they contain the sentiments about childhood, storytelling, and presumably universal human conditions like loneliness or homecoming that make both volumes of *Persepolis* intelligible to American readers.

Another reason why *Persepolis* became such an overnight success in the American book market is connected to the political context of its reception, and to the interest liberal-minded Americans began to develop in the Middle East because of changes in American foreign policy—an interest that helped to create a specific market for memoirs by Iranian women living in exile in the United States or Europe. Since the overthrow of the American and British-backed Shah of Iran in 1979, Iran had been considered an enemy of the United States. It had been considered this way longer than any other nation in the Middle East (Hooglund 2006). But in 2003, when Americans learned that their country was at war with Iraq, the image of Iran as a principle enemy of the United States began to shift. Previously, American foreign policy had been to support Iraq, which was often at war with Iran, as a way to isolate Iran in the Middle East. A succession of American presidential administrations had done this to maintain an uneasy balance of power in the oil-rich region. When Jimmy Carter was the president of the United States in the 1970s, his administration had regarded any attempt to gain control of the Persian Gulf after the Soviet invasion of Afghanistan as an act against American interests and a threat to American access to oil reserves (Metz 2–3). A major problem for American foreign policy, therefore, was Iran. Iran had been considered an enemy of the United States since 1979, when the Iranian revolution toppled the British and American-backed Shah of Iran. During the 1980s, the Reagan administration had supported Saddam Hussein, president of Iraq, against Iran to ensure the balance of power in the Persian Gulf was preserved (Metz 6–7). But Saddam's invasion of Kuwait and his withdrawal from it after the first Gulf War meant that Iraq had also become an enemy of the United States. Although Saddam had not successfully invaded Kuwait, he had not been definitively defeated. The new Clinton administration of 1993 sought to deal with this by creating the policy of "dual containment" in which Iran and

Iraq would be diplomatically and economically isolated from the rest of the world (Allawi 2007, 64–65). Dual containment created impoverished conditions in Iraq and, in the end, probably helped to build Saddam's resistance to American interests in the region, while it helped to create a right-wing alternative policy in the United States government (65).

When George W. Bush became president of the United States, the scene was set to change policy toward Iraq and Iran. In the wake of the 9/11 attacks, the hard-liners in the Bush administration were convinced that a hawk-like approach to Iraq was preferable to dual containment, and that Saddam had to be stopped. Their ideas about military intervention became the policy of the Bush Administration. Bush had already publicly stated in his State of the Union Address on January 29, 2002, that Iraq was a rogue state and that with Iran and North Korea, Iraq formed the "Axis of Evil" that the United States had a duty to resist. Therefore, Iran and Iraq were linked together and equally censured in American public discourse at the time, even though they are enemies of each other. This resulted in the assumption in Iran that Bush was in fact espousing an ideological opposition to the entire Islamic world. Meanwhile, neo-conservatives in the United States have described (and continue to describe) Iran as a "rogue state," a "state sponsor of terrorism," and an "outpost of tyranny" (Hooglund 2006). As American political rhetoric heated up and it became clear that the United States would go to war with Iraq, the interest of the American reading public about that part of the Middle East began to increase. But as Gillian Whitlock has observed in the case of Afghanistan, that reading took a very specific turn. Like the interest in Afghanistan, interest in Iran focused on the condition of women and particularly on the veil as the symbol of the oppression of women in Muslim countries in the Middle East. The result was an increase in memoirs by Iranian women who had been forced to leave the country. In addition to both volumes of *Persepolis* and the bestselling memoirs *Reading Lolita in Tehran* and *Lipstick Jihad*, there were at least eight other memoirs published between 1999 and 2005 by diasporic Iranian women about their experiences in Iran and in the United States. There were only four memoirs by Iranian men in the same period, and they were not as widely read.[6] Although it is possible to see the increase as an attempt by Iranian women to seize narrative control of their life stories and gain agency for themselves (Naghibi and O'Malley 2005), Amy Malek suggests that we should look critically at the market demand for these kinds of stories. She says that "the fact that there was an eager market for these memoirs is a point that should not be overlooked or underestimated. Amidst the popularity of memoirs in general, and women's memoirs, in particular, the post-9/11 atmosphere has created a level of curiosity towards Iran.... as Americans and others around the world seek insight into a country and a people that have been deemed 'evil' and an imminent threat to Western society" (360–62). Malek goes on to say that Iranian women like Satrapi who wanted to work against the prevailing view of Iran as an "evil" nation turned to the memoir genre, a genre that Iranian women were not traditionally encouraged to use, as a way to make their stories heard, particularly after the success of *Reading Lolita in Tehran*. But the problem with this is that Iranian women cannot enter the public sphere in any other way. The demand for their "experiences" means that they are unable to create other terms of recognition for themselves and for their work. As Malek says, this creates a situation where Iranian women are asked to act as native informants, constantly "unveiling" their country in non-fictional texts and films as part of the ongoing economy of East and West estrangement and curiosity:

> while Iranian women's voices may appeal to readers in this particular moment for a variety of reasons, they are still confined and pigeonholed within the memoir genre by an industry unable—or unwilling—to recognize them beyond their perceived status as "formerly oppressed third-world women," and rather for their real intellectual, literary, and artistic talents. This only perpetuates several frustrations in Iranian exile culture within the larger Western culture: memoir and film have become the only two creative vehicles through which mainstream Western consumers can view Iran and Iranians outside of the one-dimensional view provided by commercial news outlets. These two outlets have become further embedded in the Othering of the Iranian experience by giving a voice to Iranian artists and writers, while keeping them within these limited genres, thus further Othering them, though this time using their own supposed non-fictive voices. (363)

Here is the problem of genre that Whitlock detailed in the case of Afghan women's narratives: the market demand for a particular kind of life story means that these narratives must follow a logic of western storytelling in order to be rendered intelligible, but in the process the only narratives that fulfil the needs of American curiosity about "the enemy" are those that restage the "problem" of the Middle East as the subjugation of women behind a veil that only life stories can lift. The immediate popularity of *Persepolis: The Story of a Childhood* in 2003 is part of this economy of spectatorship, one that Satrapi used for her own ends to get her message out, but one that has also served to blunt the political messages of the memoir and what it asks its readers to do when "otherness" and exile appear at home.

When they are taken together, however, the volumes of *Persepolis*, as many critics have observed, do move beyond the sentimentality of their reception and render highly complex the political history of Iran, the position of Marji as a child narrator, and issues connected to the image of the west in *Persepolis* (N. Miller 2007a; Malek 2006; Tensuan 2006). One of the ways Satrapi addresses the political history of Iran is to explore what citizenship in democracies and in non-democratic countries can mean. To do this, she combines personal stories with an exploration of the relationship between Iran, Europe, and the United States in a specific critique of citizenship as a problem. *Persepolis: The Story of a Return* contains a counter-narrative about citizenship that serves to indict any form of national belonging founded on patriotism or the idea of otherness in nation formation.

At the end of *Persepolis, The Story of a Childhood*, Marji is seen off at the airport by her parents and her grandmother. She is being sent to Vienna, Austria, because after she denounces her religion teacher at school, her parents are afraid that she will be jailed, raped, and executed (144–46). Her parents make sure to tell Marji that she will be happier in Europe. Before she leaves, her grandmother tells her to "always keep your dignity and be true to yourself" (150). At the airport, Marji turns around to say goodbye to her parents and sees that her mother has fainted. The last panel, however, does not show this from Marji's point of view. Marji is in the background, separated from her parents by a wall of glass. In the foreground of the panel, Marji's mother is lying in her husband's arms, a foreshadowing of an image of young soldier who—like the image of Jesus in the Pietà—appears in *Persepolis 2: The Story of a Return* lying dead in the arms of his mother, martyred and innocent (127). The image here is of the trauma of separation that recasts Marji's mother as a true martyr for her country because she has had to let her daughter go. The images in the volume are of the airport where people escape, of Iran as a country that will not allow a young girl like Marji to speak the truth and so it must be left behind.

And so *Persepolis* ends with this—the picture of Iran—as the negative place of imprisonment and of Europe as a positive place of freedom and opportunity. But the opening panels of *Persepolis 2: The Story of a Return* quickly dispel this impression. Marjane (she now refers to herself by her adult name) is lying on a bed, thinking about her predicament: "I had come here [to Austria] with the idea of leaving a religious Iran for an open and secular Europe and that Zozo, my mother's best friend, would love me like her own daughter. Only here I am! She left me at a boarding house run by nuns" (1). From this point, Marjane encounters many difficulties in Austria, including language problems because she does not speak German, conflict with the nuns, and an inability to fit into European life. Her friends are outcasts who like her, but they make little attempt to understand Marjane on her home terms. They even fail to see that during holidays she would have nowhere to go. Marjane tries to adapt: she gradually learns about Western sexual attitudes, dresses like a punk, and even begins to take drugs to try to fit in, but there is little in her life to diminish the sense of alienation she feels. She describes her difficult and painful mental transformation into a "European" as an equivalent to her physical transformation in the chapter called "the Vegetable." Much like her awkwardness at trying to fit into to Austrian society, Marjane's own body literally does not "fit" her as she begins a growth spurt. She sees herself as physically monstrous and pictures herself as "The Incredible Hulk." In an emotional and cultural way too, she begins to see herself not as human, but as a vegetable, which is the word her parents use to describe a drug-addicted acquaintance (38). Marjane's attempts to assimilate only heighten this sense of her inauthenticity: "the harder I tried to assimilate," she writes, "the more I had the feeling that I was distancing myself from my culture, betraying my parents and my origins" (39). She lies to her parents and feels guilty that she takes drugs and knows about sex "while they are being bombed every day" (39). At a low point, Marjane tries to forget her past in Iran and she denies her identity as an Iranian because "at the time, Iran was the epitome of evil and to be Iranian was a heavy burden to bear" (41) but the lie only results in feelings of guilt because she forgot her grandmother's advice. Marjane redeems herself and reclaims her citizenship as an Iranian, however, when she screams at a group of girls who criticize her that she is proud to be Iranian . This brings her a measure of pride and relief (43).

But Marjane still struggles on her own in Austria. She has several unfulfilling relationships, becomes part of a drug culture, and, consumed with self hatred and disappointment, does not do well at school. When she discovers that her boyfriend has been cheating on her, she breaks down in a chapter called "The Veil," an ironic reference in part to her first experience of wearing a veil when she was a schoolgirl in Iran in the opening chapter of *Persepolis: The Story of a Childhood*. But now, the veil becomes a way to achieve authenticity and personal growth. It is not a symbol of subjection. At the top of two panels, Marjane talks about her despair at being left alone in a foreign country: "I had just lost my one emotional support.... I had no family or friends. I had counted on this relationship for everything" (79). Underneath the panels, her landlady comes into her room where Marjane is crying and accuses her of stealing a necklace. This proves to be the breaking point for Marjane, who leaves and with nowhere to go and no one to turn to, lives on the street. By day she rides the trams of Vienna, which are represented as a maze of looping paths to show that her life is without direction (84). Finally, she becomes ill and is hospitalized, and then she asks her parents if she can come back to Iran.

The trajectory of Marjane's time in Europe ends with her statelessness: she is a homeless person without a job, a purpose, or a sense of identity. Until she becomes ill, no one cares much about her or tries to understand her. Unlike the image of western Europe as a place of freedom and opportunity, for Marjane in *Persepolis: The Story of a Return* the West appears as a brutal, uncaring society and as the place where she feels monstrous. In the end, she feels nothing but shame, "shame at not having become someone ... the shame of having become a mediocre nihilist" (90). The last panel of "The Veil" shows Marjane unhappily wearing her headscarf as she looks into a mirror, thinking bitterly to herself that individual liberties mattered less than going home.

But in *Persepolis: The Story of a Return* home is not a place of belonging either, and Marjane experiences the same sense of statelessness that she had in Europe. After an absence of four years, Marjane herself has changed, while the country she left has become more entrenched in fundamentalist thinking. To resist, young women she meets imitate the makeup and hairstyles of Western television actresses, and they do not understand why Marjane herself does not do this (105). Marjane experiences such dislocation that she tries to kill herself (119), but she survives. She becomes an art student and secretly gets engaged, but she struggles with the restrictions at the art school and with the problems of living in a fundamentalist society where she and her friends are under constant scrutiny. Satrapi describes the atmosphere as so oppressive that thinking like a citizen was no longer possible. She draws two representations of herself asking questions: one contains questions that the regime forced women to ask of themselves such as "Are my trousers long enough?" and "Are they going to whip me?" rather than questions that citizens should ask about themselves and their country, shown in the second panel, where the questions include "Where is my freedom of thought?" and "What's going on in the political prisons?" (148). Satrapi shows here that the effect of the constant oppression of women in Iran was a focus on the self and the "proper" appearance of the body as well as on everyday problems, rather than on the ability to ask more abstract questions about the body politic or one's public life, and she sees this inability to think as a citizen as widespread. When the first Persian Gulf war against Iraq begins, Satrapi pictures many kinds of reactions by "people in the street" to the war. From the soldier who was injured in the Iranian war with Iraq who wants Saddam dead, to a man who says, "Now our economy will finally pick up!" no one (except for Marjane's parents) thinks about the issue critically. As Satrapi shows in a panel with a happy Iranian nuclear family surrounded by soldiers and gun barrels, "the regime had absolute power ... and most people, in search of a cloud of happiness, had forgotten their political conscience" (169).

But Marjane cannot forget her political conscience for long and as she says, she "changed her life" (173). Learning what citizenship and belonging can mean is central to this change. Encouraged by her parents and her psychologist, she reads about Iran and begins to learn from Iranian intellectuals about the political problems with her country. She works with Reza, her husband, on a design for a theme park based on Persian mythological heroes, but the proposal fails because the regime will not allow powerful Persian woman warriors to be represented (177). Frustrated by this setback, appalled by the sexism of Iranian society and trapped in a loveless marriage that came about in part as a response to Iranian social restrictions, Marjane decides to leave Reza to emigrate again, this time to France. But the circumstances of leaving have changed: Marjane decides to go because she is not allowed to be a citizen in Iran: "Not having been able to build anything in my own country," she writes, "I prepared to leave it once again" (185). She says goodbye to the Iranian landscape, visits the grave of her Uncle Anoosh, who had died for his political beliefs, to promise him that she will be honest, and then leaves her parents and her grandmother at the airport.

The airport scene is arranged in the same way as the one that ends *Persepolis: The Story of a Childhood*: Marjane is again behind the glass waving goodbye to her family, except that this time she and her parents are smiling. Unlike the separation of mother and daughter pictured at the end of *Persepolis: The Story of a Childhood*, the focus here is on a different kind of intergenerational separation, although at least one commentator does read it as a scene about mother-daughter leave-taking.[7] There is no Pietà tableau of a grieving mother. Satrapi comments that "the goodbyes were much less painful than ten years before when I embarked for Austria: there was no longer a war, I was no longer a child, my mother didn't faint and my grandma was there, happily ..." (187). Here, Satrapi disrupts her commentary with the airport drawing where her grandmother, wearing a veil and in tears, is now the focus. She continues "... happily, because ... she [her grandmother] died January 4, 1996 ... freedom had a price." Satrapi pictures the scene as happy because she leaves to be the kind of citizen of whom her mother and her grandmother can be proud (her mother forbids her to return to Iran), and because the scene of leaving includes her grandmother, whom she will soon lose.

Although the scene is marked by future grief because her grandmother will die two years later, political freedom and personal integrity are pictured as good choices. They are the ones her grandmother always encouraged her to make. Throughout the *Persepolis* series, Marjane's grandmother is pictured as the most radical member of her family and a symbol of the need to be authentic. She refuses to wear a veil unless she is forced to and always remembers the sacrifices her husband and Anoosh, her elder son, made as a political prisoners. She reacts to news that Marjane wants to leave her husband with pragmatism and the advice to divorce him. As we have seen, it is her words that help Marjane to regain her pride in her Iranian heritage when she is in Austria. She is also the one who upbraids Marjane for putting a young Iranian man in danger when she first returns to Iran: her grandmother accuses her of a lack of integrity and angrily reminds her of the sacrifices her family had made for others (137). She does not forgive this until Marjane goes back to art school, where she learns more about freedom and independence (140). Marjane's grandmother, therefore, symbolizes the importance of freethinking in Iran as part of its true political heritage, and of the need to be authentic in public and private life. It is fitting that "The Story of a Return" ends with a focus on Marjane's grandmother, because it is her grandmother who asks her to return to her true beliefs. "The return" in *Persepolis: The Story of a Return* is not, therefore, about Marjane's return to Iran from Austria or even about her return to Europe, but about her symbolic return to her roots as the descendent of those who fought for their ideals and a return to her need to fight for what is right. It is a return to thinking about Iran as "Persepolis," the capital of a civilization that had values worth remembering in the present. In the end, *Persepolis* is the story of Marjane told as a prodigal narrative about her loss of integrity as a woman and a citizen because she loses her memory of what Iran had once been, and her regaining of this integrity through memory so that no matter where she lives, she will be personally and politically authentic. It is not possible in the *Persepolis* series to consider one form of authenticity without the other, and it is memory that keeps them together.

When *Persepolis: The Story of a Childhood* and *Persepolis: The Story of a Return* are read together, the themes of childhood and return retain their political force and ask readers to think about the investment Western people often have in the romance of a certain kind of Middle East. But the initial reception of the first volume of *Persepolis* as an apolitical story about childhood with "universal" values ensured its popularity with American readers, as it avoided the more complex presentation of identity and history that Satrapi intended for its new readership. The marketing of the book as a specific kind of memoir by a mainstream press, therefore, helped to create the very kind of barrier to reading the story that Satrapi wished to surmount. The reception of another book published by Random House that year, *A Million Little Pieces*, shows how the intervention of a publisher in the generic marketing of a book can create the conditions of its acceptance for a specific reading public, and also create the conditions of its failure.

KEEPING OPRAH AWAKE: *A MILLION LITTLE PIECES* AND THE PROBLEM OF NATIONAL TRUTH(INESS)

"I learned the strength of words and I used them."

– James Frey, *A Million Little Pieces*

James Frey's *A Million Little Pieces*, a bestselling account about Frey's time in rehabilitation as he battled against drug and alcohol addictions, is now synonymous with literary fraud. It has been discussed with an equal amount of bemusement and contempt in the popular press, and is associated with the limits of Oprah Winfrey's philosophy of transformation. But the circumstances that led to Frey's account being published as a memoir in 2003, and the reception of the book in 2005 when it was chosen as an Oprah's Book Club selection, are more complex than most journalists and commentators have pointed out. The book's meteoric rise to bestselling non-fiction book of 2005 (it also sold more copies than any other book except for *Harry Potter and the Half-Blood Prince*), Frey's subsequent fall from grace after *The Smoking Gun* website discovered that he had fabricated his arrest record and, finally, Winfrey's defence of Frey followed by her assertion on television that Frey is a liar makes for a dramatic story in itself. But the Frey controversy also points to the limits and tensions of a specific part of Lauren Berlant's intimate public sphere: as the book emerged and then fell afoul of conflicting expectations of memoir as genre, it also became part of a public debate in the United States about the meaning of truth, the image of the addict in American culture, and the value of personal experience in the public realm. The trajectory of the book's acceptance and then rejection roughly traces a path in American public discourse about what is true and what Americans should believe. It appeared in 2003 when public support for the war in Iraq and the popularity of the president, George W. Bush, were very high, and it became a runaway bestseller in 2005, the first year of Bush's second term. By 2006, when the Frey controversy was at its height and Winfrey denounced him as a liar, Bush's popularity was slipping, and Americans were beginning to publicly question many of the things that the Bush administration had been saying about the need for the war in Iraq (Pew Research Center 2008). The moral panic created in the wake of the revelations about the book shows that at the time when it began to be widely accepted that the Bush administration was not being truthful, exposing a public lie was of great interest to many Americans.

A Million Little Pieces is a relatively rare example of a memoir about addiction for a mainstream audience that appeared during a time of change in American drug-trafficking policy, a change that shifted images of addiction from a consideration of the addict's experiences to addiction as a matter of national security. The War on Drugs, a controversial program to stop drug use and drug trafficking instituted by Richard Nixon in 1969 and supported by every presidential administration since then was on the wane,[8] just as the War on Terror produced an unintended effect. Before the conflict in Afghanistan began, the Taliban—which is strongly against drug use and trafficking—had managed to gain control of the poppy-farming industry and put it out of business. But the removal of the Taliban from government meant that poppy growing for the heroin trade was on the rise again. In 2004, the Bush administration asked the United States Congress for $780 million dollars to crack down on cultivation and trafficking in Afghanistan, thereby bringing the methods used in the War on Drugs directly to a foreign country where American soldiers were already fighting what the Bush administration called the War on Terror (Willems 2005). A Million Little Pieces appeared, became wildly popular and then became the centre of a moral panic about truth-telling and addiction at the same time as the methods and the messages of the Bush administration were beginning to be called into question, and when the War on Drugs became part of the War on Terror.

The political climate in the United States at the time shows how A Million Little Pieces itself and the media firestorm that resulted from Oprah's denunciation of the book work as a model for a specific kind of citizenship and an urgency about its expression, one that emphasizes self-reliance and truth to facilitate personal transformation from a "bad" citizen (an addict) to a good citizen (someone who has recovered and gives back to the community) back to a "bad" citizen (someone who lies about something as important to Americans as addiction). But the controversy surrounding the genre of the book and its truth claims meant that in the public sphere *A Million Little Pieces* eventually became associated with "truthiness," which as I have mentioned, is Stephen Colbert's term for the emotional belief in politics that does not require facts to be considered true. It is important to remember that Colbert meant for "truthiness" to be a critique of contemporary political events: one of his examples of the term in action was the tendency of the Bush administration to defend the war in Iraq on purely ideological grounds and for the tendency of right-wing media in the United States to support Bush's position without questioning it. This is important, because as Nancy K. Miller points out in "The Entangled Self," truthiness became the byword for talking about *A Million Little Pieces* and its reception by readers, particularly with regards to whether the American public believes everything it is told (2007a). The reception of the book on the *Oprah Winfrey Show* also sketches the character and limits of a specific paradigm of reading and epistemology most recently made popular by Oprah's Book Club. *A Million Little Pieces* tested Winfrey's ability to collapse the public and the private together as she reads in concert with her large fan base. Ultimately, this method of reading was found wanting when the production of memoir for mass markets was revealed and the need for "truth" in the public sphere outstripped the importance of other kinds of knowledge that are in the book. The Frey controversy shows how important non-fictional personal accounts, or "true stories," have become in popular culture, and how their reception raises political questions about who is allowed to tell the truth, and why.

"Truthiness" was eventually applied to *A Million Little Pieces* in light of the defences Frey and his publisher made: as I will show below, both of them argued that what they call the higher truths of the book should mean more than factual inaccuracy. This argument is often made for truth-telling properties of fiction, and it is the argument Oprah herself used when she initially defended Frey. But truthiness as a way of reading and of responding is also part of the ideology of Oprah's Book Club and of the *Oprah Winfrey Show* itself, in which personal experience and integrity become central to any reaction to public events. It is what makes Oprah's endorsement, defence, and then rejection of Frey and *A Million Little Pieces* so interesting. Oprah's initial endorsement of *A Million Little Pieces* can be read as a specific type of response within an intimate public sphere that is "a space of mediation in which the personal is refracted through the general [and for its consumers] a space of recognition and reflection" (Berlant 2008, viii). In *The Female Complaint*, Berlant expands the idea of the intimate public to include the emergence of "women's culture" during the nineteenth century in the United States, with its emphasis on sentimentality as a response to political conditions without having to be political. Through the consumption of goods and images, women in an intimate public could "feel" connected to each other in a loose way: "it [women's culture] sees collective sociality routed in revelations of what is personal, regardless of how what is personal has itself been threaded through mediating institutions and social hierarchy. It marks out the non-political situation of most ordinary life as it is lived as a space of continuity and optimism and social self-cultivation. If it were political, it would be democratic" (2009, 10).

But as Berlant goes on to say, this manifestation of the intimate public in the United States is not political, although it gestures to political spheres. It often stresses the importance of a fantasy of vague social belonging and a sense of a shared past of injustice rather than a critique of the conditions of belonging. It involves what Berlant calls "relief from the political" (10) because to be political would require "women's culture" to actively challenge such a loose consensus. The concept of "sisterhood" would be part of this idea of the intimate public, since sisterhood has come under critique within feminism but not within Berlant's understanding of women's culture.

The *Oprah Winfrey Show* is an excellent example of the persistence of an intimate public sphere that gestures to political issues at times but responds to them within the frame of intimacy. Much of the *Oprah Winfrey Show*'s power comes from forging connections between a public type of intimacy that Winfrey herself models, a belief in affective types of knowing and finally a sense of the citizen (and especially the female citizen) as someone who *knows* something publicly because she *feels* its truth and witnesses to others who *feel the same way*. In other words, identification with Winfrey and with others is an important element of trust within the context of the *Oprah Winfrey Show* and its spinoff projects, such as *O Magazine*. Whether the topic is what to read, what to buy, or how to respond to an issue of the day, the *Oprah Winfrey Show* is the engine of an intimate public that aims to create belonging. In the context of the Frey controversy, the engine stalls when Frey and his memoir challenge the aims of this public.

In Oprah's Book Club, the reading paradigm Winfrey uses most often combines enthusiasm for a work, personal identification with the characters and social issues of a book, and an emphasis on group connections between readers and writers (Konchar Farr and Harker 2008). In addition to this, the role of reading on the *Oprah Winfrey Show* aims to produce affective bonds of recognition between Winfrey and other readers, and between one reader and another. This approach to reading is not new: women's book clubs had been employing at least some of these ways of reading for a long time. Winfrey's use of the discourse represents a highly successful contemporary adaptation of book-club culture for the television market, with interesting results. As Harker and Konchar-Farr point out, contemptuous backlash against them as "merely" feminine have been part of the women's book club movements in the United States for over a century. The ferocity of negative reactions to Oprah's Book Club as the enemy of avant-garde reading practices and the advent of non-critical approaches to reading can be understood as part of a long-standing pattern of popularity, dismissal, and contempt (3–4). But the Frey controversy took a different turn from the usual attack on Oprah Winfrey and the values of Oprah's Book Club. As the media firestorm about Frey's increased its intensity, Winfrey abandoned her usual reading paradigm for a different kind of response as a reader-citizen who has a more jurisdictional approach to truth. In effect, the controversy about *A Million Little Pieces* caused Winfrey to move from her original intervention on behalf of "truthiness" to a much more legalistic idea about what truth is in the public sphere. Winfrey laid the blame for her "misreading" of *A Million Little Pieces* not just on Frey himself, but also on the publishing industry, which she accused of not labelling the genre of their "product"—that is, memoir— accurately. This created a situation of genre boundary policing that, in an unusual way, laid bare the role of publishers in creating genre expectations in the reading public and connected issues about genre directly to the workings of a market economy.

As in the case of *Persepolis: The Story of a Childhood*, the publication history of *A Million Little Pieces* set the stage for the reception of the work. James Frey began writing an account of his time in a rehabilitation centre in 1997. As he said in his 2006 interview on *Larry King Live*, he offered it to a number of publishers as a novel but it was turned down.[9] Frey said to King that he found success by changing the generic categorization of his book: Nan Talese, a vice-president at Doubleday, which is a publishing company owned by industry giant Random House, read the manuscript and suggested that the book be published as a memoir. Here is a case of genre "coaxing" as Smith and Watson describe it because Talese's assumption caused Frey to change the book's genre, presumably because she thought that a factual account about addiction would sell better than a fictional one. As it turned out, Talese was right: the public did want to read the story because it was true, not just because it was a good story.

Why were these kinds of conditions placed on a story about addiction and why did they work so well at first? The answer lies in the ways in which certain kinds of memoir appear within a politics of recognition. When authors do not have access to one or more privileges that allow stories to be accepted as true, or even as good literature, they must write their stories as memoirs of survival in order to get recognition. The way in which the experiences of these authors enter the public realm, then, are as unusual accounts packaged for mainstream audiences, since in "ordinary" circumstances there would be little interest in their lives. It is why, I believe, that many of the stories about marginal life published for a mainstream readership have a sensational element to them, and why so many of them are about the survival of a trauma. In other words, what Deborah Britzman has called the "difficult knowledges" of suffering and recovery (1998) have to be at the core of stories by people whose race, sexuality, class, language, cultural background, or gender somehow combine to make them, and their stories, unintelligible in other registers. Whether the subject is the survival of a mountaineering accident as in Joe Simpson's *Touching the Void*, the many narratives about atrocities in Nazi death camps, Harima Bashir's memoir *Tears of the Desert: A Memoir of Suffering in Darfur* or Greg Mortenson's account (which itself has now been publically challenged) of building schools in Afghanistan in *Three Cups of Tea*, the public interest in these unknown people who survive or accomplish something extraordinary has to do with identification (the protagonists of the story are seen to be ordinary like themselves), dis-identification with the event (the event did not happen to all or most of the readers), and an attachment to the protagonist *through* the account's veracity (the event's status as a "true story" makes the protagonist into someone heroic). The account is interesting not because it is well written—although this can be the case—but because the *pressure* of the event makes the identity of the author important in relation to the event itself. The classic *Reader's Digest* feature column "Drama in Real Life" with its stories of people who survive accidents of various kinds is an example of this kind of narrative pressure. Memoirs by famous people or fictional stories do not have to respond to this kind of singular pressure: other imperatives can create a compelling story.

Memoirs about these kinds of extraordinary events are subject to different kinds of rules about veracity and accuracy because the writers are always ordinary (that is, they were not public persons before their stories were published) and often marginal and marginalized, and the situations they describe are often seen as extreme. As Leigh Gilmore argues about a different set of scandals about memoirs and truth-telling, when life stories about trauma by marginalized authors make their way from the private to the public sphere, the result is often a demand, which she calls an "autobiographical jurisdiction," that the truth claims in the text be absolute and even be legally verifiable (2003, 695–96). Gilmore's examples of the problems that can result include the case of Rigoberta Menchú, a Quiché Indian from Guatemala. Her memoir—written, she said, by a collaborator because she herself was unschooled—is about atrocities perpetuated against her people in Guatemala. *I Rigoberta Menchú* became a bestseller worldwide, and the book was part of the reason why she won the Nobel Peace Prize in 1992. Anthropologist David Stoll subsequently questioned the veracity of many of the book's assertions after conducting extensive research (1999). In an example like this, the text and the author (which are seen as inseparable) are subject to very rigorous truth claims, and Stoll concludes that Rigoberta Menchú lied. Gilmore argues from this example that legal definitions of truth claims are, in effect, put on trial in an extra-legal sphere: "Both the text itself and the public sphere it enters can be understood as jurisdictions; indeed, thinking of the public sphere in this way elucidates the mechanisms of judgment that pervade it, the contest of authorities that can arise around oppositional texts, and the levering forward of ethics, truth-telling, and scandal as the language through which such extra-judicial "trials" unfold (2003, 696).

Unlike Rigoberta Menchú, James Frey would not normally be regarded as a marginal subject. He is male, from an upper-middle-class background, able-bodied, white, and print-literate. He did not have to live through a war or other mass trauma, and he was not subjected to forms of physical or sexual abuse when he was a child. But as an addict, Frey joined the category of the undesirable people who typically cannot have a place in any public because, as one of the earlier models of addiction in the United States has suggested, addiction is the result of social deviance and moral weakness.

In this model, addiction afflicts some groups more than others, and so the urban poor, recent immigrants, African Americans, homosexuals, or prostitutes were thought to be predisposed to addiction and therefore a threat to American life. This threat had to be legally controlled, and addicts had to be put away for the public good. There was little sense that an addict could, or even should, be cured.[10] In *A Million Little Pieces*, James Frey identifies himself as this kind of addict, even though he did not belong to any of the "predisposed" groups. Frey does not believe that he has a curable disease or even that he has a disease at all—addiction as a disease was an idea that was developed when middle-class white people began to experiment with drugs (Muzak 2007, 257–58). Rather, Frey decides that addiction is what identifies him with those without power, and it gives his story the power of an insider's tale. In many places in the memoir, Frey repeats to himself, almost as if it were a mantra, that he is "an Alcoholic and a Drug Addict and a Criminal" with each word in capital letters (74), particularly when he thinks that he will not survive. Although he writes *A Million Little Pieces* after he has recovered, Frey's sense of himself during the time of the narrative is that he is so far removed from normal society that he cannot be helped. For him, addiction has eradicated any privileges he had, and it creates in him a sense that he has the most in common with the Mafia boss, the prostitute, and the thieves he befriends while he is in treatment. His violent behaviour during the first half of his treatment and his stubborn refusal to accept the twelve-step program's notion of cure during the second half of the book mean that in *A Million Little Pieces*, Frey appears as an example of the model of addiction that was prevalent *before* the 1960s recasting of addiction as an illness that "affects" the middle class as well.

Therefore, Frey's account of himself as socially marginal in *A Million Little Pieces* has the effect of moving the narrative into the realm of the jurisdictional and its demands for veracity and accuracy. The story cannot be read as an account of recovery within a middle-class frame of reference, and so Frey becomes a subject who, like Rigoberta Menchú, would not have a public hearing unless the story he had to tell involved trauma. The searing descriptions of illness, violence, and anger in *A Million Little Pieces* make it a narrative of trauma in which, as he later told Oprah Winfrey, Frey wants readers to feel what he felt at the time. And so, Frey's memoir is more than just a life story. The truth matters in *A Million Little Pieces* and that is why it sells. It is unsurprising, then, that Nan Talese assumed when she read it that a trade book with this portrait of the addict as utterly abject and not middle-class could *not* be read with sympathy unless it were a "true" story about recovery.

This is unlike what happened to Hunter S. Thompson's 1971 *roman à clef* called *Fear and Loathing in Las Vegas* and William S. Burroughs' 1952 semi-autobiographical tale *Junky: Confessions of an Unredeemed Drug Addict* (called *Junkie* in some later editions), although those exceptions prove the rule. Thompson's story of his drug-fuelled journey to Las Vegas appeared first as a story for *Rolling Stone* magazine. It was published in book form as a novel and has been read as one, but he later characterized it as "gonzo journalism" to emphasize that the countercultural nature of his drug experiences blurred the boundaries between fiction and journalism (Banco 2007, 130). Burroughs published his book through Ace Books, a pulp publisher that catered to subway riders. The book first appeared in a "double" edition that included a previously published novel called *Narcotic Agent*, thus providing "2 for 1" value for only 35 cents. The format combined nonfiction and fiction together in a single set of lurid tales. The original cover featured the addict as a violent, unsavoury character who could have been drawn from the dime-store detective thrillers of Mickey Spillane (Harris 2003, 47–48).

For this kind of format, *Junky* did not need to be verifiably true. It just had to be thrilling during a boring subway ride. *Fear and Loathing in Las Vegas* did not have to be verifiable either, since its author had already claimed that parts of it were fictionalized and even invented a term—and an explanation that was aesthetic and cultural—for his technique. But *A Million Little Pieces* was published as a trade book by a major publisher and not as a mass-market paperback or a magazine article, and so the literary and jurisdictional stakes were considerably higher for it before it even appeared. The narrative had to be well written, but it also had to have at least the appearance of a true story, as in the case of another bestselling memoir that appeared around the same time, Augusten Burroughs' *Running with Scissors* of 2002. That account also had its veracity challenged in a 2005 lawsuit.[11]

But at first, the publishers of *A Million Little Pieces* did not understand what it meant to have a memoir become jurisdictional, and what the risks could be. When the controversy broke, Nan Talese said on the January 26, 2006, episode of the *Oprah Winfrey Show* that *A Million Little Pieces* succeeds as a book because of the impact it has on a reader, and so it should not matter whether facts have been altered or not.[12] In another interview, Talese alludes to the problem of WMDs in an effort to downplay the Frey controversy, saying that "we are not talking about weapons of mass destruction.... Memoir writing is not like mathematics. I am not at all dismayed. The truth is that the book has helped people enormously.... There might be some facts missing" (qtd. in Rieder 2006, 6). In effect, Talese argues that memoir can and should be read like a novel for its "higher" truths rather than for factual accuracy. As we shall see, Talese's claim was not understood to be convincing, in part because—as she probably knew— the book could only have succeeded in attracting the middlebrow readership it needed if it were published as a memoir and read as one. The jurisdictional discourse that was activated during the Frey controversy meant that Talese's more generous reading of the genre is not the one that was acceptable in the public sphere. The furor over WMDs *did* link to the debate about Frey's book.

When *A Million Little Pieces* appeared in 2003, it was reviewed in mainstream publications that included *GQ, Times Literary Supplement*, and *Publisher's Weekly*, garnering critical attention from important reviewers (Valby 2003). Reviews were generally positive and stressed the "honest" way that Frey told his story (Burns and Bell-Russel 2003; *Publishers Weekly* 2003; Reese 2003; Santella 2003), with the exception of James Browning in the *Village Voice*, who thought that Frey's style was amateurish and that his account of dental surgery was not credible (Browning 2003). But when the book was chosen as an Oprah's Book Club selection two years later, Frey and *A Million Little Pieces* were placed squarely in the public eye. The well-known power of Oprah's Book Club to create bestsellers from its selections meant that *A Million Little Pieces* immediately vaulted to the top of bestseller lists produced by *The New York Times, USA Today*, and *Publisher's Weekly* and stayed there for months. Oprah herself reported this fact with pride on her October 26, 2005, show dedicated to *A Million Little Pieces* called "The Man Who Kept Oprah Awake at Night."[13]

The selection of *A Million Little Pieces* for Oprah's Book Club is interesting for a number of reasons. Oprah's Book Club had already undergone a number of changes. In 2001, Jonathan Franzen had commented negatively on Oprah's Book Club after his novel, *The Corrections*, was selected because he felt that the book club's reputation for choosing middlebrow selections would tarnish his literary reputation. His book was deselected and Oprah's Book Club was suspended (Konchar Farr 2008, 33–35). Oprah's Book Club returned in 2003 with an emphasis on reading classic fiction. This was an excellent way for Oprah Winfrey to deflect criticism that many of her selections were not of high enough literary quality, and the strategy worked (Rooney 2005). From 2003 until 2005 the book club featured classics by Tolstoy, Pearl S. Buck, and William Faulkner, among others. The selection of *A Million Little Pieces* is all the more remarkable because it was the first book to signal a turn away from the classics (it followed several works by Faulkner) and it marked a return to a focus on contemporary works. Jaime Harker thinks that this represented a return to Oprah Winfrey's previous formula of middlebrow selections designed to elicit an affective response (2008, 323–24).

But was it? *A Million Little Pieces* does not at first glance look at all like something suitable for Oprah's Book Club. It was not a story that most of Oprah's audience and book club readership, which is female and middlebrow in its general orientation, would be able to passionately identify as their own.[14] The style of *A Million Little Pieces* is, as Harker has pointed out, aggressively pro-masculinist and echoes other stories of addiction that make use of "hard-boiled" images and characterizations from pulp fiction like *Naked Lunch* by William S. Burroughs or Hunter S. Thompson's *Fear and Loathing in Las Vegas* (2008, 326–30). Frey's rejection of the twelve-step model and the transformation it promises would seem to be at odds with the values of the *Oprah Winfrey Show*, which emphasizes the importance of self-transformation. The story itself is full of profanity and grisly details, including Frey's description of undergoing dental surgery without anaesthetic, his graphic descriptions of vomit, crack houses, and the suffering of his fellow patients, the use of profanity through the story, and Frey's portrayal of himself as aggressive, violent, and confrontational. As Harker observes, the book is so masculine that it seems to verge on camp (2008, 325).

Why would it be chosen? I suggest that with this selection Oprah's Book Club began another alteration, one where non-fiction would help the followers of Oprah's Book Club to read for identification and personal transformation. The *Oprah Winfrey Show* already featured writers of self-help narratives about relationships, finances and other issues. Now those narratives about the need for self-improvement could also be part of the book club. Since *A Million Little Pieces,* two memoirs have become part of the selections for Oprah's Book Club, Eli Wiesel's *Night,* his memoir about Auschwitz, and a memoir by African-American actor Sidney Poitier. In 2009 the book club selected Echart Tolle's *A New Earth,* another non-fiction book that emphasizes the need for personal growth. Although one classic novel did appear as a selection in 2007, there have been no others since. Oprah's Book Club appears to have moved back to an emphasis on contemporary fiction, but accompanied this time by non-fiction that can foster the values of the *Oprah Winfrey Show* more generally. Although Oprah's Book Club ended with the end of the *Oprah Winfrey Show* in 2011, by 2012 an online version of the club—Oprah's Book Club 2.0—continued this emphasis on non-fiction with its first selection, Cheryl Strayed's memoir *Wild.*[15] Memoirs can be read as honest records of the lives of others so that the work of personal transformation can be carried out and carried on by readers. In this understanding of what memoirs are, it does not matter whether they are "literary" or not, but whether they are true or not and whether they faithfully report experiences from which others can learn.

The qualities that did make *A Million Little Pieces* a good beginning for this change in focus were the emphasis on the personal integrity of its author as he details his stay in a treatment centre and finally, his own plan for rehabilitation. In the memoir, Frey recovers from severe addictions to alcohol and drugs not because of the twelve-step program that is key to the centre's treatment plan, but because of his friendships with some of the staff and patients, and the help of his family and friends. *A Million Little Pieces* is neither a narrative about addictions to drugs and alcohol nor a narrative of confession as this appears in the twelve-step program, but an argument for personal honesty, self-reliance, and a community as the keys to recovery.

In *A Million Little Pieces,* Frey also appears as someone who understands the truth about himself from the beginning, and he is willing to portray himself in a negative light as part of this commitment to the truth (Harker 2008, 325). The style of the book is terse and direct, both of which provide a sense that the events happened as he described them. Frey is also willing to be honest and emotionally open in the memoir with himself and with others as long as others are honest with him: as he thinks on two occasions, "the truth is all that matters" (Frey 2004, 108, 178) about addiction. He believes that without this commitment to honesty, recovery is not real recovery. He even refuses to accept the twelve-step program's religious elements because he thinks that it is false to pretend that a higher power exists and that religion itself is addictive (223–25). When his parents visit him, he tells them in a therapeutic session that it is not their fault that he is an addict, and that only he can take responsibility for what has happened (251). This approach does fit into the therapeutic narratives of the *Oprah Winfrey Show*, which emphasize the importance of honesty, self-reliance, and personal responsibility in all areas of life.

Frey appeared on the October 26, 2005, *Oprah Winfrey Show*. Before he was interviewed, Oprah Winfrey emphasized the book's therapeutic qualities and the potential for readers to either identify with the narrative and be transformed, or be transformed by it because they are family or friends of addicts. The title of the show, "The Man Who Kept Oprah Awake at Night," is a reference to the story's impact on readers: Winfrey repeatedly emphasized that the book was so powerful that she had to stay up late to finish it. This image of Oprah Winfrey as someone who cannot "control" her behaviour shows how the story's "power" as a book has the potential to turn her into a reading addict. Winfrey's "admission" of her addictive reading behaviour also paves the way for her confession—not for the first time—that she is a food addict. Her reading of *A Million Little Pieces* models two reading strategies: recognition and transformation. She offers a third reading strategy for those who cannot identify with Frey: she opens her show about Frey with a message for the parents of addicts, saying that *A Million Little Pieces* will help them understand the mind of an addicted person, and she mentions "thousands of emails" she has received about the book as proof that the book has had the power to help many people understand addiction.

Although Oprah Winfrey does interview Frey briefly in the show about his opposition to twelve-step discourse (which Frey downplays), much of the discussion is about the power and honesty of the book and its ability to change lives. Frey talks about how he was able to write such an accurate account when Winfrey asks him how he could remember everything that had happened to him: he says that he kept a diary and had access to his own medical files. In response to Winfrey's questions about why he is so negative about himself in *A Million Little Pieces*, Frey replies that "if I was going to write a book that was true, that was honest, I would have to show myself in very, very negative ways." This kind of interview emphasizes how important honesty is to Frey. In video vignettes, the focus is on Frey's past as an addict and his previous status as a bad kid, and his present life as a happy family man in order to show the audience that he has recovered and now leads a normal life.

The majority of the episode's content is not about Frey himself, however. On a show about an Oprah's Book Club selection, it might seem surprising that there is no discussion of the style or ideas in the book. Instead of this kind of discussion, the second half of the show is about responses to the book. The theme here is the power of the book to affect others and to create change. We meet "Sandy," an addict who reads *A Million Little Pieces* and writes to Frey for help on the Oprah.com website. In response to his advice, she goes into treatment and starts to recover. In a video made for the *Oprah Winfrey Show*, Frey meets with Sandy while she is still in treatment and tells her, as he often tells himself in his book, to "hold on." Here Frey's rehabilitation comes full-circle because he helps someone else "thirteen years to the day" that he went into treatment, with the help of the *Oprah Winfrey Show* itself. Back in the studio, women in the audience are in tears as they watch the video, and some openly wonder how to help their relatives. Frey's parents and his brother are also in the audience, and Oprah Winfrey asks them for their views of addiction. The show then moves to a focus on the staff at

Harpo, the company that produces the *Oprah Winfrey Show*, with individual employees talking about how moving the book was. "We all loved the book so much," Winfrey says.

At this point, Frey's memoir is operating squarely within the discourse of the intimate public as it appears on the *Oprah Winfrey Show*. Winfrey herself models how to read the book as a transformation narrative, and then provides her audience with examples of reading transformation (the staffers who are moved by the narrative and the thousands of emails she receives), life transformation (the story of "Sandy"), and family renewal (Frey's family and the parents of addicts in the audience). Berlant's idea of women's culture within an intimate public framework fits this situation well. The Oprah's Book Club viewers who watched the program, read *A Million Little Pieces*, or did both could find ways to either identify with the experiences Frey describes or see someone they loved in the narrative. They could see that others felt as they did, including Winfrey herself, and that the book was about "real" issues to do with addiction but on a personal level rather than on a political level. That personal level is about the workings of women's culture and its affirmation of social belonging, affect, and intimacy rather than an exploration of the problems with addiction. With the exception of Frey, his father (who does not speak), and his brother (who only says that he didn't think that Frey was in that much trouble), all of the models for reading the book and all of the people who are moved by it are female. As I mentioned earlier, Winfrey does ask Frey about his opposition to twelve-step rehabilitation because as she says, many of the responses to Frey take up that question. Frey's answer does not shed light on the problems of the model, however, and Winfrey does not inquire further. There is no wider discussion in the show about social issues connected to addiction and substance abuse, and little attempt to provide historical contexts for thinking about addiction. The community of manhood that, as we shall see, is key to Frey's understanding of healing in the book, is never mentioned. Instead, *A Million Little Pieces* becomes the occasion for *female* personal recognition within this intimate public, an affirmation of other women in a reading community who feel the same way, and an opportunity to affirm the importance of emotional responses to reading itself. In order to do this, Frey's own tendency to highlight how important the truth is becomes central to the interpretation of the book in Oprah's Book Club. This emphasis on "truth" above all else in the memoir contributes to Frey's undoing and to Oprah Winfrey's public chastisement of him.

On January 8, 2006, the website *The Smoking Gun* reported that in its attempt to obtain a mug shot of James Frey for its online collection, its researchers had discovered that Frey had exaggerated the conditions of his arrest in Ohio, a key event in *A Million Little Pieces*. Frey had written that he was wanted in three states, two for drug possession and the third for a conflict with police in Ohio. In the memoir, he often says that he is wanted in three states as a way to tell himself that he is a criminal (171). Although he learns that the possession charges will be dropped, by the end of his stay in the treatment facility he finds out that he could be jailed for up to three years for jumping bail in Ohio, where he said that he spent time in jail for hitting a police officer with his car while he was high on crack. He tells his parents that he resisted arrest and so "they beat my ass with billy clubs and arrested me" (250). In the memoir, his friends Leonard (a Mafia boss) and Miles (a judge) arrange for the charges to be reduced, and Frey learns that he only has to serve a few months when he gets out of the treatment centre (369–70). In fact, *The Smoking Gun* discovered that Frey had not resisted arrest, and a mugshot of him showed that he had not been beaten. He spent a few hours in jail rather than the 87 days he reported, and he was not arrested for any charges except for driving under the influence. He could not have served another three years for these charges. The website also reported that Frey had exaggerated other parts of his arrest record, invented a role for himself in a train accident that killed a classmate of his, and changed the manner in which Lilly, his girlfriend at the treatment centre, had died (*The Smoking Gun* 2006; *Word Info* 2006). At first, Frey insisted that all details in the book were true, but as the controversy built in intensity, Frey appeared with his mother on the CNN interview program *Larry King Live* on January 11, 2006, to answer the accusations.

Larry King begins the show by asking if *A Million Little Pieces* was fraudulent, and outlined *The Smoking Gun*'s investigation as well as Oprah Winfrey's endorsement of the book. Frey replies to the allegations with a definition of memoir that would set the stage for the fierce debate about non-fiction to follow on the *Oprah Winfrey Show*. When King asks Frey for his side of the story, the following dialogue follows:

FREY: My side is I wrote a memoir. I never expected the book to come under the type of scrutiny that it has. A memoir literally means my story, a memoir is a subjective retelling of events.

LK: But it is supposed to be factual events. The memoir is a form of biography.

FREY: Yes. Memoir is within the genre of non-fiction. I don't think it's necessarily appropriate to say I've conned anyone.[16]

Frey goes on to say that "there is a great debate about memoir" with respect
to whether it is a subjective account or like journalism. He concludes that
his story is truthful, but also that it is his version of events. King repeats
that memoirs are supposed to be factual and that "people reading a memoir
expect a true story."

Although they use terms such as "biography" loosely, the debate
between Frey and King does have a long history. As I have written about
elsewhere, memoir has been understood most often by scholars of auto/
biography to be the record of a public life, a life story that includes a life of
another person, or a record of public events. Unlike autobiography, which
was defined as a more creative account of the growth of the writer's personality, memoir was often referred to by critics like Georges Gusdorf or Georg
Misch as a secondary genre by non-professional writers. It was "merely"
factual or self-aggrandizing, while autobiography was often described
as the place where higher truths can be found much as they are in fiction
(Rak 2004a, 306–10). But within the last decade and particularly in North
America, "memoir" as a term has replaced the term "autobiography" in
the popular press and in the marketing of personal narratives, and it has
become associated with subjective accounts of events much as Frey argues
(Rak 2004a, 324).

However, most of the reading public does not see it this way. As Philippe
Lejeune argued in "The Autobiographical Pact" decades before, the
assumption that there is a connection between a text and an author begins
in a store where the consumer looks for a correspondence between the "signature" or proper name on the cover, the first-person narrator on the first
page, and a real person who exists in the world. If any of these elements of
the "pact" between reader and text breaks down, the work is fiction and is
not autobiography (1983, 44). Lejeune's autobiographical pact has been critiqued on a number of fronts, but what is often overlooked is that Lejeune
is describing a consumer's relationship to autobiography as an object at the
moment of purchase. What is the author "selling" and how has he or she
created an identity that is for sale in the first place? What is it about the narrative that makes someone want to purchase it? As Lejeune pointed out in
"The Autobiography of Those Who Do Not Write," the key assumption for
the consumer looking at a text like this is that the narrative is true and accu-

rate. But the relationship between text and world is unsteady, and it creates ethical problems as well as unfulfilled desires for the whole story:

> What the public consumes is the personal form of a discourse assumed by a real person, responsible for his writing as he is for his life. We consume the full-fledged "subject," which we want to believe is true ... the public finds itself in an ambiguous situation, a situation of bad faith, always ready both to suspect the authenticity of a text and to yell "scandal" ... and at the same time always prepared to lend itself to the games of illusion and not see through the transparent veils that cover the production of the text, the essential being to enjoy it. (Lejeune 1989, 194)

Lejeune admits that the life writing of any author contains necessary fictions, but the reading public both *wants* and *needs* the narrative to be factual and *is suspicious* when the production of the illusion is revealed.

In other words, the argument that an autobiography (or now, a memoir) is fictional has the potential to create problems with authenticity and with its own audience's expectations. Larry King points this out in his debate with James Frey. For him, the truth of a memoir is factual, and he says that people do "expect" a true story. For Frey, a memoir is about subjective experience, and so it does not need to be factual. Autobiography's interpretation by the Romantic writers as a story about the self and the personality that the author both reveals and constructs does make autobiography look much like fiction when it focuses on character development. Frey replies in the Romantic tradition when he says that memoir is subjective, and yet is about a higher truth. But the position of *A Million Little Pieces* within a jurisdictional framework means that King's version of what memoir is cannot be dismissed. The decision Frey's publisher made to publish and market the book as a memoir means that now, the pact between Frey, his text, and his readership has been broken.

During the interview with James Frey on his program, Larry King received a phone call from Oprah Winfrey, who wanted to support Frey. Winfrey's comments show that she sees the autobiographical pact as a guarantee made between the publisher, who indicates whether the book is a memoir or not, the author, and the reader. The scene of genre identification is for Winfrey the scene of consumer purchase, the bookstore. She supports Frey's version of what memoir is and stresses the importance of the underlying message of the book. But she also says in the phone call that reading generically in the literary marketplace means that she trusts publishers to give her the product she seeks:

> So, I'm just like everybody else. I go to the bookstore. I pick out a book I love. If it says memoir, I know that—that maybe the names and dates and the times have been compressed, because that's what a memoir is. And I feel about *A Million Little Pieces* that although some of the facts have been questioned—and people have a right to question, because we live in a country that lets you do that, that the underlying message of redemption in James Frey's memoir still resonates with me. And I know that it resonates with millions of other people who have read this book and will continue to read this book.[17]

Winfrey's comments strike that ambivalent balance Lejeune highlights between thinking of a memoir as consumer product with a label and thinking of memoir as a creative work that is not strictly factual. She even asks if this kind of memoir represents a new category for publishing, a comment that given the history of autobiography and memoir, is not accurate. But Oprah's question does show that *A Million Little Pieces* had the potential to open up a public debate in the United States about what telling the truth in the public sphere could mean, and even what the relationship between genre and capitalism had become.

This potential was not realized. On January 26, 2006, Oprah Winfrey abruptly reversed her position and embraced a jurisdictional interpretation of *A Million Little Pieces*. In the episode "James Frey and the '*A Million Little Pieces*' Controversy," a clearly angry Winfrey begins by saying that she cancelled the planned show for the day because she has never had "this" problem in her nineteen years of television broadcasting experience. She apologizes to her audience for her comments on the *Larry King Live* show, saying that "I left the impression that the truth does not matter" and that the thousands of emails she received from her viewers had "clouded her judgment." James Frey arrives on set, and Winfrey sits down with him to find out, she says, whether the allegations against him were true. The interview she does with Frey and with his publisher, Nan Talese, is in fact about the breakdown of the autobiographical pact. Winfrey begins by saying "James Frey is here and I have to say it is difficult for me to talk to you because I feel really duped. But more importantly, I feel that you betrayed millions of readers. I think it's such a gift to have millions of people to read your work and that bothers me greatly. So now, as I sit here today I don't know what is true and I don't know what isn't." Winfrey's assertion that she has been fooled by Frey and betrayed millions of readers shows the limits of this intimate public, since Frey has to be seen as honest in order for the memoir to function as an Oprah's Book Club selection. Winfrey's own position as a figure of trust within this public had also been questioned both within this public and by members of other publics. Winfrey confronted Frey very aggressively as a way to win this trust back. Influenced as she later said by a *Washington Post* op-ed piece on the controversy and by angry messages on her own website (Leider 2006), Winfrey asked Frey "Why did you lie? Why did you have to lie about the time you spent in jail? Why did you do that?" By the end of the interview, Winfrey tells Frey that "the truth will set you free" after forcing him to admit that he had lied. Winfrey then asks Nan Talese, Frey's publisher, why she and her company had not realized that the book contained untruths, an allegation that Talese tries to address by saying that it seemed to ring true for her and for the colleagues who read the manuscript. Winfrey dismisses Talese's argument and argues that it is the publisher's responsibility to give consumers the right product. As I discussed in another context in chapter 1 of this book, Oprah Winfrey makes a direct appeal to publishers as the *moral* arbiters of genre: "But if you're publishing it as a memoir, I think the publisher has a responsibility because as the consumer, the reader, I am trusting you. I'm trusting you, the publisher, to categorize this book whether as fiction or autobiographical or memoir. I'm trusting you."

I have already discussed what it means to ask for trust from an industry in chapter 1, but in the context of Oprah Winfrey's own reputation, the image of the trusting consumer-reader is also key. As the means of creating an intimate public, the *Oprah Winfrey Show* is built on trust and honesty as important values. Winfrey herself creates trust in her viewers by revealing aspects of her personal life to them, and they in turn trust her advice about books, makeup, and political issues, among other things. The movement in the *Oprah Winfrey Show* between the individual as a consumer and the individual as a citizen is based on this trust. Therefore, any breakdown of trust threatens the underlying basis for the *Oprah Winfrey Show* and its success. Talese's attempts to shift the discussion to what a memoir is do not address Winfrey's jurisdictional demands because Talese does not understand why she would be asked about trust at all. When Talese says "a novel is something different than a memoir. And a memoir is different from an autobiography. A memoir is an author's remembrance of a certain period in his life. Now, the responsibility, as far as I am concerned, is does it strike me as valid? Does it strike me as authentic?" Winfrey agrees wholeheartedly as her audience cheers her, implying that Talese's failure to fact-check the book constitutes a failure to do her job. What the interview shows is that Winfrey and her studio audience do not need to think critically about genre. They know what a memoir is, because when they purchase one they know what they should get. What they need to do is affirm the importance of trust as the bond that holds together the intimate public of the *Oprah Winfrey Show*, whether they are readers, citizens, or consumers in that moment (*Oprah Winfrey Show* 2006a).

The Frey controversy, as it became known, was widely discussed in the media in the wake of the interviews, and Random House reported that it would print disclaimers in subsequent printings of *A Million Little Pieces*. In an unusual move that supported Oprah Winfrey's view of non-fiction genres as economically generated categories within capitalism, consumers who were not satisfied with the "truth" of the memoir could return page 163 in the hardcover or the first page of the paperback for a full refund (Rich 2006). At first, Winfrey's dramatic advocacy for "truth" and repudiation of "truthiness" found wide support in the media, particularly because unlike other figures in the public sphere, she was willing to be honest when others were not. This irony was not lost on many journalists. The Frey controversy caused Howard Kurtz of *The Washington Post* to ask questions about the ethics of suppressing information about the war in Iraq in light of what he saw as hazy moral standards in the publishing world (Kurtz 2006). The January 27, 2006, editorial in *The New York Times* said that "Ms. Winfrey did what we have so often waited for public figures to do: she admitted openly that she had made a mistake in supporting Mr. Frey. Then she did her best to force him, and Ms. Talese, to admit the extent of his deception and the publisher's failure" (*New York Times* 2006). Maureen Dowd, a columnist for *The New York Times*, said in an interview with Keith Olbermann on *Countdown* that "it was fantastic to see Oprah stand up for truth, as opposed to truthiness" and compared Oprah's castigation of Frey to the need for George W. Bush to confess that he too had lied about the existence of WMDs: "When Oprah was clinging to supporting Frey, she was doing it for the reason of emotional truth, that millions of people could be helped by his story of redemption. And Bush, with Iraq, said that we, even if it turned out not to be true, the reasons we went to war, it was right because millions of Iraqis would be liberated. But you cannot, you know, do things that start with a lie, and they just lead to trouble down the road" (Dowd 2006).

Dowd clearly states that Oprah Winfrey's usual use of "emotional truth" as her touchstone had to give way to a jurisdictional approach to truth, and that is what the President of the United States should do too. In examples like this, Winfrey's treatment of Frey and Talese were read as a template for contemporary political events, and the failure of *A Million Little Pieces* in one intimate public sphere spilled over into the debate about deception in American politics, if only because to many commentators, it appeared that Oprah Winfrey had acted with more integrity than the political leaders of the country. This accounts for why Winfrey's actions were supported so strongly. The jurisdictional demands that had propelled *A Million Little Pieces* into print and then into Oprah's Book Club were too strong to sustain any argument about literary merit, a special status for memoirs, or the role of publishers. For a time, Oprah's version of truth, and not truthiness, gained her support. The political climate in the United States by 2006 helped to create this climate of censure about *A Million Little Pieces* and a rare discussion about the problems of self-disclosure and truth-telling in the public sphere.

As time passed, questions began to be raised about Winfrey's treatment of Frey and Talese. *Entertainment Weekly* thought that Winfrey had fatally confused the rules of literary criticism (here understood as criteria for literary taste) with her desire to help others (Tucker 2006), while Rebecca Keegan wrote in *Time* magazine that Winfrey had "shredded" Frey, implying that she had been too hard on him (Keegan 2006), and *The Wall Street Journal* reported that editors and publishers cannot afford the kind of fact-checking that Winfrey said should have been required (Trachtenberg 2006). During a book convention in 2007, Talese stated that Winfrey had asked Frey and her to come to the show under false pretenses by saying that they were to participate in a panel called "Truth in America," and she said that during the interview Winfrey showed "fiercely bad manners" and should apologize (Hylton 2007). In May 2009, it was revealed that Oprah Winfrey had called James Frey in 2008 and apologized to him for what she had done (Luscombe 2009). On May 17, 2011, as part of the closing episodes of the *Oprah Winfrey Show*, called "Oprah's Most Memorable Guests," Oprah Winfrey brought back James Frey for a final interview because, as she claimed, she had experienced a revelation while she was meditating that she had to apologize for what had happened. This time, the interview took place in Frey's home, and Winfrey conducted the interview with utmost seriousness, not as a talk-show host would with frequent pauses to involve the audience, but as a journalist would, where the interview subject is the source of attention. Over the course of the discussion, Winfrey apologized to Frey for the way she had acted, although Frey insisted that he should take responsibility for miscategorizing the book as a memoir. Winfrey also apologized for her staff, because as Talese had said, Frey and Talese were invited back to the show under false pretences. Although Winfrey said that she did not know of the subterfuge at the time, she took full responsibility for the actions of her staff. Frey acknowledged this, but said that he had moved past his anger and shock at what had happened (James Frey 2011).

It is hard now to read *A Million Little Pieces* without thinking about its existence within an autobiographical jurisdiction. But a key part of the book that the controversy elided still lies in its critique of twelve-step discourse and methods, and in its evocation of a community of the marginal as the way to overcome addiction. As Stanton Peele points out, Frey's critique of the twelve-step model and Alcoholics Anonymous points out how powerful AA discourse is in the United States: "That the crucial, original part of Frey's book—the heartfelt and accurate part—has not been heard indicates how difficult it is to break the AA hegemony in the United States. The worst thing about AA—and the experience Frey underwent at Hazelden—is its denial of the existence of valid alternative paths for ending addiction. We have reached an impasse until more people who end their addictions quietly, on their own terms, come forward to reveal their personal experiences" (Peele 2006, 449).

According to Robin Room, the popularity of the twelve-step model's premise that the addict is powerless to change himself or herself until the addiction is confessed connects the image of American citizenship and its promises of self-reliance and individual freedom to a picture of the addict as a failed citizen who cannot behave properly: "The ideas that good behavior is a matter of individual self-control, and that the individual is responsible for control of his or her own life, are very much embedded in a particular cultural matrix. They make sense in a culture where individuation and individualism are taken for granted, where each citizen has the right to 'life, liberty, and the pursuit of happiness'" (Room 2003, 225–26).

Twelve-step discourse therefore serves to connect confessional discourse from religious traditions to a recovery program that stresses the value of the individual and his/her own story. As Robyn Warhol and Helena Michie point out, confessional stories are part of the AA tradition, and they are central to fulfilling most of the twelve steps. These stories, called "drunkologues" in the AA terminology, involve making an inventory of the negative behaviours and actions caused by addiction and telling another person about them, sometimes in an AA meeting and sometimes by other means. The twelve steps themselves and the means of telling one's story as part of following the twelve steps are repeated constantly so that community members "learn" how to create a story within the framework. The result is a type of story collective where there is some allowance for individuality, but the outlines of the story are not capable of much deviation (1996, 330–31). Warhol and Michie call this non-autobiographical in the sense that the twelve-step story is not individual in the Western tradition of autobiography. It is, however, much like the tradition of religious confessional in its reference to powerlessness, the need for a higher power, and the reproduction of group narratives rather than individual stories as part of its therapy (1996, 347). In American twelve-step discourse, the two touchstones are the idea of citizenship and the pursuit of happiness that comes from self-reliance and control over one's life, and religious confession in some Western traditions, which emphasizes the powerlessness of a person and his/her need to confess past wrongs and live within a collective story of past and present experiences. In the case of addiction, the story of triumph is the story of sobriety. The combination of a political and a religious discourse within the narrative of AA, then, makes it very powerful and difficult to resist. Stanton Peele says that the model is so influential that it has been widely applied as a problem-solving mechanism in American society: "AA is the most successful combination of a social movement/public relations organization in twentieth-century America. It has cornered the addiction treatment market—indeed, its 12 steps have been applied to virtually every unhealthy habit Americans can have" (2006, 458). When it is combined with prevailing beliefs about addiction as disease, it can be a very difficult narrative to resist.

In *A Million Little Pieces*, Frey is told that the twelve-step recovery model is the only way to combat an addiction to drugs and alcohol. He reads *The Big Book of Alcoholics Anonymous* and concludes that its religious emphasis means that it is only an addiction replacement: "replacement of a chemical for God and Meeting. The Meetings themselves made me sick. Too much whining, too much complaining, too much blaming. Too much bullshit about Higher Powers" (2003, 76). He rejects the model because he wants to recover on his own, but the prospect frightens him: "If what the Doctor says at the beginning [of the book] is true, and joining AA is the only way to cure me, then I'm completely fucked. Fucked. Fucked. Fucked" (78). But the treatment program at the centre offers him no options, and so Frey becomes resistant to any attempt to make him believe in the twelve-step model. Most of the lectures at the centre are about the power of AA to change lives: Frey experiences these lectures as false and hypocritical. He and his friends often do not pay attention at these lectures or they actively resist them by booing or laughing (99, 165, 198). In one lecture, a famous rock star claims that the twelve steps have saved him, but this infuriates Frey, who thinks that he is lying about the level of his addiction (177–78). In the first graduation ceremony he sees, Frey says that Roy and his friend, who are graduating, have "the glazed eyes of the Converted" (99). Roy is thought by the clinic staff to be a model patient who will successfully reintegrate into world outside, but in fact he is violent and manipulative. Frey thinks that he will not stay sober. When Roy re-enters the clinic in a mad rage, swinging a bloody club and unable to even recognize his real name, the ineffectiveness of AA and the blindness of the staff are clearly linked (181–84). Any institutional attempt to make Frey accept the twelve steps goes awry: he mocks the Goal Board (199) and the twelve-step workbook (200) because he thinks that they insult his intelligence. The staff's attempts to argue with him are unsuccessful (205). In a lecture where he learns that addiction is an incurable disease and only AA and twelve-step treatment are effective against it, Frey rejects what he is told: "I would like to stand up and scream bullshit this is all fucking bullshit, but I don't do it. I don't believe that addiction is a disease ... a disease is a Medical condition that must be dealt with using Medical technology. It cannot be dealt with by using a Group or a set of Steps.... It is not a genetic disease. Addiction is a decision" (291). Frey also hears that even AA does not work well, and decides that "smiles and prayers aren't going to change reality. Eighty-five percent of us are fucked" (292).

How then does Frey recover? As Jeffrey Roth points out, Frey does make use of some of the twelve-step principles but does not experience administrative recognition or support when he puts them into practice (2006, 116). Instead of the New Testament or *The Big Book*, Frey discovers principles of serenity and detachment in the *Tao Te Ching*, a book his brother gives him (Frey 2004, 179–80). He receives support from friends and family members who talk to him on the phone and visit him (x). Joanne, the therapist he trusts, allows him to express his distrust of AA and finally gets him to do family therapy with his parents, a process where he is able to speak honestly with them, and which allows them all to heal (246–55). Instead of group testimonials, Frey learns how to recover by sharing difficult stories about the past and about addiction with fellow addicts who are honest about their struggles. The non-institutional nature of these bonds begins to change Frey from the more cartoonish spectre of macho anger that he exhibits when he first comes to the clinic to an embracing of masculinity that has community, not violence, as its core feature.

These people show him that mutual respect and honesty are the marks of community. He forges friendships with Hank, a staff member who was a fellow addict and who drives him to the dentist, Lilly—a prostitute and crack addict who he is not supposed to befriend and with whom he shares painful stories about his past (210–11), and other male patients in the treatment facility who also do not believe in the power of the twelve steps. Most important of these is Leonard, who shares his story with Frey (190–91) and convinces him not to leave the centre. Leonard gives him the advice to "hold on" (194) whenever the desire to use drugs or alcohol strikes. As he prepares to leave the centre, Leonard offers to treat Frey as the son he never had, an affirmation of continued support and love as they both finish treatment (389). Leonard, Frey, and other men spend significant amounts of time in the cafeteria sharing their stories of addiction and talking about their problems in an attempt to dispel their pain and try to learn from each other. They also joke about their experiences, which is not presented as something that occurs in twelve-step discourse (256, 384). Through them, Frey learns to express emotions as a man and not be ashamed of who he is. He begins to be part of this community, and give back. When he hugs his roommate Miles, a court judge who is deeply ashamed of his addictions, he says, "He is a man who needs a friend and I can be his friend" (244). Near the end of the memoir, Leonard throws a party for all the male patients in a joyous affirmation of this community. The party is also a celebration of masculinity, as the men eat traditional American southern food and watch a boxing fight on television in a temporary suspension of the emasculating effects of addiction and treatment. As Frey says, "we are not in a Treatment Center and we are not fucked up. We are men eating and having fun and getting ready to watch the fight. I want food myself but watching this is beautiful. Beautiful" (375). The party is supported by the treatment centre's staff but is financed and run by Leonard in a reversal of roles: for a time, the patients at the facility are the means of healing and they have the power to be full persons. From this point, Frey accepts some of the advice the staff give him (394), because the centre has adapted to the needs of its population. He accepts, for example, that his hearing loss as a child may have affected his ability to bond with others, but he refuses to blame the condition for what he has done (306). He decides to fight the addiction through his own willpower (340–42) and by confronting the seductive power of alcohol in one last test, in a bar after he leaves the centre. He is successful, and the narrative ends in victory, with his brother slapping him on the back (428–30).

Frey's story of overcoming his addictions creates a dialectic between the institutional interpretation of AA and the non-institutional supports he receives. With help from these, he rejects the "group identity" of the twelve-step method as emasculating in favour of a reliance on community and a form of self-discipline based on a strong commitment to honesty. Ironically, this very commitment is what gets Frye into trouble, since it means that his account *about* honesty was in danger of being read as *an honest account*. This is in fact what occurred, and so Frey's argument that there is more than one way to overcome an addiction to drugs and alcohol and that a community of marginalized men (with a few women) sharing stories can be more therapeutic than a medicalization of addiction as a disease has not been discussed publicly in the way it could have been. Although it is easy to dismiss Frey's account as clownishly masculine, as many journalists and at least one scholar have done (Hamilton 2007), a careful reading of the idea of community and therapy in *A Million Little Pieces* shows that Frey learns another kind of masculinity as he recovers, and that this is the key to his own healing. This aspect of Frey's changing attitudes to masculinity is also what Oprah Winfrey's book club, with its commitment to a specific type of feminine intimate public, inevitably misses or appears to misread. Frey's picture of what the potential of a community is means that in effect, *A Million Little Pieces* is about what it means to be a citizen of a certain type of counter-public, one that organizes itself around a resistance to institutions and the narratives of addiction that they perpetuate.

The Frey controversy meant that this aspect of Frey's memoir did not reach a wider public. But the controversy did act as a sounding board for the reverberations of truth, lies, and genre in the political sphere in interesting and complex ways. In his conclusion to his discussion of therapy and *A Million Little Pieces*, Jeffrey Roth wonders about the parallels between George W. Bush, a former alcoholic who also resisted AA treatment, and the backlash against James Frey for abusing the public trust: "We might even ask ourselves if James Frey might be taking a beating on behalf of another nationally known figure who is known to have used drugs and alcohol, and now proclaims himself recovered without benefit of Twelve-Step Programs. With poetic precision, the other nationally known figure was addressing the nation at exactly the same time that James Frey was being repudiated by Oprah Winfrey" (2006, 120).

The radio address that interrupted the *Oprah Winfrey Show* that day was George W. Bush's endorsement of Judge Sam Alito, an address designed to ensure that Alito, a conservative who was supportive of legislation to limit civil liberties, was appointed to the U.S. Supreme Court. Less than a week later, Bush gave a State of the Union Address. In the address, Bush said that members of al Qaeda sought to gain power in Iraq "and arm themselves with weapons of mass murder," that there will be victory in Iraq and that to fight terrorism at home, the Patriot Act should be reauthorized.[18] During a time when many Americans began to wonder if what George W. Bush said was true, it is interesting, and ironic that James Frey was held to account for betraying the trust of millions.

Conclusion

CITIZEN SELVES AND THE STATE OF THE MEMOIR BOOM

If the *New York Times* Bestseller lists are to be believed, the memoir boom lasted the entire first decade of the twenty-first century, and it shows no signs of stopping during the second decade. The hardcover non-fiction list for the week of December 19, 2010, listed seven memoirs in the top fifteen entries (*New York Times* 2010a). These included—unsurprisingly—*Decision Point*, by George W. Bush, in top spot, followed by memoirs that showed different currents in the production of memoir in the last decade. The first volume of *The Autobiography of Mark Twain* (by the first modern celebrity author in the world) was in second place. Twain's plan not to release his autobiography until one hundred years after his death—and even then, to release the volumes one at a time—turned out to be a good marketing strategy. As Loren Glass points out in *Authors Inc.*, Twain was fully aware of autobiography's powers of promotion: "no American writer more completely and enthusiastically embodied this overlap between the cultural performance of authorial personality and the general reliance on authorial autobiography than the man known as Mark Twain" (2004, 57). Twain's decision to place control of his intellectual property under the trusteeship of one of New York's largest investment banks in the form of the Mark Twain Foundation (Glass 2004, 58) shows that Twain also understood copyright to be essential to the control of his own celebrity in ways that prefigure how memoir is connected to the idea of public identity and capitalism today.

Other bestsellers on the list included memoirs by public figures: Keith Richard's tell-all, ghostwritten by James Fox, appeared alongside Sarah Palin's second memoir, *America by Heart*, and a memoir by hip-hop star Jay-Z. These books are part of the celebrity culture in the United States that allows musicians such as Richards and Jay-Z to produce memoirs that purport to reveal intimate details about their lives and their careers, but that also allows a political figure like Sarah Palin to become visible *in the same way* in the public sphere. This can happen in the United States because, as I have written about elsewhere, celebrity culture has become a grammar of knowing for the American public. This grammar of knowing consists of an economy of public visibility and private "revelations" that have driven American forms of celebrity since the advent of the motion picture industry at the beginning of the twentieth century. Americans have come to recognize this form of celebrity as the condition for public identity of any kind (Rak 2010). Politicians like Palin must now trade themselves within this economy in order to achieve visibility, despite the risks to public reputation that she must run as she turns herself—through her production of her life story—into a commodity. Memoir has become one of the mediums of exchange in this economy because of its long association with the market and with the liberal democratic ideal of sharing one's life in the public sphere. There are memoirs on this list that also fulfil other fears of the memoir boom's critics that memoir is only and always about sensationalist events: one is a tell-all story of one-night stands; another is a grisly account of a mountaineering accident. But they do not constitute the majority of the memoirs that are finding audiences today.

Some of the hardcover memoirs on the list that particular week in December 2010 were not by public figures and did not deal with potentially sensationalist subjects. Their presence shows how the memoir boom, despite complaints to the contrary, is still producing stories by ordinary people that others want to read. An example of this trend is Nora Ephron, a screenwriter and director who co-wrote *Sleepless in Seattle* and directed *Silkwood*, who has become a popular non-fiction writer. Her latest book, *I Remember Nothing*, a memoir about aging, was ninth on the list, possibly because Ephron is already well known for the bestselling *I Feel Bad about My Neck: And Other Thoughts about Being a Woman* (2008) and a collection of her magazine articles called *Wallflower at the Orgy* (2007). Another interesting example was Justin Halpern's *Sh*t My Dad Says*, formerly number one on the hardcover list, a memoir about Halpern and his family fashioned from an original list of aphorisms by Halpern's father that Halpern originally posted on a Twitter feed. The popularity of this book (it even spawned a short-lived CBS network television show starring William Shatner) shows that the production of personal narratives on the Internet did not necessarily displace more traditionally published memoirs. The remediation of online life writing to other forms of life narrative in older media has had the effect of supporting the publishing industry, as it did in the case of *Julie and Julia*, a film (directed by Nora Ephron) based on a book that was in turn based on a blog by Julie Powell, who cooked all the recipes in Julia Child's first cookbook in a single year.

Paperback bestsellers for that week revealed similar patterns: number one was still Elizabeth Gilbert's account of travelling as part of a spiritual awakening called *Eat, Pray, Love*, while Patti Smith's *Just Kids*, her memoir of her time with Robert Mapplethorpe, was at number three (*New York Times* 2010b). Most of the other memoirs are by relatively unknown authors whose stories feature dramatic premises: including Jeannette Walls' memoir about growing up in an eccentric, poverty-stricken family *The Glass Castle*, and Greg Mortenson's memoir—now partly discredited—about his pledge to build schools in Pakistan, called *Three Cups of Tea*. Both memoirs highlight different aspects of the boom. *The Glass Castle* is a critical as well as a commercial success, and it highlights social inequity in the United States in ways that do not resolve this story into a narrative of triumph or a resolution of the American dream. *Three Cups of Tea*, like *Persepolis: The Story of a Childhood*, owes much of its popularity to the American fascination with the Middle East, but it also tells a story of altruism and social change that has the potential to be a meaningful intervention in the public debates about America's relationship with Pakistan and Afghanistan. In this sense, Walls' and Mortenson's memoirs are also memoirs about different kinds of citizenship, and they are clearly popular because—as Thomas Larson observed—the liberal discourse on which memoir is founded can be used to critique received notions about American life and even America's relations with other nations. In the four examples I discuss in chapter 3 and in countless more titles, memoir is a genre by, for, and about citizenship of specific kind. It is this quality, I suggest, that has helped to fuel public interest in the books of the memoir boom, and that has caused some of the more public debates about the relationship of memoir writing to the ideas of truth and accuracy.

MEMOIR AS CITIZENSHIP TECHNOLOGY

Genre provides the terms of production, recognition, and consumption that help to make memoir a product and a technology of and for identity. But genre alone cannot explain why memoir's movement between public and private has come to mean as much as it does in early twenty-first century America. One of the terms of recognition that has clearly become important for American readers is citizenship as a way to describe a state of belonging, and a way of belonging within a state that is not always subject to the liberal requirements that the state may place upon its citizens. This version of what citizenship is departs from traditional ways to understand citizenship from classic liberal thought as the expression of rights a person within a state has, and the responsibilities that a citizen within that state. This is the essence of citizenship as it appears in Rousseau's *Social Contract*. In the classic liberal picture of citizenship that developed since Rousseau himself created the notion of rights and responsibilities, a citizen has been pictured as having relatively passive relationship to the state because the citizen exists in relation to the state, which provides security in exchange for individual freedoms (Petersen et al. 1999, 17). There are now attempts—on the left and on the right—to think of citizenship in more active ways so that people can be encouraged to participate in the public sphere more fully (Petersen et al. 1999; Kymlicka & Norman 2001).

However, even Rousseau saw citizenship as something more than a description of participation, rights, or protection. In *The Social Contract*, Rousseau famously expressed citizenship as the condition of *giving away* freedoms for the public good where "finally, each man, in giving himself to all, gives himself to nobody" to maintain his freedom and the security of the people (1975, 123). The contract does not work unless an individual participates in this act of giving away, trusting that he or she will not lose his ability to be a private, and free, person. This act of giving away means that Rousseau understood citizenship as an expression of loss that, nevertheless, must be enacted in order for a social body to work. In his other writing, Rousseau saw citizenship not as a condition of being subject to a state but as an emotional expression of belonging. He wrote about this extensively in *The Confessions* when he talks about a citizenship of the road, which is a romantic feeling for place that he feels most keenly when he is in exile from Geneva (Rak 2004c). Recently, other theorists have begun to explore what citizenship can mean to people beyond its functionalist roles. These theorists see citizenship as a subjective experience that can exceed the conditions set for it by a state or that is an expression against the loss of community and even of the self. Citizenship is closely connected to other discourses of affect, because citizenship is the condition of feeling that one belongs to a greater public, or even a nation. This picture of citizenship owes something to Habermas' original idea of a public as a group of private citizens who are not controlled by the state (1996, 29). But contemporary thinking about citizenship takes Habermas' initial formulation and lifts it away from a location or sphere. Citizenship becomes a way to express a need for any kind of public belonging, and a way to articulate an individual's imagined relationship with others in a public sphere. For Michael Warner, citizenship is the expression of belonging in what he calls a "counterpublic," a creation of an oppositional citizenship by its members who have been excluded from a greater public (2005). For Toby Miller, cultural citizenship is a way to register what he calls a "crisis of belonging" in the United States and to investigate how mass media, especially television, monitor this crisis and hold it in check (2007, 1). Other theories of citizenship insist that there is a political dimension to this belonging and that new forms of citizenship have arisen as groups of people excluded from citizenship's privileges begin to organize against this exclusion. Henry Giroux's conception of "social citizenship" specifically refers to the activity of resisting neoliberal social formations in everyday locations such as government, workplace, and school (2001, 9). In a slightly different way, "cultural citizenship" refers to the efforts of dissident groups to agitate for full rights in a state that has marginalized them and denied these rights to them (Rosaldo 1999, 255). In Lauren Berlant's thinking, citizenship is an expression of intimacy, particularly during the Reagan era in American politics (1997, 6–7). Even when citizenship does not appear in the rhetoric of daily life, Berlant says that it does inform the way that public life appears, because "the rhetoric of citizenship does provide important definitional frames for the ways people see themselves as public, when they do" (2008, 10). Citizenship, in other words, works much like a genre. It sets the terms for thinking about individuality and public life for many Americans in quiet, invisible ways. But it is not simply about patriotism, which is an active expression of belonging. In her subsequent work on publics, Berlant characterizes what she calls an "intimate public" as a grouping of individuals that is held together by the need of the individuals to belong to something greater. It is not, Berlant stresses, a political movement necessarily, but "if it were political, it would be democratic" (2008, 10). Since an intimate public often stresses the importance of a fantasy of vague social belonging and a sense of a shared past of injustice rather than a critique of the conditions of belonging, it is loose in character and not a radical formation. But expressions of citizenship like Barack Obama's statement "my story is part of the American story" have an intensity in an intimate public because they invoke that picture of belonging, particularly for those who have been outsiders.

These approaches offer different ways to analyze citizenship's function in contemporary societies, but they do share an important feature: they all closely connect citizenship to the idea of personal identity, an identity that is not—for a variety of reasons—entirely a creation of a state but that gestures to the sense of belonging that a state cannot provide. This picture of citizenship lifts it away from descriptions of functionalist connections between a person and a state. The figure of the person as a citizen has the potential to be an expression of that person's public life, but this public life has an affective dimension, and even a gesture against some kind of loss—of community, of self, even of a nation. It is an expression of a relation between competing demands to be private and public at the same time. In this sense, citizenship appears as the tension between what a subject experiences and thinks about a state and his/her place within it, and how a state constructs rights and responsibilities for it. Memoir is one of the genres of writing that is about the movement from private to public. For this reason, it often contains ideas about citizenship, and it is taken up within other debates about the meaning of individual experiences in the public realm. Thomas Larson's question about the American public shows how a debate can unfold: "How much were we taken in—at least, in the moment—by the sonorously familiar. How many of us believed President Clinton when he said, 'I did not have sex with that woman?' How many of us were convinced by President Bush's 2003 claim, 'Mission accomplished?' We always want to believe more than we want to question. . . . I would argue that memoir is taking the lead, among other dissenting voices, against any form of media misrepresentation" (2007, 188).

Thomas Larson's image of memoir as a way to represent the self that could contain a counter-discourse about public life at the same time is one way to show how, in the United States, there can be no representation of individual life without a gesture, whether it is to a counter-public or an intimate public, to citizenship as an expression of public and private intimacy.

The memoir boom, then, may not be a boom at all but an indication of a shift in American reading publics toward a serious interest in personal stories of all types that continue to explore—and upset—the balance between public and private, personal, and political. As Americans continue to read and think about politics in their lives, or even think about their lives as an expression of politics, memoir's uneasy position as a commodity and as a practice of going public remains a way for many people to access the life and experiences of another, in order to think through affective ties of belonging in what Lauren Berlant says we should call the affective dimension of citizenship. Citizenship as a lived identity with others and for others is therefore a mode of reading as well as thinking that is sometimes radical, and sometimes conservative, but always is in excess of what the state asks of its citizens. Here is where memoir can be viewed not as a practice of identity in a loose sense, but as a genre that is socially produced, negotiated, negated, and embraced because technologies of identity are present within it. Whether it reinforces normative ways of thinking and being, or whether it creates new ways to imagine affective ties, justice, and even new ways of being social, memoir remains a technology of the self and citizenship that fascinates, infuriates, educates, and inspires its readers. It promises to remain an important way of understanding identity as a commodity and as a practice for at least the next decade of the twenty-first century.

NOTES

NOTES TO INTRODUCTION

1 This is a technical term for autobiographical and biographical life writing that acknowledges or combines both aspects of these genres. See Smith and Watson, *Reading Autobiography*, 2nd ed. (2010, 256).

2 In the United Kingdom, sales of celebrity memoirs were down in 2011, although memoirs by non-celebrities appear to be unaffected. See Richard Lea, "Celebrity Memoirs Lose Star Power at the Tills" (2011).

3 For an account of the history of memoir in criticism, see Julie Rak, "Are Memoirs Autobiography?" (2004a).

4 See Helen Buss' argument for memoir as a lyrical form in *Repossessing the World* (2002) and Nancy K. Miller's discussion of memoirs as a postmodern form of elegy that moves between private and public in *Bequest and Betrayal* (2000).

5 In an interesting twist to Frey's attempts to distance himself from memoir and the controversy about truth-telling, he has attempted to reinvent himself as a literary figure and an entrepreneur who seeks to produce genre fiction for young adults in the hopes that the books sell as well as the *Harry Potter* and *Twilight* series. For a full account of Frey's attempt to mass produce genre fiction, see Suzanne Mozes' "James Frey's Fiction Factory" in the online version of *New York Books* (2010). Thanks to Daphne Read for providing this reference.

6 For the blurb see Nancy Pearl's "Happy Holidays, Voyeurs," *NPR Books* (2010). The audio file for the program is available through http://www.npr.org/ 2010/12/03/131392774/happy-holidays-voyeurs-nancy-pearl-picks-memoirs.

7 See David Hesmondhalgh's discussion of the reasons it is necessary to move beyond Adorno's and Horkheimer's critique in his introduction to *The Cultural Industries*, 2nd ed. (2007, 15–17).

8 The exception is the area of rhetoric, where Bakhtin's work on speech-genres has been used to argue that genre is part of every social process. See Amy J. Devitt, *Writing Genres* (2004, 33–34); John Frow, *Genre* (2006, 12); Aviva Freedman and Peter Medway, "Locating Genre Studies" (1994, 1); and Richard M. Coe et al., "Genre as Action, Strategy, and *Différance* (2001, 2–3).

9 For general accounts of genre from the field of rhetoric, see Heather Dubrow's summary in chapter 4 of *Genre* (1982). Also see John Frow's discussion of the development of genre studies in *Genre* (2006, 70–71); and David Duff's introduction to *Modern Genre Theory* (2000, 8–19).

10 There is no word for non-fiction in French, and it is not commonly used as a way to categorize material in French bookstores. Terms such as *essais* [topical studies] or *témoignages* [testimonies] are more common. Personal communication with Philippe Lejeune (2010).

11 There are a number of ways that autobiography and life writing scholars have tried to rethink the idea of genre as discursive or rhetorical. Smith and Watson in the 2010 edition of *Reading Autobiography* use the term "the autobiographical" and "autobiographical acts" to stress the non-generic quality of this kind of representation: they devote a chapter to discussing acts as a situated instance of rhetoric. Leigh Gilmore makes a case for studying autobiography as a confessional discourse (1994), as do I in *Negotiated Memory* (2004b) for texts that are not published or written. Laura Marcus makes a strong case for thinking about all autobiography discursively (1994). Others have said that autobiography should be considered as a discourse that appears in a wide range of "non-autobiographical" popular media such as cookbooks (Goldman 1991), comics (Egan 1999), zines (Poletti 2008), or home movies (Lane 2002). Still others have stressed how popular autobiography is the "autobiography" people produce in their everyday lives, but not anything that is mass-produced (Smith and Watson 1996; Stanley 2000). Caren Kaplan has argued that genre cannot be used to describe autobiography: instead, discussion should turn to "outlaw genres" that are hybrid and that can be used as part of political resistance narratives (1992).

NOTES TO CHAPTER 1

1 See the *826 National* website for details: http://826national.org/stores/.
2 My thanks to Greg Hollingshead for the original account of the story. For accounts of the workshops in print, see Steve Dulin, "Pirates and Writers in Training," *The Oregonian* (February 24, 2008): 1–2; and Dianne Dunkelburger, "Conquest of the World Masters," *Benefit Magazine* (November/December 2006).
3 For a discussion of the origins of memoir, see Julie Rak, "Are Memoirs Autobiography?" (2004a).
4 Beth Luey argues in *Expanding the American Mind* that the book appealed to middle-class mothers, but she does not support this assertion (2010, 13–14). See chapter 1 in Kenneth Davis, *Two-Bit Culture* (1984) for an alternative view of the market for *Baby and Child Care*.
5 See John B. Thompson, *Merchants of Culture* (2010, 112–17) for details about the publishing house mergers, acquisitions and holdings as of 2008.
6 See chapter 2 of John B. Thompson's *Merchants of Culture* (2010) on literary agents for a more complete discussion.
7 See Vicky Myron, *Dewey: The Small-Town Library Cat Who Touched the World* (2008) and Vicky Myron's follow-up book, *Dewey's Nine Lives: The Legacy of the Small-Town Library Cat Who Inspired Millions* (2010).

NOTES TO CHAPTER 2

1 Professional journals include the United Kingdom publication *Publishers Research Quarterly* and the American magazine *Publisher's Weekly*, both of which include discussions of the ongoing marketing rivalry between large chains and independent stores (Trachtenberg 2005; Laing 2005; Milliot 2008). In Canada, the Association of Canadian Publishers has sponsored studies like Lorimer and Shaw's *Book Reading in Canada* (1983). Heritage Canada has sponsored the study *The Book Retail Sector in Canada* (2007).
2 I kept my study within Canada, and in English-language bookstores in order to keep my sample manageable, and because history of the book trade in Canada differs in some significant ways from that of the United States. With the exception of the Toronto Women's Bookstore (which did have a lot of generalist content), I chose self-described "generalist" stores because they most closely resembled the operation of Chapters Indigo. My sample included stores from almost every region of Canada: the western provinces, Atlantic Canada, and central Canada. I interviewed only one store manager

from Chapters Indigo because, as she told me, the classification systems for each store are centrally managed: there is no difference between each store. Interviews were conducted with open-ended questions at eleven independent stores and one branch of Chapters Indigo. Interviews were taped either at the store location or in a café nearby. They ran from one to two hours.

3 "Big-box" stores are chain stores that are not based in strip malls or covered malls, but are warehouse-like stores with very large square footages. They are able to combine warehouse functions and retail functions in a single location. The success of these environments depends on their ability to significantly discount merchandise while providing choice for consumers. Big-box stores are usually located near each other (often on the outskirts of an urban centre) to draw more consumers to them.

4 On March 27, 2008, Susan Delean cited Chapters Indigo as a major factor in the closing of her Toronto bookstore, Ballenford Books (*blog t.o.* 2008). For a more recent example of this kind of argument, see Daniel Tencer, "In the Twighlight of the Independent Bookstore, Chapters Looms" in *This Magazine* January 8, 2010. http://this.org/magazine/2010/01/08/death-of-independent -bookstore/.

5 For the purposes of this discussion, I understand store image to be the physical appearance of the store itself, and store culture to be the result of interactions between store image, work practices, customer behaviour, and employee/customer beliefs about the meaning of the store environment as a whole.

6 Interview with Heidi Hallett, Halifax, Nova Scotia, October 27, 2006.

7 Interview with Michael Hamm, Halifax, Nova Scotia, October 27, 2006.

8 Interview with Bruce Cartledge, Montreal, Quebec, October 30, 2006.

9 Interview with Sheila Koffman, Toronto, Ontario, November 1, 2006.

10 Interview with Kristen Hogan, Toronto, Ontario, November 1, 2006.

11 Toronto Women's Bookstore, "About Us," http://womensbookstore.com/about/. Accessed July 18, 2008.

12 The Facebook group called "We Love the Toronto Women's Bookstore" is no longer active and has been replaced by the more common Facebook "page," but you can still access the original at https://www.facebook.com/groups/3147545437/.

13 Since the closure of Pages, the website content has changed on the "About Pages" webpage, http://pagesbooks.ca/about.php. Accessed July 20, 2008.

14 Interview with Gregory King, Toronto Ontario, November 3, 2006.

15 "About Pages."

16 Interview with Mika Bareket, Toronto, Ontario, November 3, 2006.

17 Interview with Sharon Budnarchuk, Edmonton, Alberta, June 20, 2007.

18 Book Warehouse has since been sold to Black Bond books and the website content has changed. "About Book Warehouse," http://www.bookwarehouse.ca/aboutUs.php. Accessed April 2008.

19 Interview with Gary Crompton, Vancouver, British Columbia, November 6, 2006.

20 West End Community Network, "Book Warehouse Story," http://www.westendcommunitynetwork.com/home/community-businesses/book-warehouse-story. Accessed July 18, 2008. This website no longer contains this content.

21 Interview with Ria Bleumer, Vancouver, British Columbia, November 6, 2006.

22 Interview with Katherine Connaught, Edmonton Alberta, September 15, 2007.

23 ChaptersIndigo Trusted Advisor Health, http://www.chapters.indigo.ca/books/Trusted-Advisor-mainpage/ta_main-bq.html. Accessed July 30, 2008. This website is no longer active.

24 Indigo Books. 2012. Website. http://www.chapters.indigo.ca. Accessed December 2012.

25 "Techne" is originally the Greek word for art or craft. Michel Foucault uses the word to indicate a material practice which is deployed for a specific aim. See Foucault, *The Order of Things: An Archaeology of the Human Sciences* (1994).

26 See *Pages Beyond Bricks and Mortar,* http://pagesbooks.ca/home.php.

NOTES TO CHAPTER 3

1 *Modern Library,* "About Modern Library," accessed December 2010. http://www.modernlibrary.com/about/.

2 *Gale Directory of Company Histories,* s.v. "Random House," accessed December 2010. http://www.answers.com/topic/random-house.

3 Ibid.

4 *Random House,* "About Us," accessed December 2010. http://randomhouse.com/history.html

5 See John B. Thompson's *Merchants of Culture* (2010), chapters 3 and 4 for a detailed look at corporate structuring in publishing.

6 *Random House,* "Our Publishers," accessed December 2010. http://randomhouse.biz/ourpublishers.

7 Ibid.

8 *Knopf Publishers,* accessed December 2010. http://knopf.knopfdoubleday.com/. The content on the Knopf website changes regularly to reflect current titles.

9 *Pantheon Books*, accessed December 2010. http://pantheon.knopfdoubleday
   .com/.

10 *News Corporation*, "Books," accessed December 2010. http://newscorp.com/
   operations/books.html/.

11 *HarperCollins Publishers*, accessed December 2010. http://www.harpercollins
   .com. The content on this page changes regularly.

12 For a pilot study I analyzed an additional seven titles by Random House, but
   the reading criteria set for that study differed from the criteria used for the
   larger sample, and so these were excluded from this study. The method used
   for selection was random sampling, where every tenth book on the list was
   selected.

13 As indicated earlier, the rubrics used by both publishers do not always refer
   to commonly understood definitions of memoir, autobiography, or biography
   as genres, and rubrics are not common to both publishers. To make a clearer
   analysis in this part of the discussion, I used the rubrics by publishers and
   the summaries of books found on their back covers to determine whether a
   book was a memoir or autobiography, or whether it was a biography. For the
   purposes of this distinction, memoir and autobiography are narratives where
   the author and protagonist are the same person, and a biography is a narrative
   by one person about another person's life.

14 Ejovi Nuwere's life and career is chronicled on his website, *Ejovi Nuwere: An
   American Entrepreneur and Technologist*, accessed December 2010. http://
   www.ejovi.net/about/.

15 *The Crown Publishing Group*, "Broadway Books," accessed December 2010.
   http://www.randomhouse.com/crown/broadway-books/.

16 See the comments on Amazon.com for *Cosmopolitan*, accessed December
   2010. http://www.amazon.com/Cosmopolitan-Bartenders-Life-Toby
   -Cecchini/product-reviews/0767912098/.

17 The reviews on Amazon.com are the only record I could find of a response
   to *Where the Birds Never Sing*. All are overwhelmingly positive. Some are by
   survivors of Dachau. http://www.amazon.com/Where-Birds-Never-Sing
   -Liberation/product-reviews/0060096667/.

NOTES TO CHAPTER 4

1 There is not a consensus in the scholarly or the creative communities about
   what to call comic art which appears in a bound format. See Rocìo G. Davis'
   discussion of the history of the term in her note 3 (2005). Since the narratives I refer to here are non-fictional, I call these narratives graphic books, as

opposed to graphic novels, which is the most common generic term in the publishing industry.

2 For a detailed genealogy of the politics of memoir and the development of an aesthetics for autobiography, see my article "Are Memoirs Autobiography? A Consideration of Memoir and Public Identity," in *Genre: Forms of Discourse and Culture* (2004a).

3 There were other memoirs published by major publishers in 2003 that became bestsellers, notably Asar Nafisi's *Reading Lolita in Tehran* by Random House, the international hardcover bestseller *A Royal Duty* (a tell-all book by Princess Diana's butler Paul Burrell published by Putnam), and Hillary Rodham Clinton's *Living History* by Simon & Schuster. Mitch Albom's *Tuesdays with Morrie* was published a year earlier by Knopf Doubleday but in 2003 was still on most bestseller lists.

4 "David B." is David Beauchard, one of the founders of *L'Association*, who at the time was probably the best-known comic memoirist in France. He helped to get Satrapi her start as a graphic memoirist. Beauchard's endorsement of Satrapi via his introduction was designed to signal to dedicated readers of French comics that her work is worth serious consideration. Thanks to Bart Beaty for this information.

5 In fact, the image was cropped from a photograph of two women reading a newspaper together. See the original image at http://weekly.ahram.org .eg/2006/797/sc07.jpg.

6 See Amy Malek's "Memoir as Iranian Exile Cultural Production" (2006) for a complete list and a detailed discussion of these memoirs.

7 Although Nancy K. Miller's study gives some space to Satrapi's "non-conformist" grandmother, she devotes more time to thinking about Satrapi's feminist mother and about feminist readings of the mother–daughter relation. She reads the last scene as a an injunction to remember all three generations, but her focus is on the mother–daughter relation in the last panel, and it remains primary in her analysis (2007b, 27).

8 The War on Drugs took a number of different forms, including efforts to prosecute users and prevent illegal drugs from entering the United States. During the Nixon administration in 1969, it operated as a prohibition campaign that aimed to stop the importing of marijuana. Other efforts to stop drug production included the capture of General Manuel Noriega, the leader of Panama in 1989, overseen by George H.W. Bush, and the spraying of crops in Columbia from 2000–2006, overseen by the Clinton administration, to inhibit the production of coca, the plant used to make cocaine. One of the more interesting campaigns in the War on Drugs on the home front included the production

of television advertisements, aimed at young people, that were designed to make drug use seem distasteful, and tax-supported incentives for television programs to incorporate anti-drug messages into popular prime-time shows. For more information about the War on Drugs, see Arthur Benavie's *Drugs: America's Holy War* (2009) and Cornelius Friesendorf's *U.S. Foreign Policy and War on Drugs* (2007).

9 The complete transcript of the *Larry King Live* show is available through CNN.com at http://transcripts.cnn.com/TRANSCRIPTS/0601/11/lkl.01.html. All references to the Larry King interview are to this transcript.

10 For an overview of the social history of addiction in the United States, see Joanne Muzak's "'They Say the Disease Is Responsible': Social Identity and the Disease Concept of Drug Addiction" (2007) and Wayne Morgan's *Drugs in America: A Social History 1800–1980* (1982).

11 Burroughs was sued in 2005 by the family portrayed in the memoir. In the settlement, Burroughs agreed to call his work a "book" and not a memoir in an afterword, but he later said in an online interview that "it's still a memoir, it's marketed as a memoir." The transcript of this interview is at http://en.wikinews.org/wiki/Augusten_Burroughs.

12 All references to the January 26, 2006, episode of the *Oprah Winfrey Show* called "James Frey and the *A Million Little Pieces* Controversy" are to the original program.

13 All references to the October 26, 2005, episode of the *Oprah Winfrey Show* called "The Man Who Kept Oprah Awake at Night" are to the original program.

14 By "middlebrow" I mean the term that describes pejoratively from the 1920s onward the cultural activities of people (mainly women) who are thought to be neither intellectually gifted nor socially adept, although they may have pretensions to be both. The term is not completely identified with "middle class," since working-class people with middlebrow pretensions were often lampooned in print. See Janice Radway's description of middlebrow book culture in chapter 7, "The Scandal of the Middlebrow," in her *A Feeling for Books* (1997). Oprah's Book Club has been described as a false intellectual environment for undereducated women in similar ways.

15 Oprah's Book Club 2.0. 2012. Web site. http://www.oprah.com/packages/oprahs-book-club-2.html.

16 All references are to the transcript of the January 11, 2006, episode of the *Larry King Live* show. See note 9 for the reference.

17 Ibid.

18 The text of the January 31, 2006, State of the Union address can be found at http://georgewbush-whitehouse.archives.gov/stateoftheunion/2006/.

REFERENCES

Adorno, Theodor, and Max Horkheimer. 1997. "The Culture Industry: Enlightenment as Mass Deception." In *Production of Culture/Cultures of Production*, edited by Paul Du Gay, 105–11. London: Sage.

Akroyd, Peter. 2001. *London: The Biography*. London: Vintage Books.

Ali, Dominic. 2000. "Fear & Trembling at BookExpo America." *Vancouver Sun*, June 17, 2000. http://www.domali.com/feartrembling.htm. Accessed April 2008 (link no longer active).

Allawi, Ali A. 2007. *The Occupation of Iraq: Winning the War, Losing the Peace*. New Haven: Yale University Press.

Althusser, Louis. 1990. *For Marx*. Translated by Ben Brewster. London: Verso.

Arsenalia. 2010. "Bookseller Feature: Ria Bleumer, Sitka Books and Art." *Arsenalia*, September 17. http://www.arsenalia.com/bookseller-feature-ria-bleumer/.

Association of American Publishers. 2012. "Bookstats Publishing Categories Highlights." Association of American Publishers. http://www.publishers.org/bookstats/categories/.

Banco, Lindsey Michael. 2007. "Trafficking Trips: Drugs and the Anti-Tourist Novels of Hunter S. Thompson and Alex Garland." *Studies in Travel Writing* 11, no. 2 (September): 127–53.

Beaty, Bart. 2007. *Unpopular Culture: Transforming the European Comic Book in the 1990s*. Toronto: University of Toronto Press.

Beeman, William O. 2003. *The "Great Satan" vs. "the Mad Mullahs": How the United States and Iran Demonize Each Other*. Chicago: University of Chicago Press.

Benavie, Arthur. 2009. *Drugs: America's Holy War*. New York and London: Routledge.

Benjamin, Walter. 1973. "The Work of Art in the Mechanical Age of Reproduction." In *Illuminations*. Edited by Hannah Arendt, translated by Harry Zohn, 211–44. London: Fontana Press.

Berlant, Lauren. 1997. *The Queen of America Goes to Washington City: Essays on Sex and Citizenship*. Durham, NC: Duke University Press.

———. 2008. *The Female Complaint: The Unfinished Business of Sentimentality in American Culture*. Durham, NC: Duke University Press.

Bertelsmann. 2009. *Annual Report 2009*. Gütersloh, EU: Bertelsmann. http://www
.bertelsmann.com/bertelsmann_corp/wms41/customers/bmcorp/pdf/2009_
ENGL_Annual_Report.pdf.

———. 2010. Press Release. "Bertelsmann Raises Its Forecast for 2010 after a First-half Leap in Profits." August 31. http://www.bertelsmann.com/bertelsmann_
corp/wms41/bm/page_popup.php.

Bethel, Wendy. 2001. Review of *Stuffed: Growing Up in a Restaurant Family*, by Patricia Volk. *Library Journal* 26, no. 8: 84.

blog.TO/Toronto Blog. 2008. "Ballenford Books to Close." March 27. http://www
.blogto.com/books_lit/2008/03/ballenford_books_to_close/.

Bourdieu, Pierre. 2000. "The Field of Cultural Production." In *The Field of Cultural Production: Essays on Art and Literature*, edited by Randal Johnson, 29–73. Cambridge, UK: Polity.

Britzman, Deborah P. 1998. *Lost Subjects, Contested Objects: Towards a Psychoanalytic Theory of Learning*. Albany, NY: SUNY Press.

Browning, James. 2003. "The Crack-Up." *Village Voice* 48, no. 16 (April 16): 47.

Burgess, Steve. 1999. "A Better Mousetrap: The Chapters Man. He Has Scruples. He Doesn't Buy Books from Those Dirty Rats, but He Likes the Coffee and, Hey, Nice View …" *Vancouver Sun*, July 17.

Burns, Ann, and Danna Bell-Russel. 2003. Review of *A Million Little Pieces*, by James Frey. *Library Journal* 128, no. 19 (November 15): 115–16.

Buss, Helen. 2002. *Repossessing the World: Reading Memoirs by Contemporary Women*. Waterloo, ON: Wilfrid Laurier University Press.

Butler, Judith. 1999. "Gender Is Burning: Questions of Appropriation and Subversion." In *Feminist Film Theory: A Reader*, edited by Sue Thornham, 337–48. Edinburgh: Edinburgh University Press.

———. 2004. "Imitation and Gender Insubordination." In *The Judith Butler Reader*, edited by Sarah Salih with Judith Butler, 119–37. Oxford: Blackwell.

Canada. 2007. Canadian Heritage. *The Book Retail Sector in Canada*. Vancouver: Turner-Riggs. http://www.pch.gc.ca/pgm/padie-bpidp/rep/rapp-rep_07/
rapport-pdf-report-eng.pdf.

Cecchini, Toby. 2003. *Cosmopolitan: A Bartender's Life*. New York: Broadway Books.

Cerf, Bennett. 1977. *At Random: The Reminiscences of Bennett Cerf.* New York: Random House.

The Coast. 2008. "Frog Hollow Books." http://www.thecoast.ca/AcctListing -93977.112113_Frog_Hollow_Books.html.

Cobley, Paul. 2001. *Narrative*. London: Routledge.

Coe, Richard M., Lorelei Lingard, and Tatiana Teslenko. 2001. "Genre as Action, Strategy and *Differance*: An Introduction." In *The Rhetoric and Ideology of Genre: Strategies for Stability and Change*, edited by Richard M. Coe, Lorelei Lingard, and Tatiana Teslenko, 1–12. Cresskill, NJ: Hampton Press.

Colbert, Stephen. 2006. "Interview with Stephen Colbert, by Nathan Rabin." *The Onion's A.V. Club*, January 25. http://www.avclub.com/articles/stephen -colbert,13970/.

Collins, Robert. 2010. "After the Celebrity Memoir Gold-Rush ..." *The Telegraph*, January 13. http://www.telegraph.co.uk/culture/books/6982776/After-the -celebrity-memoir-gold-rush....html.

Constantino, Manuela. 2008. "Marji: Popular Commix Heroine Breathing Life into the Writing of History." *Canadian Review of American Studies* 38, no. 3: 429–47.

Couser, G. Thomas. 2012. *Memoir: An Introduction*. New York: Oxford University Press.

Dann, Sam, ed. 1998. *Dachau 29 April 1945: The Rainbow Liberation*. Lubbock: Texas Tech University Press.

Darnton, Robert. 2002. "What Is the History of Books?" In *The Book History Reader*, edited by David Finkelstein and Alistair McCleery, 9–26. New York and London: Routledge.

Davis, Kenneth C. 1984. *Two-Bit Culture: The Paperbacking of America*. Boston: Houghton Mifflin.

Davis, Rocìo G. 2005. "A Graphic Self: Comics as Autobiography in Marjane Satrapi's *Persepolis*." *Prose Studies* 27, no. 3 (December): 264–79.

de Certeau, Michel. 1984. *The Practice of Everyday Life*. Berkeley: University of California Press.

De Man, Paul. 1979. "Autobiography as De-Facement." MLN 94, no. 5 (December): 919–30.

Devitt, Amy J. 2004. *Writing Genres*. Carbondale: Southern Illinois University Press.

Dimock, Wai Chee. 2007. "Introduction: Genre as Fields of Knowledge." PMLA 122, no. 5 (October): 1377–88.

Dixon, Christopher M., Lynn McKechnie, Laura J. Miller, and Paulette M. Roth-bauer. 2001. "Latte Grande, No Sprinkles: An Exploratory Observational Study of Customer Behavior at Chapters Bookstores." CAIS/ACSI Conference Proceedings, 165–74. http://www.cais-acsi.ca/proceedings/2001/Dixon_2001.pdf.

Dowd, Maureen. 2006. "Oprah: Separating Fact from Fiction: Interview with Maureen Dowd." By Keith Olbermann. *Countdown with Keith Olbermann*, January 27. http://www.msnbc.msn.com/id/11060546/.

Dubrow, Heather. 1982. *Genre*. London: Methuen.

Duff, David. 2000. Introduction to *Modern Genre Theory*. Harlow, UK: Longman.

Dyer, Richard. 2004. *Heavenly Bodies: Film Stars and Society*. 2nd ed. London: Routledge.

Eakin, Paul John. 1992. *Touching the World: Reference in Autobiography*. Princeton, NJ: Princeton University Press.

Egan, Susanna. 1999. *Mirror Talk: Genres of Crisis in Contemporary Autobiography*. Chapel Hill: University of North Carolina Press.

Eichler, Leah, 2001. "Study Shows Chapters' Dominance in Retail Market." *Publishers Weekly* 248, no. 27: 17.

Elien, Shadi. 2009. "Former Duthie Books Manager to Open New Independent Bookstore in Vancouver." *straight.com*, July 5. http://www.straight.com/article-332398/vancouver/former-duthie-books-manager-open-new-independent-bookstore-vancouver.

Epstein, Jason. 2002. *Book Business: Publishing Past, Present, and Future*. New York and London: W.W. Norton.

Fawn, Rick. 2006. "The Iraq War: Unfolding and Unfinished." In *The Iraq War: Causes and Consequences*, edited by Rick Fawn and Raymond Hinnebusch, 1–20. Boulder, CO, and London: Lynne Rienner.

Fetherling, George. 2001. Preface to *The Vintage Book of Canadian Memoirs*. Toronto: Vintage Canada.

Feuer, Jane. 1992. "Genre Study and Television." In *Channels of Discourse, Reassembled: Television and Contemporary Criticism*. 2nd ed, edited by Robert C. Allen, 138–60. Chapel Hill: University of North Carolina Press.

Finkelstein, David. 2009. "The Globalization of the Book, 1800–1970." In *A Companion to the History of the Book*, edited by Simon Eliot and Jonathan Rose, 329–40. Chichester, UK: Wiley-Blackwell.

Finkelstein, David, and Alistair McCleery. 2005. *An Introduction to Book History*. New York and London: Routledge.

Fiske, John. 1989. *Understanding Popular Culture*. New York: Unwin Hyman.

Foroohar, Rana, Tracy McNicoll, Mary Acoymo, Mark Russell, and Kay Itoi. 2005. "Comic Relief." *Newsweek* 146, no. 8 (August 22).

Foucault, Michel. 1980. *Power/knowledge: Selected Interviews and Other Writings, 1972–1977*. Edited by Colin Gordon. New York: Pantheon.

———. 1984. *The Foucault Reader*. Edited by Paul Rabinow. New York: Random House. 101–120.

———. 1994. *The Order of Things: An Archaeology of the Human Sciences*, New York: Vintage. First English translation published in 1970 by Pantheon.

Freadman, Anne. 1994. "Anyone for Tennis?" In *Genre and the New Rhetoric*, edited by Aviva Freedman and Peter Medway, 43–66. London: Taylor & Francis.

Freedman, Aviva, and Peter Medway. 1994. "Locating Genre Studies: Antecedents and Prospects." In Freedman and Medway, *Genre and the New Rhetoric*, 1–22.

Frey, James. 2004. *A Million Little Pieces*. New York: Anchor Books. First edition published in 2003.

Friesendorf, Cornelius. 2007. *US Foreign Policy and the War on Drugs: Displacing the Cocaine and Heroine Industry*. New York and London: Routledge.

Frow, John. 2006. *Genre*. New York: Routledge.

———. 2007. "'Reproducibles, Rubrics, and Everything You Need': Genre Theory Today." *PMLA* 122, no. 5 (October): 1626–34.

Fulford, Robert. 2000. "The Turmoil over Chapters Book Chain." *National Post*, July 21. Accessed April 7, 2008, at http://www.robertfulford.com/Chapters.html.

Gamson, Joshua. 2001. "The Assembly Life of Greatness: Celebrity in Twentieth-Century America." In *Popular Culture: Production and Consumption*, edited by C. Lee Harrington and Denise D. Beilby, 259–82. Malden, MA: Blackwell.

Gardiner, Juliet. 2002. "Reforming the Reader: Internet Bookselling and Its Impact on the Construction of Reading Practices." *Changing English: Studies in Reading and Culture* 9, no. 2 (October): 161–68.

Genette, Gerard. 1997. *Paratexts: Thresholds of Interpretation*. Translated by Jane E. Lewin. Cambridge: Cambridge University Press.

Gentile, Catherine. 2007. Review of *Persépolis*. *Sitartmag*. http://www.sitartmag.com/msatrapi.htm.

Gilmore, Leigh. 1994. *Autobiographics: A Feminist Theory of Women's Self-Representation*. Ithaca, NY: Cornell University Press.

———. 2001. *The Limits of Autobiography: Trauma and Testimony*. Ithaca, NY: Cornell University Press.

———. 2003. "Jurisdictions: *I, Rigoberta Menchú, The Kiss*, and Scandalous Self-Representation in the Age of Memoir and Trauma." *Signs: Journal of Women in Culture and Society* 28, no. 2: 695–718.

———. 2010. "American Neoconfessional: Memoir, Self-Help, and Redemption on Oprah's Couch." *Biography: An Interdisciplinary Quarterly* 33, no. 4 (Fall): 657–79.

Giltrow, Janet. 1994. "Genre and the Pragmatic Concept of Background Knowledge." In Freedman and Medway, *Genre and the New Rhetoric*, 155–78.

Giroux, Henry A. 2001. "Cultural Studies as Performative Politics." *Cultural Studies—Critical Methodologies* 1, no. 1: 5–23.

Glass, Loren. 2004. *Authors Inc.: Literary Celebrity in the Modern United States, 1880–1980*. New York: New York University Press.

Gold, Sarah F., Emily Chenoweth, Lynn Andriani, and Jeff Zaleski. 2003. Review of *Where the Birds Never Sing*. *Publishers Weekly* 250, no. 32 (October 11): 268.

Goldman, Anne. 1996. *Take My Word: Autobiographical Innovations of Ethnic American Working Class Women*. Berkeley and Los Angeles: University of California Press.

Gowlings. 2004. "Canadian Booksellers Association Abandons Amazon.ca Case." *Intellectual Property Report Online*. http://www.smithlyons.ca/news/index.asp.

Greco, Albert N. 1996. "Shaping the Future: Mergers, Acquisitions, and the U.S. Publishing, Communications, and Mass Media Industries, 1990–1995." *Publishing Research Quarterly* 12, no. 3 (Fall): n.p.

———. 2000. Market Concentration Levels in the U.S. Consumer Book Industry: 1995–1996. *Journal of Cultural Economics* 24: 321–36.

———. 2004. *The Book Publishing Industry*. Mahwah, NJ: Lawrence Erlbaum Associates.

Greco, Albert N., Clara E. Rodriguez, and Robert M. Wharton. 2006. *The Culture and Commerce of Publishing in the 21st Century*. Palo Alto, CA: Stanford University Press.

Habermas, Jürgen. 1996. "The Transformation of the Public Sphere's Political Function." In *The Habermas Reader*, edited by William Outhwaite, 28–31. Cambridge: Polity.

Hall, Stuart. 1981. "Notes on Deconstructing 'the Popular.'" In *People's History and Socialist Theory*, edited by Raphael Samuel, 227–40. London: Routledge & Kegan Paul.

Hamilton, Geoff. 2007. "Mixing Memoir and Desire: James Frey, Wound Culture, and 'the Essential American Soul.'" *Journal of American Culture* 30, no. 3 (September): 324–33.

Harker, Jaime. 2008. "Afterword: Oprah, James Frey, and the Problem of the Literary." In *The Oprah Affect: Critical Essays on Oprah's Book Club*, edited by Cecilia Konchar Farr and Jaime Harker, 321–34. Albany, NY: SUNY Press.

Harris, Mark. 2000. "New World Bookselling: Despite the Inundation of Mega Bookstores, at Least One Independent Is Flourishing—Call It Chapters Petite." *Vancouver Sun*, September 2.

Harris. Oliver. 2003. *William S. Burroughs and the Secret of Fascination*. Carbondale: Southern Illinois University Press.

Hart, Melissa. 2010. "'What's at Stake?': How an *Agent's* Key Question about Characters Improved the Quality of a Published Memoir." *Writer* 123, no. 8: 39–40.

Hawkins, Harriet. 1990. *Classics and Trash: Traditions and Taboos in High Literature and Popular Modern Genres*. Toronto: University of Toronto Press.

Hellekson, Karen, and Kristina Busse. 2006. *Fan Fiction and Fan Communities in the Age of the Internet: New Essays*. Jefferson, NC: McFarland.

Hesmondalgh, David. 2007. *The Cultural Industries*. 2nd Ed. London: Sage.

Hoashi, Lisa. 2007. "Fluency in Form: A Survey of the Graphic Memoir." *Missouri Review* 30, no. 4 (2007): 159–74.

Hoogland, Eric. 2006. "Iran: Wary Neutral." In *The Iraq War: Causes and Consequences,* edited by Rick Fawn and Raymond Hinnebusch, 173–86. Boulder, CO, and London: Lynne Rienner.

Hylton, Hillary. 2007. "Oprah vs. James Frey: The Sequel." *Time/CNN.com.* July 30. http://www.time.com/time/arts/article/0,8599,1648140,00.html.

Jones, Ken, and Michael Doucet. 1999. *The Impact of Big-Box Development on Toronto's Retail Structure*. Toronto: Centre for the Study of Commercial Activity, Ryerson Polytechnic University.

Jones, Jeffrey. 2003. "Americans Cite Weapons, Liberating Iraqis as Good Reasons for War." March 19. *Gallup.com.* http://www.gallup.com/poll/8029/Americans-Cite-Weapons-Liberating-Iraqis-Good-Reasons-War.aspx.

Kaplan, Caren. 1992. "Resisting Autobiography: Out-law Genres and Transnational Feminist Subjects." In *De/Colonizing the Subject: The Politics of Gender in Women's Autobiography*, edited by Sidonie Smith and Julia Watson, 115–38. Minneapolis: University of Minnesota Press.

Karr, Clarence. 2000. *Authors and Audiences: Popular Canadian Fiction in the Early Twentieth Century*. Montreal and Kingston: McGill-Queen's University Press.

Keegan, Rebecca. 2006. "O.K., Now He's in a Million Little Pieces." *Time* (June 6): 71.

Kelly, Christopher. 2003. *Rousseau as an Author: Consecrating One's Life to the Truth*. Chicago: University of Chicago Press.

Keyes, John T.D. 2000. "Out of the Woods: Her Chain of Family Bookstores Is History, but Celia Duthie Is Back with a Grand New Experiment: The Readers' Retreat." *National Post*, May 6.

King, Stephen. 2000. *Secret Windows: Essays and Fiction on the Craft of Writing*. New York: Book-of-the-Month Club.

Kingwell, Mark. 2001. "Writers and the Big, Bad Booksellers." *National Post*, May 16.

Konchar Farr, Cecilia. 2008. "Talking Readers." In *The Oprah Affect: Critical Essays on Oprah's Book Club*, 33–54.

Konchar Farr, Cecilia, and Jaime Harker, eds. 2008. *The Oprah Affect: Critical Essays on Oprah's Book Club.* Albany, NY: SUNY Press.

Kurtz, Howard. 2006. "In the Fog of War, a Moral Haze." *Washington Post*, January 16. http://www.highbeam.com/doc/1P2-90915.html.

Kymlicka, Will, and Wayne Norman. 2001. "The Return of the Citizen." In *Democracy: A Reader*, edited by Ricardo Blaug and John Schwarzmantel, 220–27. New York: Columbia University Press.

Lacey, Nick. 2000. *Narrative and Genre: Key Concepts in Media Studies.* New York: St Martin's Press.

Lahey, Anita. 1999. "Celebrating Canada." *Quill and Quire* 65, no. 9 (September 1): 27.

Laing, Audrey. 2005. "Extend the Market or Maintain the Loyal Customer? The Dilemma Facing Today's Booksellers." *Publishing Research Quarterly* 21, no. 2: 19–29.

Lane, Jim. 2002. *The Autobiographical Documentary in America.* Madison: University of Wisconsin Press.

Langan, Celeste. 1995. *Romantic Vagrancy: Wordsworth and the Simulation of Freedom.* Berkeley: University of California Press.

Larson, Jeannette. 2003. "Subject Roundup: Memoirs." *Booklist* (October 1): 340.

Larson, Thomas. 2007. *Memoir and the Memoirist: Reading and Writing Personal Narrative.* Athens, OH: Swallow Press/University of Ohio Press.

Lea, Richard. 2011. "Celebrity Memoirs Lose Star Power at the Tills." *Guardian Online*, December 2. http://www.guardian.co.uk/books/2011/dec/02/celebrity-memoirs-lose-alan-partridge?newsfeed=true.

Leavis, Q.D. 1932. *Fiction and the Reading Public.* London: Chatto & Windus.

Leider, Paula. 2006. "Oprah Confrontation 'Very Intense.'" *The Early Show*, January 27. http://www.cbsnews.com/stories/2006/01/27/earlyshow/main1244853.shtml.

Lejeune, Philippe. 1975. *Le pacte autobiographique.* Paris: Seuil.

———. 1983. "Le Pacte autobiographique (bis)." *Poetique: Revue de Theorie et d'Analyse Litteraires* 14, no. 56: 416–34.

———. 1989a. "The Autobiographical Pact (bis)." In *On Autobiography.* Edited by Paul John Eakin. Translated by Katherine Leary, 119–37. Minneapolis: University of Minnesota Press.

———. 1989b. "The Autobiography of Those Who Do Not Write." In *On Autobiography*, 185–215.

Lockheed, Gordon. 2003. "What's Wrong in the Book Trade?" *Dooney's Café* (blog), September 28. http://www.dooneyscafe.com/archives/250.

Lorinc, John. 2000. "Indigo Bid Tests Competition Policy Again: 35% of the Market?" *National Post*, November 29.

Lorimer, James, and Susan M. Shaw. 1983. *Book Reading in Canada: The Audience, the Marketplace, and the Distribution System for Trade Books in English Canada*. Toronto: Association of Canadian Publishers.

Luey, Beth. 2009a. "Modernity and Print III: The United States 1890–1970." In Eliot and Rose, *A Companion to the History of the Book*, 368–80.

———. 2009b. "The Organization of the Book Publishing Industry." In *The History of the Book in America*. Vol. 5, *The Enduring Book: Print Culture in Postwar America*, edited by David Paul Nord, Joan Shelley Rubin, and Michael Schudson, 29–54. Chapel Hill: University of North Carolina Press.

———. 2010. *Expanding the American Mind: Books and the Popularization of Knowledge*. Amherst and Boston: University of Massachusetts Press.

Luscombe, Belinda. 2009. "World's Most Shocking Apology: Oprah to James Frey." *Time/CNN.com*, May 13. http://www.time.com/time/arts/article/0,8599,1897924,00.html.

Lyall, Sarah. 2010. "Celebrities Sell Books in Britain (Talent Optional)." *New York Times*, January 22.

Malek, Amy. 2006. "Memoir as Iranian Exile Cultural Production: A Case Study of Marjane Satrapi's *Persepolis* Series." *Iranian Studies* 39, no. 3 (September): 353–80.

Marcus, Laura. 1994. *Auto/biographical Discourses: Theory, Criticism, Practice*. Manchester: Manchester University Press.

McMurdry, Deidre. 2001. Last-Minute Credit Rescues Publisher: Chapters' Sad Story Resonates within the Book Industry. *Edmonton Journal*, November 6.

Metz, Steven. 2008. *Iraq and the Evolution of American Strategy*. Washington, DC: Potomac Books.

Milbank, Dana, and Jim VandeHei. 2003. "No Political Fallout for Bush on Weapons." *Washington Post*, May 17.

Miller, Anna. 2008. "Who's Afraid of the Big Bad Box-Store? Not These 'Indies'; Small Booksellers Carve Out Niche against Giants." *National Post*, April 5.

Miller, Carolyn. 1994. "Genre as Social Action." In Freedman and Medway, *Genre and the New Rhetoric*, 3–42.

Miller, Laura J. 2000. "The Best-Seller List as Marketing Tool and Historical Fiction." *Book History* 3: 286–304.

———. 2007. *Reluctant Capitalists: Bookselling and the Culture of Consumption*. Chicago and London: University of Chicago Press.

Miller, Mark Crispin. 1997. "The Publishing Industry." In *Conglomerates and the Media*. By Patricia Aufderheide, Erid Barnouw, Richard M. Cohen, Thomas Frank, David Lieberman, Mark Crispin Miller, Gene Roberts, and Thomas Shatz. New York: New Press. 107–34.

Miller, Nancy K. 2000. *Bequest and Betrayal: Memoirs of a Parent's Death.* Bloomington: Indiana University Press.

———. 2002. *But Enough about Me: Why We Read Other People's Lives.* New York: Columbia University Press.

———. 2007a. "The Entangled Self: Genre Bondage in the Age of Memoir." PMLA 122 (March): 537–48.

———. 2007b. "Out of the Family: Generations of Women in Marjane Satrapi's *Persepolis.*" *Life Writing* 4, no. 1 (April): 13–29.

Miller, Toby. 2007. *Cultural Citizenship: Cosmopolitanism, Consumerism, and Television in a Neoliberal Age.* Philadelphia: Temple University Press.

Milliot, Jim. 2008. "Chains, Internet Ruled Bookselling in 2007." *Publishers Weekly* 255, no. 15: 8.

Minzesheimer, Bob. 2008. "Everybody Has a Story to Tell, so Memoirs Sell." *USA Today*, February 27. http://www.usatoday.com/life/books/news/2008-02-27 -memoirs_N.htm.

Mittell, Jason. 2004. *Genre and Television: From Cop Shows to Cartoons in American Culture.* New York and London: Routledge.

Moore, John. 2001. "Down, but Not Out: Our Small, Feisty Bookstore Struggle to Stay Afloat in the Leviathan's Wake." *Vancouver Sun*, April 7: H24.

Morgan, H. Wayne. 1982. *Drugs in America: A Social History.* Syracuse: Syracuse University Press.

Mozes, Suzanne. 2010. "James Frey's Fiction Factory." *New York Books*, November 12. http://nymag.com/arts/books/features/69474/.

Muzak, Joanne. 2007. "'They Say the Disease Is Responsible': Social Identity and the Disease Concept of Addiction." *Unfitting Stories: Narratives of Disease, Disability, and Trauma*, edited by Valerie Raoul, Connie Canham, Angela D. Henderson, and Carla Paterson, 255–64. Waterloo, ON: Wilfrid Laurier University Press.

Naghibi, Nima, and Andrew O'Malley. 2005. "Estranging the Familiar: 'East' and 'West' in Satrapi's *Persepolis.*" *English Studies in Canada* 31, nos. 2–3: 223–47.

Nelson, Miranda. 2009. "Independent Bookstore Duthie Books Set to Close." *straight.com*, January 19. http://www.straight.com/article-281190/vancouver/ independent-bookstore-duthie-books-set-close.

Newport, Frank, and Lydia Saad. 2002. "Americans' View: U.S. Should Not Go It Alone in Iraq." *Gallup.com*, September 24. http://www.gallup.com/poll/6874/ Americans-View-US-Should-Alone-Iraq.aspx.

New York Times. 2007. "On Oprah's Couch." Editorial, January 27. http://www .nytimes.com/2006/01/27/opinion/27fri3.html.

———. 2010a. "Best Sellers: Hardcover Nonfiction." December 16. http://www .nytimes.com/best-sellers-books/2010-12-19/hardcover-nonfiction/list.html.

———. 2010b. "Best Sellers: Paperback Nonfiction." December 19. http://www
.nytimes.com/best-sellers-books/2010-12-19/paperback-nonfiction/list.html.

News Corporation. 2009. *Annual Report 2009*. http://www.newscorp.com/
Report2009/index.html.

Niagara Falls Review. 2001. "Small Bookstores Benefit from Chapters' Turmoil."
July 12.

Nickson, Elizabeth. 2004. "A Depressing Chapter in Our Development." *National
Post*, February 13.

Nord, David Paul, Joan Shelley Rubin, and Michael Schudson, eds. 2009. "General
Introduction: The Enduring Book in a Multimedia Age." *The History of the
Book in America*. Vol. 5, *The Enduring Book: Print Culture in Postwar America*,
1–24. Chapel Hill: University of North Carolina Press.

Nuwere, Ejovi, with David Chanoff. 2002. *Hacker Cracker: A Journey from the
Mean Streets of Brooklyn to the Frontiers of Cyberspace*. New York: William
Morrow/HarperCollins.

Obama, Barack. 2004. "2004 Democratic National Convention Keynote Address."
American Rhetoric Online Speech Bank, July 27.

Ohmann, Richard. 1996. *Selling Culture: Magazine, Markets, and Class at the Turn
of the Century*. London: Verso.

Oprah Winfrey Show. 2005. "The Man Who Kept Oprah Awake at Night." Originally aired October 26. http://www.oprah.com/dated/oprahshow/
oprahshow_20051026.

———. 2006a. "James Frey and the *A Million Little Pieces* Controversy." Originally
aired January 26. http://www.oprah.com/dated/oprahshow/oprahshow_
20060126.

———. 2006b. "Oprah's Questions for James." Transcript for *The Oprah Winfrey
Show*, January 26. http://www.oprah.com/oprahshow/Oprahs-Questions-for
-James/10.

———. 2011. "James Frey, Five Years Later, Part 2." Originally aired May 17. www
.oprah.com/oprahshow/James-Frey-Five-Years-Later-Part-2.

Pawling, Christopher. 1984. *Popular Fiction and Social Change*. London: Macmillan Press.

Pearl, Nancy. 2003. *Book Lust: Recommended Reading for Every Mood, Moment,
and Reason*. Seattle: Sasquatch Books.

———. 2005. *More Book Lust: 1000 New Reading Recommendations for Every
Mood, Moment, and Reason*. Seattle: Sasquatch Books.

———. 2010. "Happy Holidays, Voyeurs: Nancy Pearl Picks Memoirs." December 3.
http://www.npr.org/2010/12/03/131392774/happy-holidays-voyeurs-nancy
-pearl-picks-memoirs.

Peele, Stanton. 2006. "James Frey's One True Thing." *Addiction Research and Theory* 14, no. 5 (October): 453–60.

Perry, Michael. 2002. "Duthie's Is as Open as a Favourite Book." *Vancouver Sun*, December 17.

Perry, Michael W. 2000. *Dachau Liberated: The Official Report*. 2nd edition. Seattle: Inkling Books.

Petersen, Alan, Ian Barns, Janice Dudley, and Patricia Harris. 1999. "Introduction: Themes, Contexts, and Perspectives." In *Poststructuralism, Citizenship, and Social Policy*, 1–17. London: Routledge.

Pew Research Center. 2008. "Public Attitudes toward the War in Iraq: 2003–2008." March 12. http://pewresearch.org/pubs/770/iraq-war-five-year-anniversary.

Poletti, Anna. 2008. *Intimate Ephemera: Reading Young Lives in Australian Zine Culture*. Victoria: Melbourne University Press.

Ponce de Leon, Charles L. 2002. *Self-Exposure: Human-Interest Journalism and the Emergence of Celebrity in America, 1890–1940*. Chapel Hill: University of North Carolina Press.

ProCon.org. "Iran-Iraq War." 2009. http://usiraq.procon.org/viewresource .asp?resourceID=673#I.H.

Pruess, Simone. 2009. "Harper Collins Publisher Profile." *Suite 101.com*, September 5. http://www.suite101.com/content/harper-collins-publisher -profile-a145663.

Publishers Weekly. 2003. Review of *A Million Little Pieces*. *Publishers Weekly* 250, no. 27 (November 7): 27.

Radway, Janice. 1984. *Reading the Romance: Women, Patriarchy and Popular Literature*. Chapel Hill: University of North Carolina Press.

———. 1997. *A Feeling for Books: The Book-of-the-Month Club, Literary Taste, and Middle-Class Desire*. Chapel Hill: University of North Carolina Press.

Rak, Julie. 2003. "Do Witness: *Don't a Woman's Word* and Trauma as Pedagogy." *Topia: A Canadian Journal of Cultural Studies* 10 (Fall): 53–72.

———. 2004a. "Are Memoirs Autobiography? A Consideration of Memoir and Public Identity." *Genre: Forms of Discourse and Culture* 36 (Fall/Winter): 305–26.

———. 2004b. *Negotiated Memory: Doukhobor Autobiographical Discourse*. Vancouver: University of British Columbia Press.

———. 2004c. "Popular Memoir and the Roots of Citizenship: Rousseau, Mountaineering, Autobiography." In *Life Writing and the Generations, edited by Richard Freadman and John Gatt-Rutter*. Special issue, *a/b: Auto/Biography Studies* 19, nos. 1–2 (Summer and Winter): 10–18.

———. 2005. "Bio-power: CBC Television's *Life and Times* and A&E Network's *Biography on A&E*." *Life Writing* 1, no. 2: 19–45.

———. 2010. "Insecure Citizenship: Michael Ignatieff, Memoir, Canada." *Biography* 33, no. 1: 1–23.

Reese, Jennifer. 2003. "Straight Story." *Entertainment Weekly* 706–707 (April 4): 152.

Rich, Motoko. 2006. "James Frey and His Publisher Settle Suit over Lies." *New York Times*, September 7. http://www.nytimes.com/2006/09/07/arts/ 07frey.html.

Rieder, Rem. 2006. "Falling to 'Pieces.'" *American Journalism Review* 28, no. 1 (Fall/Winter): 6.

Room, Robin. 2003. "The Cultural Framing of Addiction." *Janus Head* 6, no. 2: 221–34.

Rooney, Kathleen. 2005. *Reading with Oprah: The Book Club That Changed America*. Fayetteville: University of Arkansas Press.

Root, Robert L., and Marjane Satrapi. 2007. "Interview with Marjane Satrapi." *Fourth Genre* 9, no. 2 (Fall): 147–57.

Rosaldo, Rinaldo. 1999. "Cultural Citizenship, Inequality, and Multiculturalism." In *Race, Identity, and Citizenship: A Reader*, edited by Rodolpho D. Torres, Louis F. Mirón, and Jonathan Xavier Inda, 253–61. Oxford: Blackwell.

Roth, Jeffrey D. 2006. "Editor's Bookshelf: *A Million Little Pieces.*" *Journal of Groups in Addiction and Recovery* 1, nos. 3–4: 113–20.

Rousseau, Jean-Jacques. 1975. *The Social Contract and Discourses*. Translated by G. D. H. Cole. London: Dent.

Sacco, Jack. 2004. *Where the Birds Never Sing: The True Story of the 92nd Signal Battalion and the Liberation of Dachau*. New York: Harper Perennial.

Sales, Leigh. 2010. "Well Readhead: The Memoir Boom." Australian Broadcasting Corporation. *The Drum*, March 26. http://www.abc.net.au/news/stories/ 2010/03/26/2856619.htm.

Santella, Andrew. "Picking Up the Pieces." *GQ: Gentlemen's Quarterly* 73, no. 5 (May): 38.

Satrapi, Marjane. 2003a. "Tales from an Ordinary Iranian Girlhood." *Ms.* (March).

———. 2003b. *Persepolis: The Story of a Childhood*. New York: Pantheon.

———. 2004. *Persepolis: The Story of a Return*. New York: Pantheon.

Schiffrin, André. 2001. *The Business of Books: How International Conglomerates Took Over Publishing and Changed the Way We Read*. London and New York: Verso.

Schott, Chris. 2008. "Provincialism Dooms Cosmopolitan Inventor." *New York Observer*, March 25. http://www.observer.com/2008/provincialism-dooms -cosmopolitan-inventor.

Schuessler, Jennifer. 2009. "Frank McCourt and the American Memoir." *New York Times*. July 25.

Scott, Linda M. 2009. "Markets and Audiences." In *A History of the Book in America*. Vol. 5, *The Enduring Book: Print Culture in Postwar America*, 72–90. Chapel Hill, NC: University of North Carolina Press.

Sellers, Jeff M. 1999. "Big Box Blues: Toronto's Chapters Threatens to Crush Locally Owned Bookselling Competition." *BC Report* 10, no. 17 (June 28): 36–37.

Shapiro, Susan. 2010. "13 Tips for Launching Your Memoir: Here's What You Need to Know to Get Your Book on the Shelves of this Popular Genre." *Writer* 123, no. 8 (August): 46–47.

Shatzkin, Leonard. 1982. *In Cold Type: Overcoming the Book Crisis*. Boston: Houghton Mifflin.

Shultz, Judy. 2007. "Parity Pricing Makes Cookbooks a Good Deal." *Edmonton Journal*. November 21.

Smith, Sidonie, and Julia Watson. 1996. Introduction to *Getting a Life: Everyday Uses of Autobiography*, edited by Sidonie Smith and Julia Watson, 1–26. Minneapolis: University of Minnesota Press.

———. 2010. *Reading Autobiography: A Guide for Interpreting Life Narratives*. 2nd Edition. Minneapolis: University of Minnesota Press.

The Smoking Gun. 2006a. "The Man Who Conned Oprah." January 8. http://www .thesmokinggun.com/archive/0104061jamesfrey1.html.

———. 2006b. "Memoir: Authenticity Challenged. Parts I and II." http://www .wordinfo.info/words/index/info/view_unit/3685/?letter=M&spage=4.

Squires, Claire. 2007. *Marketing Literature: The Making of Contemporary Writing in Britain*. Houndmills: Palgrave Macmillan.

Stanley, Liz. 2000. "From 'Self-Made Women' to 'Women's Made-Selves?' Adult Selves, Simulation, and Surveillance in the Rise of Public Women." In *Feminism and Autobiography: Texts, Theories, Methods*, edited by Tess Cosslett, Celia Lury, and Penny Summerfield, 40–60. London and New York: Routledge.

Steward, Gillian. 2001. "Some of the Best Books Never Written: Will the New Chapters/Indigo Be Open to Regional Publishing?" *Media* 8, no. 2: 22.

Stoll, David. 1999. *Rigoberta Menchú and the Story of All Poor Guatemalans*. Boulder, CO: Westview Press.

Tedesco, Theresa. 2003. "The Real Story Kept between the Covers: Booksellers Quietly Fume during Talks with Indigo." *National Post*, November 8.

Tensuan, Theresa M. 2006. "Comic Visions and Revisions in the Work of Lynda Barry and Marjane Satrapi." *MFS: Modern Fiction Studies* 52, no. 4 (Winter): 947–64.

Terefenko, Paul. 2009. "Pages Bookstore Going Down." *Now Magazine* 28, no. 45 (July 14–17): A1. http://www.nowtoronto.com/news/story.cfm?content=170346.

Thompson, John B. 2010. *Merchants of Culture: The Publishing Business in the Twenty-first Century.* Cambridge: Polity Press.

Thompson, Lynda M. 2000. *The "Scandalous Memoirists": Constantia Phillips, Laetitia Pilkington, and the Shame of "Publik Fame."* Manchester: Manchester University Press.

Todorov, Tzvetan. 1975. *The Fantastic: A Structural Approach to a Literary Genre.* Ithaca, NY: Cornell University Press.

Toller, Carol, and Shirley Hewett. 2000. "Vancouver Hit by Wave of Store Closures: Five Independents Have Shut Down since December." *Quill and Quire* 66, no. 4: 5.

Torontoist. 2007. "Villain: Chapters, Indigo, Coles, Smithbooks, etc." December 28. http://torontoist.com/2007/12/villain_chapter.php.

Trachtenberg, Jeffrey. 2005. "To Compete with Book Chains, Some Think Big: Independent Sellers Gain with Size and Service." *Publishing Research Quarterly* 21, no. 2: 35–38.

———. 2006. "Publishers Say Fact-Checking Is Too Costly." *Wall Street Journal* 247, no. 24 (January 30): B1–B4.

Tucker, Ken. 2006. "Frey, Frey Again." *Entertainment Weekly* 862–863 (February 10): 21.

Valby Karen. 2003. "James Frey Does Not Care What You Think about Him (Please Love Him)." *Entertainment Weekly* 703 (April 4): 60–64.

Veale, Scott. 2002. "New and Noteworthy Paperbacks." *New York Times Book Review*, October 27.

Volk, Patricia. 2002. *Stuffed: Growing Up in a Restaurant Family.* New York: Vintage.

Warhol, Robyn R., and Helena Michie. 1996. "Twelve-Step Teleology: Narratives of Recovery/Recovery as Narrative." In Smith and Watson, *Getting a Life: Everyday Uses of Autobiography*, 327–50.

Warner, Michael. 2005. *Publics and Counterpublics.* Cambridge, MA: Zone Books.

Weeks, Wendy. 2007. "The Literary Divide: Although Our Dollar Is Still Flying High, the Price Gap between American and Canadian Books Remains Huge." *Ottawa Citizen*, September 9.

Where Halifax. 2008. "Halifax Shops and Services Guide." http://www.where.ca/halifax/guide_listing~listing_id~538.htm.

Whiteside, Thomas. 1981. *The Blockbuster Complex: Conglomerates, Show Business, and Book Publishing.* Middletown, CT: Wesleyan University Press.

Whitlock, Gillian. 2005. "The Skin of the 'Burqa': Recent Life Narratives from Afghanistan." *Biography* 28, no. 1: 54–76.

———. 2006. "Autographics: The Seeing 'I' of the Comics." *Modern Fiction Studies* 52, no. 4: 965–79.

———. 2007. *Soft Weapons: Autobiography in Transit.* Chicago: University of Chicago Press.

Willems, Peter. 2005. "Blooming and Booming." *Middle East* 353 (February): 22–23.

Williamson, Milly. 2005. *The Lure of the Vampire: Gender, Fiction, and Fandom from Bram Stoker to Buffy.* London: Wallflower.

Wirtén, Eva Hemmungs. 2009. "The Global Market, 1970–2000: Producers." In Eliot and Rose, *A Companion to the History of the Book*, 395–405.

Wong, Hertha Dawn. 1992. *Sending My Heart Back across the Years: Tradition and Innovation in Native American Autobiography.* New York: Oxford University Press.

Wright, David. 2005. "Mediating Production and Consumption: Cultural Capital and 'Cultural Workers.'" *British Journal of Sociology* 56, no. 1: 105–21.

Yagoda, Ben. 2009. *Memoir: A History.* New York: Riverhead Books.

Yardley, Jonathan. 2009. "Shelve It under Navel-Gazing." *Washington Post*, November 29. http://www.washingtonpost.com/wp-dyn/content/article/2009/11/25/AR2009112502870.html.

Zboray, Ronald J., and Mary Saracino Zboray. 2005. *Literary Dollars and Social Sense: A People's History of the Mass Market Book.* New York: Routledge.

INDEX

Books in the Life Writing Series

Published by Wilfrid Laurier University Press

Haven't Any News: Ruby's Letters from the Fifties edited by Edna Staebler with an Afterword by Marlene Kadar • 1995 / x + 165 pp. / ISBN 0-88920-248-6

"I Want to Join Your Club": Letters from Rural Children, 1900–1920 edited by Norah L. Lewis with a Preface by Neil Sutherland • 1996 / xii + 250 pp. (30 b&w photos) / ISBN 0-88920-260-5

And Peace Never Came by Elisabeth M. Raab with Historical Notes by Marlene Kadar • 1996 / x + 196 pp. (12 b&w photos, map) / ISBN 0-88920-281-8

Dear Editor and Friends: Letters from Rural Women of the North-West, 1900–1920 edited by Norah L. Lewis • 1998 / xvi + 166 pp. (20 b&w photos) / ISBN 0-88920-287-7

The Surprise of My Life: An Autobiography by Claire Drainie Taylor with a Foreword by Marlene Kadar • 1998 / xii + 268 pp. (8 colour photos and 92 b&w photos) / ISBN 0-88920-302-4

Memoirs from Away: A New Found Land Girlhood by Helen M. Buss / Margaret Clarke • 1998 / xvi + 153 pp. / ISBN 0-88920-350-4

The Life and Letters of Annie Leake Tuttle: Working for the Best by Marilyn Färdig Whiteley • 1999 / xviii + 150 pp. / ISBN 0-88920-330-X

Marian Engel's Notebooks: "Ah, mon cahier, écoute" edited by Christl Verduyn • 1999 / viii + 576 pp. / ISBN 0-88920-333-4 cloth / ISBN 0-88920-349-0 paper

Be Good Sweet Maid: The Trials of Dorothy Joudrie by Audrey Andrews • 1999 / vi + 276 pp. / ISBN 0-88920-334-2

Working in Women's Archives: Researching Women's Private Literature and Archival Documents edited by Helen M. Buss and Marlene Kadar • 2001 / vi + 120 pp. / ISBN 0-88920-341-5

Repossessing the World: Reading Memoirs by Contemporary Women by Helen M. Buss • 2002 / xxvi + 206 pp. / ISBN 0-88920-408-x cloth / ISBN 0-88920-410-1 paper

Chasing the Comet: A Scottish-Canadian Life by Patricia Koretchuk • 2002 / xx + 244 pp. / ISBN 0-88920-407-1

The Queen of Peace Room by Magie Dominic • 2002 / xii + 115 pp. / ISBN 0-88920-417-9

China Diary: The Life of Mary Austin Endicott by Shirley Jane Endicott • 2002 / xvi + 251 pp. / ISBN 0-88920-412-8

The Curtain: Witness and Memory in Wartime Holland by Henry G. Schogt • 2003 / xii + 132 pp. / ISBN 0-88920-396-2

Teaching Places by Audrey J. Whitson • 2003 / xiii + 178 pp. / ISBN 0-88920-425-x

Through the Hitler Line by Laurence F. Wilmot, M.C. • 2003 / xvi + 152 pp. / ISBN 0-88920-448-9

Where I Come From by Vijay Agnew • 2003 / xiv + 298 pp. / ISBN 0-88920-414-4

The Water Lily Pond by Han Z. Li • 2004 / x + 254 pp. / ISBN 0-88920-431-4

The Life Writings of Mary Baker McQuesten: Victorian Matriarch edited by Mary J. Anderson • 2004 / xxii + 338 pp. / ISBN 0-88920-437-3

Seven Eggs Today: The Diaries of Mary Armstrong, 1859 and 1869 edited by Jackson W. Armstrong • 2004 / xvi + 228 pp. / ISBN 0-88920-440-3

Love and War in London: A Woman's Diary 1939–1942 by Olivia Cockett; edited by Robert W. Malcolmson • 2005 / xvi + 208 pp. / ISBN 0-88920-458-6

Incorrigible by Velma Demerson • 2004 / vi + 178 pp. / ISBN 0-88920-444-6

Auto/biography in Canada: Critical Directions edited by Julie Rak • 2005 / viii + 264 pp. / ISBN 0-88920-478-0

Tracing the Autobiographical edited by Marlene Kadar, Linda Warley, Jeanne Perreault, and Susanna Egan • 2005 / viii + 280 pp. / ISBN 0-88920-476-4

Must Write: Edna Staebler's Diaries edited by Christl Verduyn • 2005 / viii + 304 pp. / ISBN 0-88920-481-0

Pursuing Giraffe: A 1950s Adventure by Anne Innis Dagg • 2006 / xvi + 284 pp. (photos, 2 maps) / 978-0-88920-463-8

Food That Really Schmecks by Edna Staebler • 2007 / xxiv + 334 pp. / ISBN 978-0-88920-521-5

163256: A Memoir of Resistance by Michael Englishman • 2007 / xvi + 112 pp. (14 b&w photos) / ISBN 978-1-55458-009-5

The Wartime Letters of Leslie and Cecil Frost, 1915–1919 edited by R.B. Fleming • 2007 / xxxvi + 384 pp. (49 b&w photos, 5 maps) / ISBN 978-1-55458-000-2

Johanna Krause Twice Persecuted: Surviving in Nazi Germany and Communist East Germany by Carolyn Gammon and Christiane Hemker • 2007 / x + 170 pp. (58 b&w photos, 2 maps) / ISBN 978-1-55458-006-4

Watermelon Syrup: A Novel by Annie Jacobsen with Jane Finlay-Young and Di Brandt • 2007 / x + 268 pp. / ISBN 978-1-55458-005-7

Broad Is the Way: Stories from Mayerthorpe by Margaret Norquay • 2008 / x + 106 pp. (6 b&w photos) / ISBN 978-1-55458-020-0

Becoming My Mother's Daughter: A Story of Survival and Renewal by Erika Gottlieb • 2008 / x + 178 pp. (36 b&w illus., 17 colour) / ISBN 978-1-55458-030-9

Leaving Fundamentalism: Personal Stories edited by G. Elijah Dann • 2008 / xii + 234 pp. / ISBN 978-1-55458-026-2

Bearing Witness: Living with Ovarian Cancer edited by Kathryn Carter and Lauri Elit • 2009 / viii + 94 pp. / ISBN 978-1-55458-055-2

Dead Woman Pickney: A Memoir of Childhood in Jamaica by Yvonne Shorter Brown • 2010 / viii + 202 pp. / ISBN 978-1-55458-189-4

I Have a Story to Tell You by Seemah C. Berson • 2010 / xx + 288 pp. (24 b&w photos) / ISBN 978-1-55458-219-8

We All Giggled: A Bourgeois Family Memoir by Thomas O. Hueglin • 2010 / xiv + 232 pp. (20 b&w photos) / ISBN 978-1-55458-262-4

Just a Larger Family: Letters of Marie Williamson from the Canadian Home Front, 1940–1944 edited by Mary F. Williamson and Tom Sharp • 2011 / xxiv + 378 pp. (16 b&w photos) / ISBN 978-1-55458-323-2

Burdens of Proof: Faith, Doubt, and Identity in Autobiography by Susanna Egan • 2011 / x + 200 pp. / ISBN 978-1-55458-333-1

Accident of Fate: A Personal Account 1938–1945 by Imre Rochlitz with Joseph Rochlitz • 2011 / xiv + 226 pp. (50 b&w photos, 5 maps) / ISBN 978-1-55458-267-9

The Green Sofa by Natascha Würzbach, translated by Raleigh Whitinger • 2012 / xiv + 240 pp. (5 b&w photos) / ISBN 978-1-55458-334-8

Unheard Of: Memoirs of a Canadian Composer by John Beckwith • 2012 / x + 393 pp. (74 illus., 8 musical examples) / ISBN 978-1-55458-358-4

Borrowed Tongues: Life Writing, Migration, and Translation by Eva C. Karpinski • 2012 / viii + 274 pp. / ISBN 978-1-55458-357-7

Basements and Attics, Closets and Cyberspace: Explorations in Canadian Women's Archives edited by Linda M. Morra and Jessica Schagerl • 2012 / x + 338 pp. / ISBN 978-1-55458-632-5

The Memory of Water by Allen Smutylo • 2013 / x + 262 pp. (50 colour illus.) / ISBN 978-1-55458-842-8

The Unwritten Diary of Israel Unger by Carolyn Gammon and Israel Unger • 2013 / x + 224 pp. (b&w illus.) / ISBN 978-1-55458-831-2

Boom! Manufacturing Memoir for the Popular Public by Julie Rak + 2013 / viii + 250 pp. (7 b&w photos) / ISBN 978-1-55458-939-5

Not the Whole Story: Challenging the Single Mother Narrative edited by Lea Caragata and Judit Alcalde • forthcoming 2013 / 176 pp. / ISBN 978-1-55458-624-0

www.ingramcontent.com/pod-product-compliance
Lightning Source LLC
Chambersburg PA
CBHW020402120726
47904CB00002B/671